Praise for *Horseshoes vs. Chess*

"The life and world of a chamber executive has never been more thoroughly and enjoyably covered than it is in Dave Adkisson's book *Horseshoes vs. Chess*. From sharing very relatable real-life examples to presenting his expert counsel from his amazing career in the profession, Dave's book is a must-read for anyone considering chamber work and a great affirmation for anyone currently in chamber work. I cannot recommend it highly enough."

–Thomas Baldrige, President and CEO
Lancaster Chamber, PA

"Dave Adkisson is one of the most intelligent and thoughtful individuals I have encountered in the chamber of commerce world, so it is not a surprise he has written the definitive account of how you can improve yourself, your organization and your community through chamber work. Too often we use the term 'required reading' but for those who want to enter chamber work, advance in that career, or just be better in their organization, this book is indispensable. The only regret I have about Dave's work is that I did not have it when I started my chamber career 17 years ago."

–Gene Barr, President and CEO
Pennsylvania Chamber of Business and Industry

"*Horseshoes vs. Chess* uniquely captures the essence of the necessary skill set, ethical leadership, personality traits and adaptiveness needed to excel in chamber management. The book also provides clear and convincing examples of how successful organizations can positively transform communities, regions and states. Whether you're just starting out in this industry or an experienced professional, Dave Adkisson provides an insightful resource for all…a must read!"

–Jay Chesshir, President and CEO
Little Rock Chamber, AR

"Dave Adkisson's practical new book gives chamber professionals a sense of profound purpose and provides inspiration to leaders in the broader nonprofit world. Chamber executives from chambers of all sizes can relate to many of the lessons and vivid illustrations Dave shares. While I have known him as a personal mentor in my career, *Horseshoes vs. Chess* now allows chamber professionals across the country the chance to reflect on their own experiences through his stories about building stronger chambers and more prosperous communities."

–Amy Cloud, Executive Director
Kentucky Association of Chamber Executives

"Through the lens of a seasoned chamber executive, *Horseshoes vs Chess* provides keen insights and shares valuable leadership lessons learned. It will inform and inspire both new and long-time chamber professionals to utilize the true capacity of their chambers to make a meaningful difference for their members and communities."

–Mark Eagan, President and CEO
Capital Region Chamber, Albany, NY

"The author brings sage insights and advice to the complexities of chamber leadership gained through a lifetime of experience. It shows clearly the characteristics that lead to success and how those who embody these skills can have a fulfilling career while making a big impact in the communities they serve."

–Lew Ebert, Executive Director
Council of State Chambers

"As would be expected given his extensive personal experience and intellectual curiosity, Dave Adkisson's *Horseshoes v. Chess* is thorough and highly informative. Because the book includes constant reminders of the in-the-trenches work that a chamber of commerce must address, as well as the necessary complex strategies, it may have been appropriate to call it *Horseshoes AND Chess*. Dave succeeded in the goal he states in his introduction, i.e. to create a publication for multiple audiences: chamber of commerce chief executives, staffs, nonprofit boards of directors, and even those seeking to understand how communities are built. He is careful to back up every opinion and assertion with illustrative stories from his long and successful career in the field, but also with research and input from hundreds of peers and organization experts. It is a perfect blend of chamber how-to, why-to, and why not. Practical and inspirational."

–Mick Fleming, Retired President and CEO
Association of Chamber of Commerce Executives

"Dave's book *Horseshoes vs. Chess* is filled with compassion for the chamber industry. His ability to describe the importance of discernment throughout the manuscript is remarkable and a gift! Dave is a storyteller at heart. His genuineness is revealed from the collection of insights that comes from searching to understand, understanding with sympathy, coupled with Dave's keen practical judgement. I highly recommend *Horseshoes vs. Chess!*"

–Kelly Hall, President and CEO
Longview Chamber of Commerce, TX

"This book should be required reading for any search committee looking to find the right leader to build upon a community's strengths and opportunities. Additionally, a chamber CEO should provide this as a gift to its volunteer officers. The practical observations and insights are sure to assist in building a symbiotic relationship between the business community leaders and the professional executive leadership in establishing a path to success. Serving the chamber profession for more than 30 years, I highly recommend every executive chamber professional, regardless of length of service, read this from cover to cover."

–Nancy Keefer, President and CEO
Daytona Regional Chamber, FL

"Dave's book not only highlights the essentials needed for a strong chamber of commerce but also the core of what it takes to thrive as a chamber executive in our dynamic, ever-changing world. Never proscriptive, this guide focuses on the soul of leadership and ways to maximize community impact. A must-read for CEOs seeking to affect greater change in their role, as well as aspiring community leaders who want inspiration and guidance to get them to the helm."

–**Sheree Anne Kelly, President and CEO**
Association of Chamber of Commerce Executives

"David Adkisson hits the nail on the head about all things chamber. As I read *Horseshoes vs. Chess* I found myself constantly stopping and saying to myself 'Absolutely' in agreement with his relevant insights, advice and observations. It's a MUST-read for any chamber of commerce executive – but especially those who want to 'survive' and make chamber work a successful, long career."

–**Dave Kilby, President**
Western Association of Chamber Executives
Sacramento, CA

"When I first became CEO and President of the Chamber of Commerce of Hawaii, I was in unfamiliar territory as to how to lead a chamber effectively. This was my first leadership position. Then I met Dave. He taught me how to navigate and blaze the path forward. He has always been a mentor, an inspiration, and a sincere and genuine leader to me and others. This book will be invaluable for any aspiring emerging leader, anyone who wants to enter a Chamber career, and anyone who wants to lead a Chamber or any other organization."

–**Sherry Menor-McNamara, CEO and President**
Chamber of Commerce of Hawaii

"In all the chamber literature I've seen – board minutes, chamber annual reports, items from ACCE and its predecessor organization, chamber histories, my history and all the sources that went into it, web pages, PDFs – there might be 100,000 pages of material. Almost all of that has relevance to chambers. There is one source, however, that outshines all the others in usefulness to today's chamber executive: Dave Adkisson's remarkable new book, *Horseshoes vs. Chess*. This is the best thing we've had since 1768. It is brilliant, touching, perceptive, full of spot-on examples, and, to top it off, a great read."

–**Chris Mead, author of** *Magicians of Main Street: America and its Chambers of Commerce, 1768-1945*

"*Horseshoes vs. Chess* will be a useful guide to those entering the chamber industry, while providing helpful reminders to those currently engaged in this community-impacting work. I've known Dave for most of his career and by a complete coincidence, I observed him at all three of his chambers. We're from the same home town in Kentucky, our families lived in Birmingham at the same time and then he and I worked together at the Kentucky Chamber. I know this book project was a labor of love for him, and I predict it will be required reading for all current and future chamber professionals!"

–**Carlos Phillips, President and CEO**
Greenville Chamber, SC

"Dave is a natural leader. Everything he touches turns to gold. Luck? Hardly…no one will out-work or out-think Dave. *Horseshoes vs. Chess* will touch many lives and be a catalyst for success."

–**Bob Quick, President and CEO**
Commerce Lexington Inc., KY

"Dave does an amazing job of describing the 360-degree life of a chamber CEO, a life that sometimes feels like only if you've been there, done that, could you possibly understand the dynamics…but with this guide, one can. And candidly, those of us who have worked with Dave and other colleagues know that the gig, yes often a chess game to be good at it, is one of the best ways on the planet to help a city, a region and possibly your own home town."

–Joe Roman, President and CEO
Greater Cleveland Partnership, OH

"Working under Dave's leadership was like taking a master class on how to run a chamber. I was fortunate to learn the lessons laid out in *Horseshoes v. Chess* each and every day. Dave's leadership, vision and proactive nature inspired me, and many others, to fall in love with this 'accidental career.' Following in his rather large footsteps, there isn't a day that goes by that I don't think 'What would Dave do?'"

–Ashli Watts, President and CEO
Kentucky Chamber of Commerce

Horseshoes vs. Chess

A Practical Guide for Chamber of Commerce Leaders

DAVE ADKISSON, CCE

IGNITE
PRESS
Fresno, CA

Published in the United States by Ignite Press.
ignitepress.us

ISBN: 978-1-953655-30-1 (Amazon Print)
ISBN: 978-1-953655-31-8 (IngramSpark) PAPERBACK
ISBN: 978-1-953655-32-5 (IngramSpark) HARDCOVER
ISBN: 978-1-953655-33-2 (E-book)

For bulk purchase and for booking, contact:

Dave Adkisson, CCE
Email: dave@chamberdave.com
Website: www.chamberdave.com

Library of Congress Control Number: 2020923759

To Bonnie, Kendra and Cyrus

ACKNOWLEDGMENTS

Many colleagues have inspired me during my chamber of commerce career and supported me during this attempt to describe in writing the unique role of a chamber professional. It is with warm gratitude and lasting respect that I mention just a few who represent various milestones in my personal journey:

Chris Mead, former senior vice president of ACCE, for challenging me to document my unique career experience of managing three very different chambers and my involvement on the national level with three chamber organizations.

Diana Taylor, a friend, former newspaper reporter, and communications and policy consultant for the Kentucky Chamber, for editing several drafts of my *Horseshoes vs. Chess* manuscript and working diligently to make me appear literate.

Drew Page, now retired in South Carolina, for hiring me at my home-town chamber, immediately sending me to the U. S. Chamber's Institute for Organization Management and, as my first chamber boss, introducing me to the unique and powerful opportunity to improve my community through chamber work.

The officers and directors of the Owensboro Chamber for taking a chance on an eager beaver and promoting me from project manager to CEO of my hometown chamber at age 25.

The late Charles Herd, former president of the Louisville Chamber and former chairman of ACCE, for serving as a distinguished role model during my early career and for sharing with our state association of chamber execs the analogy of horseshoes vs. chess and suggesting it as a vivid illustration of the strategies required to lead a chamber and a community. The fact that I quote the story 40 years later reflects how profoundly it resonates with me to this day.

My informal editorial board, who as friends and chamber colleagues from across the country, agreed to review my manuscript and offer advice, even as most of them were leading their own chambers and associations. I'm deeply indebted to:

Tom Baldrige	The Lancaster Chamber, PA
Gene Barr	The Pennsylvania Chamber of Business and Industry
Kurt Bauer	WMC, Wisconsin's Chamber
Jay Chesshir	The Little Rock Chamber, AR
Amy Cloud	Kentucky Chamber of Commerce Executives
Mark Eagan	The Capital Region Chamber, Albany, NY
Lew Ebert	The Council of State Chambers (COSC)
Mick Fleming	Chamber Counselor, LLC
Kelly Hall	The Longview Chamber of Commerce, TX
Nancy Keefer	The Daytona Regional Chamber, FL
Sheree Anne Kelly	Association of Chamber of Commerce Executives (ACCE)
Dave Kilby	Western Association of Chamber Executives, CA

Sherry Menor-McNamara   The Chamber of Commerce of Hawaii
Chris Mead   *Magicians of Main Street: America and its Chambers of Commerce, 1768-1945*
Carlos Phillips   The Greenville Chamber, SC
Bob Quick   Commerce Lexington, Inc., KY
Joe Roman   The Greater Cleveland Partnership, OH
Raymond Towle   The U.S. Chamber Institute for Organization Management, Washington, D.C.
Ashli Watts   The Kentucky Chamber of Commerce

Former ACCE president Mick Fleming and my fellow ACCE board members for encouraging my active engagement with such an important association of peers and giving me the opportunity to serve in a leadership role of that organization.

Joe Crosby and Bill Kramer for their professional support of the Council of State Chambers, their personal encouragement of state chamber professionals and their friendship.

More than 30 chamber board chairs and hundreds of dedicated board members for their support, guidance and friendship during my chamber career.

My former co-workers – my "chamber family" – at the Owensboro (KY) Chamber, the Birmingham (AL) Regional Chamber and the Kentucky Chamber, including a half dozen who have gone on to serve as CEOs of their own chambers.

Countless chamber colleagues for their personal encouragement and for sharing ideas that I could implement in my own chambers and communities.

My friend, campaign manager and civic co-conspirator Rodney Berry of Owensboro, Kentucky for more than 40 years of support, counsel, an endless stream of ideas for civic improvement and above all, our lasting friendship.

And above all my wife, Bonnie, who not only gave me continuing feedback on my manuscript but who along with our daughter, Dr. Kendra Faucett, and our son, Cyrus Adkisson, supported my passion for civic engagement, my 12-year adventure in politics, and 30+ year career in Chamber World.

TABLE OF CONTENTS

PART I:
IT'S ABOUT YOU AS A CHAMBER LEADER

PART II:
IT'S ABOUT YOU AND YOUR CHAMBER

PART III:
IT'S ABOUT YOU AND YOUR COMMUNITY

PART IV:
IT'S ABOUT YOU AND YOUR CAREER

INTRODUCTION

This is a book about and for chamber of commerce professionals and volunteers. It speaks primarily to chamber CEOs and other chamber decision-makers – aspiring CEOs, senior-level chamber staffers, conscientious volunteer chamber leaders, members of chamber search committees and, especially, to young, eager chamber staffers who are "bitten by the chamber bug" and see themselves immersed in an exciting and fulfilling career as a chamber professional.

I think of this book as a letter to my younger self: What would I want to know if I were at the beginning of this career path?

My experience and a passion for the chamber business frame the perspective of this work. Having managed a relatively small city chamber in my hometown (Owensboro, KY, population 60,000 in a county of 100,000), a metropolitan chamber (Birmingham, AL, in a metro area of 1.3 million), and a state chamber (Kentucky, population 4.3 million), I have had the privilege of experiencing chamber management from three distinct angles. In addition, as the 2010 board chair of the Association of Chamber of Commerce Executives (ACCE), the 2014 board chair of the national Council of State Chambers (COSC), a founder of the national State Chamber Policy Center, a board member for six years and the education policy committee chair for three years of the U.S. Chamber, and mayor of my hometown for eight years, I have observed chambers and chamber leaders from multiple perspectives for several decades.

I've seen chambers lead their communities in profound ways, and I've seen chambers swerve into a sinkhole of dysfunction and negativity. I've seen young chamber leaders attain professional heights they never planned or expected, and I've seen capable, well-meaning chamber executives fall victim to political crosscurrents that were largely unpredictable but disruptive to their promising careers.

I've seen chambers that were well respected and professionally managed turned upside down because a casual conversation at a country club about the community's recent economic slump suddenly became a finger-pointing campaign and a desire to shake things up at the chamber. And I've seen a few brilliant chamber executives self-destruct professionally because of a particular human weakness that, at least temporarily, seemed to cancel out the sum of their career accomplishments.

This is not meant to be an instructional manual, except in the sense that it might stir a personal reaction and a thought process about how best to handle certain situations. Neither is it a scholarly work on organizational dynamics, nonprofit management or leadership. Rather, it attempts to offer particular insights about leadership in a chamber of commerce context -- to address time management, politics, group dynamics and similar matters – all within that context.

It also is meant to inspire thoughtful comparative reflection among chamber leaders – or better yet – a dialogue among chamber leaders about the unique positions of leadership and stewardship they hold and the enormous trust they can engender within a chamber of commerce and, thereby, the broader community.

Having served as a mayor midway through my chamber career, I've often offered chamber colleagues this word of encouragement: If you gave me four years to change my community, I would want to be the mayor. But if you gave me twenty years, I would want to be the chamber exec.

At City Hall, you have hundreds or thousands of employees, millions of dollars, a bully pulpit, a formal mandate, political capital, the trappings of office, quick access to the local media, legal authority – you name it – to use for the betterment of your community. In the role of chamber leader, you have the time to learn the culture and needs of the community and to put in place strategic plans that reflect an ambitious long-term agenda for prosperity. Over time, you have the ability to pull together the best and brightest business, political and civic talent in the community to achieve those goals. Short of being crowned the emperor of a city, being mayor isn't bad. But being a chamber exec is better.

If you gave me four years to change my community, I would want to be the mayor. But if you gave me twenty years, I would want to be the chamber exec!

Here's to you! To either be anointed emperor, to run for mayor, or better yet, to be a successful chamber exec!

■ ■ ■

Note: Because the chamber of commerce world is so diverse, among small-town chambers, small city chambers, suburban chambers, metropolitan chambers, regional chambers, consolidated chambers, ethnic chambers, LGBTQ chambers, state chambers and others, it is challenging to write in ways that will be relevant for the many variances. As former ACCE president Mick Fleming and other veteran chamber execs have framed it, "If you've seen one chamber, you've seen one chamber!" It's difficult to generalize across the many differences among chambers of commerce.

That being acknowledged, I hope most of my thoughts and observations will be relevant to any chamber of commerce or at least to the situations you are experiencing. I encourage you to actively translate these observations and stories for your own circumstances.

PART I:
IT'S ABOUT YOU AS A CHAMBER LEADER

While chambers of commerce are vastly different from each other and chamber leaders exhibit very different leadership styles, some interesting research on the subject and a career of observing chamber leaders convince me that there are unique traits and skills that many successful chamber leaders have in common. A discussion of those traits and skills can help us answer the question of what kind of individual can effectively manage a chamber.

CHAPTER 1
LEADERSHIP IN A CHAMBER CONTEXT

A chamber executive holds a unique leadership position in the community. Are there special personality traits and skills that characterize chamber leaders? Are there particular demands on a chamber leader who is expected to navigate the ever-changing political and economic currents to provide leadership for a chamber and, in turn, for a community?

The Only One in Town

There are dozens, hundreds, perhaps even thousands of lawyers in a community. But there is typically only one chamber CEO in a particular service area. Even if the chamber exists in a metropolitan area alongside dozens of other suburban chambers, the chamber exec has a unique position relative to his/her primary constituencies – members, business and political leaders and the broader community.

Because of the special nature of a chamber – typically the community's foremost business association – its chief executive has a distinct vantage point from which to observe, interpret and affect the political, economic and cultural currents. Although there are certainly other one-of-a-kind civic leaders in town – the mayor, the chief librarian, the United Way exec, perhaps the school superintendent – the chamber exec functions in a unique professional space, ideally as the primary convener of business leaders, a visible spokesperson for community business interests and a constant advocate for the community's economic progress.

The chamber exec functions in a unique professional space, ideally as the primary convener of business leaders, a visible spokesperson for community business interests and a constant advocate for the community's economic progress.

Not all chamber execs occupy that space as fully as others. In some cases, the exec is only expected by volunteer leaders to be the faithful steward of the organization, a cheery ambassador for the community, or a clerk for the financial and housekeeping duties required for paying the bills and keeping the doors open. If the expectations of a chamber's volunteer leaders are minimal, the bar is relatively low in terms of who can occupy the seat. If the expectations are high, however, and business leaders want a chamber exec to provide bold leadership and interact with them as a peer, the role is profoundly different and a different skill set is expected.

While chamber executives don't have the formal mandate of government positions, they are positioned well to provide leadership in their communities. They are, as columnist and author Thomas Friedman of *The New York Times* describes them, "leaders without authority". They carry the banner of the business community but don't have legal authority to impose their agenda on the community. They advance their causes by persuading, not mandating.

The Chamber Executive as a Leader in Evolving Circumstances

The effectiveness of an organization rarely exceeds the effectiveness of its leader. That maxim from business school textbooks succinctly summarizes the critical relationship between a chamber and its chief executive.

The chamber exec is generally expected to provide leadership in a subtle, behind-the-scenes way – as a workhorse, rather than a show horse. A chamber exec who misreads his/her chamber leadership role and plays it too prominently at the wrong time could quietly or conspicuously alienate the volunteer leaders and eventually pay a steep price for the mistake.

The type of leadership required of a chamber exec is relative to the special circumstances of the chamber and varies from chamber to chamber, year to year, and even board chair to board chair. A chamber exec's leadership style must be one that can adapt quickly to changing circumstances, certainly from year to year as the board chair (i.e., the boss) changes. One board chair might enjoy being in a prominent community position and be eager to be out front, speaking for the chamber and headlining activities. Another might shy away from the limelight, hoping to remain behind the scenes in a supportive role.

> *The chamber exec is generally expected to provide leadership in a subtle, behind-the-scenes way – as a workhorse, rather than a show horse.*

Communities evolve daily with new issues, new personalities and shifting political winds. Likewise, chambers are dynamic organizations with constantly emerging challenges and opportunities. A chamber executive has to be flexible and adaptable to those changing circumstances while holding steady to advancing the interests of the business community.

Chamber Executives as Surrogate Leaders

Today's business people have great pressures to meet bottom-line expectations in their day jobs and have less time to tackle complex community issues as civic volunteers. Therefore, they are increasingly willing to invest in talented and specialized chamber professionals to act as their surrogate civic leaders and are willing to delegate much of the heavy lifting.

A friend once commented that some communities – especially in metro areas – are willing to invest in chamber executives by paying professional salaries that are often above typical nonprofit salaries because, in effect, they are "buying" surrogate leaders. He had observed that communities are much more complex than in the past because issues are more intricate and the number of nonprofit groups, interest groups and government agencies involved in decision making has multiplied dramatically. Moreover, the electoral process often doesn't yield office-holders (e.g. mayors, county commission presidents, governors) who are comfortable with or adept at managing change.

As a result, a cadre of professional civic operatives has emerged. Planning directors, transportation engineers, public health specialists, industry recruiters, facilitators of entrepreneurism and regional growth advocates, to name a few, have become essential for communities to move forward. Chamber executives should be at the center of this professional cadre, serving as trained and qualified change agents – professionals who are skilled at managing change, articulating the aspirations for growth that are rooted in the business community, convening multiple stakeholders to achieve shared goals and serving as the community's most consistent and effective advocates for economic progress.

Playing Horseshoes vs. Chess: Managing Complexity

Perhaps the most distinguished chamber executive I've known, Charles Herd, led the Louisville, KY Chamber in the 1970s and early 1980s and chaired the Association of Chamber of Commerce Executives (ACCE) in 1979. Being in my 20s at the time and in awe of Mr. Herd, I remember vividly the specific illustration he offered in a speech to our state association of local chambers about the special nature of our task as chamber and community leaders. It was, he said, like playing horseshoes vs. playing chess. When playing horseshoes, almost anyone can step up, swing back and toss a horseshoe toward the opponent's stake. The rules are simple – almost self-evident. Get closest to the stake and you get a point; land a ringer and you get three points. Whoever gets the most points wins.

Chess, on the other hand, is much more complex. You have to know the capabilities of individual pieces (pawns vs. rooks vs. bishops vs. queens). You have to calculate what a particular move will mean in terms of setting up your next move and the one after that. It's a contest of mental focus, anticipation of multiple scenarios and intricate strategy. To make his point about the relevance of chess to the requirements of leading a chamber and, by extension, leading a community, Mr. Herd extended his analogy to the individual chess pieces by associating them with various aspects of community life: a pawn might represent tourism, a rook transportation, other pieces education, health care, recreation, the arts, economic development and so forth. The goal of the game is to "win" economic prosperity and a better quality of life for your community, but getting there is a challenge of constantly surveying the entire board, knowing the distinct capabilities of each piece, assessing your opponent's position, deciding when there is a precise

Chess is much more complex. It's a contest of mental focus, anticipation of multiple scenarios and intricate strategy.

opportunity for a move that gives you a timely advantage toward your goal. The game is not designed to allow all the pieces to move at one time. In the analogous realm of your community, the timing, external forces and scenarios created on the game board dictate when and what kind of opportunities you can seize for your advantage.

Constantly surveying the game board – the community landscape – and where the players are is an essential aspect of a chamber exec's ability to provide leadership for the chamber and, in turn, for the community.

The Consuming Nature of Chamber Leadership

One of the allures of life in Chamber World is the sheer variety – the amazing assortment of experiences and exposure it offers. Your work immerses you in a vast array of community issues and personalities. I've sometimes compared the life of a chamber exec to that of a journalist: Every day is a new assignment to dig into some new corner of the community, meet new people and encounter a new set of issues. Very few occupations offer that assortment of experiences.

That's the good news. The bad news is the other side of that coin: The stimulation of such a wide variety can swallow you up. Virtually every issue that emerges in a community seems to have an implication for the business community, at least according to the advocates for those issues. Someone wants to provide winter coats for school children. Why wouldn't the chamber make that a priority for the business community? The community theater needs to replace worn-out seats. Why wouldn't the chamber exec serve on the campaign committee and solicit prominent businesses in town for a donation? A local businessman believes eighth-graders should understand the concepts of free enterprise and the stock market. Why wouldn't the chamber agree to recruit volunteers from other businesses to teach those principles in middle school classrooms?

Every chamber executive who has served more than a year or two can tell eye-rolling stories about the expectations that come to the doorstep of a chamber and the chamber executive. The chamber is considered by many citizens to be an all-encompassing do-good agency that exists to serve the community and, more specifically, to endorse, embrace and implement the latest great idea that a chamber member – or frequently a non-member – has imagined for the community. Nearly all those issues have some tangential connection to the business community, at least according to the advocates behind those causes. And there is nothing wrong with a chamber getting involved in them, unless they pull the chamber away from things it is better suited to accomplish for a community.

While many of these ideas and proposals can be turned back with a quick and polite bit of guidance, the pressures are non-stop, and there is a constant drumbeat of legitimate ideas that a chamber must wade through to avoid trying to be everything for everybody – the ever-present curse of life in Chamber World. The likelihood of attracting those proposals and the temptation to take on more and more initiatives are inherent to a chamber organization, especially if the chamber is known for its effectiveness and enjoys a prominent profile.

Obviously, some suggestions are good ones. I remember being approached one Sunday at church by a friend of mine – a state Supreme Court justice – who had watched a television show that featured a bluegrass music festival. Why, he asked, didn't our community – located next door to the birthplace of the Father of Bluegrass Music, Bill Monroe – have a bluegrass festival? That seed of an idea com-

> *There is a constant drumbeat of legitimate ideas that a chamber must wade through to avoid trying to be everything for everybody – the ever-present curse of life in Chamber World.*

pelled me to convene an informal lunch at the chamber a few weeks later for four local people loosely connected to the music business. That discussion led to bigger ideas, eventually to a master plan, more success, more growth and now an institution that will figure prominently in the cultural life and the brand identity of the community for decades to come. Today, more than 25 years later, a new $15 million National Bluegrass Music Hall of Fame stands on the riverfront, adjacent to the convention center in my hometown. The seed planted by the judge, watered by the chamber and fed by a separate nonprofit that was created to implement the vision, grew into something much greater than the judge or the chamber initially imagined.

The temptation to take on yet another worthwhile project and the tendency toward mission creep (an ever-expanding interpretation and watering down of the chamber's mission and purpose) are perhaps two of the greatest hazards for a chamber and a chamber exec. A chamber exec who is truly passionate about his/her work in the community will often be inspired multiple times a day to imagine more and take on more. That tendency, if not tempered, can lead to diminished organizational effectiveness, an erosion of the chamber's reputation and burnout of the chamber exec and, perhaps, the organization's volunteers.

Counterbalancing these consuming tendencies requires a solid mission statement – created or at least embraced by the chamber's volunteer leaders – along with a regularly updated long-term strategic plan and annual business plans that define the chamber's goals and objectives and establishes its "to do" list.

Chamber Leadership as an Ideal: Catalytic Leadership

What is the basic function of a chamber executive? Is the person expected to simply perform administrative functions for the organization as mandated by the volunteer leadership or to serve as a dynamic change agent for the community? Is it some combination of those two extremes? Expectations obviously vary from chamber to chamber. A chamber that believes it has been damaged by an overly aggressive, strong-willed and abrasive executive may rebound by hiring someone more docile, someone who is simply expected to follow directions. Or the pendulum may swing in the opposite direction after a period of perceived stagnation.

The term "catalytic leader" has gained traction as the ideal characteristic of the chamber professional, especially after ACCE's exploration of the nature of chamber leadership in its Horizon 2025 project (addressed in more detail in chapter 12). By definition, a catalyst is something added to a mixture of elements to accelerate a chemical change in the mixture. A catalytic chamber leader is someone added to the mix of a chamber and its community to accelerate and improve outcomes. In other words, a catalytic leader is one who adds value and accelerates the process of community growth and development.

> *A catalytic chamber leader is someone added to the mix of a chamber and its community to accelerate and improve outcomes.*

Aspirational Leadership

Clearly, chamber execs with different personalities can be successful, but at the core, a chamber leader must have a strong motivation – to the point of being driven – to find ways for his/her community to be successful. In short, a successful chamber exec is aspirational – a leader who exists in a state that UPS founder Jim Casey called "constructive dissatisfaction," always aspiring to achieve a better tomorrow, waking up in the morning and going to bed at night wanting to accomplish one more thing for the chamber and for the community. Whether that aspiration expresses itself through personal achievement or through carefully managed, behind-the-scenes empowerment of staff and volunteers, an aspirational drive is the fundamental motivation that distinguishes a successful chamber exec.

A fellow chamber executive put it more bluntly. He divided chamber execs into two categories – those who are aspirational and those who are placeholders who don't strive for what is bigger and better. In his view, being aspirational is a personality trait, rooted in a person's basic motivations, rather than a skill; he doubted that aspiration can be learned. I have a somewhat different view. It's my observation that as a chamber professional experiences more, learns more and practices more, aspiration can emerge and gain momentum. Success breeds success and can increase one's appetite for more success.

A successful chamber exec is aspirational – a leader who is always aspiring to achieve a better tomorrow, waking up in the morning and going to bed at night wanting to accomplish one more thing for the chamber and for the community.

Hopefully, the volunteer leaders of a chamber also have an aspirational leaning for their mission and their work. They should be driven by a predisposition that things can and should be made better. They are not mere caretakers of a passive organization; they seek to use the organization as a vehicle for improvement. They want the chamber to become stronger and more effective, and they want to employ a catalytic leader as their CEO to make that happen. If both the chamber and its exec aspire to provide catalytic leadership, the combination creates a grand opportunity to provide bold leadership that can shape their community.

The Servant Leader

Perhaps no concept of leadership describes an effective chamber leader's ideal disposition better than the term "servant leadership." That odd combination of words seems at first to be an oxymoron. While the word servant denotes a level of subservience – perhaps even obedience – the word leadership carries the meaning and gravitas of being in charge and commanding. But putting the two words together provides a rich definition of subtle, nuanced and sophisticated leadership – a concept of providing leadership, not always by marching out front but by articulating a direction and empowering people to move of their own volition toward a mutually accepted goal.

Effective chamber leaders must be able to lead from behind but also able to be out front for the organization and the community when needed. Finding the right balance is critical. While the notion of servant leadership has received a lot of attention in recent years, it is especially relevant in nonprofit and religious settings. Not unlike the role of a minister in a congregation, the chamber leader is expected to perform certain administrative functions and to lead in specific ways. That leadership role will expand and become more prominent as the minister or the chamber executive builds trust, earns respect and becomes known for making sound decisions that don't require oversight and which advance his/her organization's mission.

I remember meeting with my three-member performance review committee and telling them that I depended on them to help me gauge what kind of profile they wanted me to have. I said, "I realize this is not 'The Dave Show'." One of them, the president of a Fortune 500 company, shot back with a friendly, "Hell, I want it to be the 'The Dave Show'! That's what we pay you to do!" The others chimed in with similar comments. While they were generous with their comments, I realized that my profile had to be different in different settings to avoid overstepping my bounds.

The boundaries for a chamber exec's profile are sometimes defined formally, such as in a job description, but are frequently informal and unwritten. Those parameters can unexpectedly change on a dime, and a chamber exec must be able to read the interpersonal subtleties of his/her environment. A person who can't perceive and understand the diverse motivations and desires of individual volunteer leaders will probably have some uncomfortable or even career-threatening situations as a chamber exec.

Being truly dedicated to a cause bigger than oneself – the cause of building an effective chamber and improving one's community – is the best underlying indicator of a true servant leader. Having volunteers, staff, chamber peers, spouses, confidants and family members who will provide candid feedback about how we are perceived can help us calibrate our standing, enhance our roles, sustain our momentum and expand our effectiveness. In a later section on professional development opportunities, I discuss ways to improve self-awareness and strengthen our abilities as servant leaders.

> *Being truly dedicated to a cause bigger than oneself – the cause of building an effective chamber and improving one's community – is the best underlying indicator of a true servant leader.*

"Aggressive Incrementalism" as a Leadership Style

Some chamber execs emerge as strong leaders at a specific point in time when a crisis occurs or some other situation creates a moment in which the chamber exec is called upon to provide bold leadership. Some are most effective in the early months or years of their tenure – during a honeymoon period when they are new, fresh, unblemished by previous battles, and well-positioned to serve as change agents. Still others build their credibility and political capital over time and find their effectiveness gaining momentum as their tenure extends over years or even decades.

External forces have a lot to say about how those opportunities arise or fade over time but clearly a person's leadership abilities play a decisive role as well. In my three chamber CEO positions, I found that the two where I served longer and had years to gain knowledge, experience and more credibility, were the most productive, and I grew into being more effective. On the other hand, the 5 ½ years I spent at the Birmingham Chamber before taking an unanticipated opportunity to return to my home state chamber were, in retrospect, not enough to build the momentum needed to make the significant strides that characterized my other two assignments. On a personal level, Birmingham was an extremely enjoyable professional experience that I was reluctant to leave; I am proud of the accomplishments we made internally by strengthening the chamber and externally in the metro region. But looking back, a longer tenure would have probably produced greater momentum and allowed more signature accomplishments by our chamber.

Having spent more than four decades in and around chambers, I developed a philosophy of chamber leadership I call "aggressive incrementalism." In other words, aggressively and tirelessly pursuing the hundreds of incremental moves needed to achieve greater prosperity for our communities. It was my experience that chamber execs are rarely in a position to create overnight, dramatic changes that alter the course of a community or region. Without the formal authority of elected officials or the armies that military leaders have at their command, our work is more often in the trenches, and our effectiveness increases over a longer term. It's the shoulder-to-the-wheel hard work of building a respected chamber that is prepared to address problems and seize opportunities. It's seeing multiple pieces on the chessboard in front of us, surveying the positions of our opponents and thoughtfully, incrementally advancing our moves. This is not to suggest that we won't orchestrate pivotal accomplishments that forever shape our communities. With hard work over time, we can look back on signature achievements – a

Chamber leadership involves aggressively pursuing the hundreds of incremental moves needed to achieve greater prosperity for our communities.

major new industry, a transformational downtown renaissance or a critical election that sparked an era of progress – that were engineered by the chamber through countless incremental moves.

Chamber Leaders as Civic Entrepreneurs

Much has been made of the role of entrepreneurs in creating businesses and wealth, especially in the Information Age with innovative high-tech solutions to the challenges of commerce. Many chambers routinely recognize their local entrepreneurs based on such factors as conspicuous success and the relative market value of their enterprises. While celebrating business success is clearly appropriate for chambers of commerce, I wonder why the notion of "civic entrepreneur" has not gained comparable status in our communities.

Chamber executives who convene stakeholders to address community issues, who often take high-profile risks to innovate on behalf of their communities and who are actively importing and adapting ideas from other communities for their local situations, are providing the role model for civic entrepreneurism. Everyday citizens – lay leaders in the civic life of a community – can likewise provide amazing civic innovation.

Chamber executives who take high-profile risks to innovate on behalf of their communities and who are actively importing and adapting ideas from other communities are providing the role model for civic entrepreneurism.

When I was mayor of my hometown, I had a college intern in my office who came to me with a bold idea. He had recently visited Memphis and had come back enamored with the decorative, "necklace" lighting on the bridges that spanned the Mississippi River. He thought we should do the same for our 1930s bridge that extended across the Ohio River from our downtown to Indiana.

I loved the idea but, because I was in my fifth or sixth year of office and had pushed the envelope with several beautification and downtown improvement projects, I told him, "If I spend money on one more beautification project, they are going to run me out of town!" I was feeling increasing pushback in the community for such extravagance, and I was essentially vetoing the intern's idea.

He persisted and a few days later asked, "What if we raised the money privately?" I finally relented – tentatively – and suggested he get some sort of cost estimate. Because I had the power of appointments over the local utility board, the general manager agreed (while probably rolling his eyes) to have his engineering department respond to my intern's request. The estimate was $150,000 for the fixtures and wiring, if the utility donated its labor for the installation.

"What? $150,000! There's no way!" was my reaction. But my intern wouldn't take no for an answer. He was too young and idealistic to know what he couldn't do. He came back a week or so later and had a new scheme: sell the bulbs for $500 apiece and let the buyer honor a friend or loved one with their name permanently displayed on a bronze plaque on the riverfront. He topped off his sales pitch by saying he "and his committee" (I'm not sure he had a committee) had decided to name the first bulb in my honor. He presented me with a certificate and thereby bestowed on me the honor of the first bulb. I was impressed and humbled by his approach (manipulative as it was) and responded by writing a personal check for $500, naming the second bulb in honor of my parents.

He worked tenaciously for four years to raise the $150,000 and his amazing persistence paid off. A huge ceremony and fireworks show on New Year's Eve commemorated the ceremonial "flipping of the switch," and the old structure took on a gorgeous new life as an amazing nighttime attraction on the city's riverfront. A young civic entrepreneur had overcome a ton of hurdles, including my pessimism, to improve his community.

I have often thought of that young intern, who later became the marketing manager for the local tourism board and who passed away prematurely in 2019, as someone who would have prospered in the right chamber role at the right time. I wish I could have given him that opportunity to expand his skills as a civic entrepreneur from a position at one of my chambers, but I never had the right opening at the right time. His passions could have blossomed in a chamber environment.

The entrepreneurial skills that characterize many chamber executives (not just CEOs) and many citizen leaders who are driven to civic success should be recognized, celebrated and nurtured. I suggest that chambers lead the way by adding the category of "civic entrepreneur" to their annual awards program and recognize those individuals – from corporate executives to nonprofit leaders to college interns – who push the envelope of progress in their communities and succeed at civic innovation.

■   ■   ■

Chamber executives occupy a unique position within their communities and must be able to adapt to constantly changing circumstances. Motivated by an aspirational drive to improve their communities and the disposition of a servant leader, they can master the "chessboard of community dynamics" and provide catalytic leadership that gains momentum over time. Rarely is a chamber leader in a position to simply flip a switch and make immediate progress occur. But with a forward-leaning determination and an aggressive, passionate approach to their work, they can incrementally build their chambers and help shape their communities for decades to come. They are uniquely positioned to become models of civic entrepreneurism.

CHAPTER 2
THE PERSONALITY OF A CHAMBER LEADER

The stereotypical notion of a chamber exec is someone who is a gregarious, ever-optimistic civic booster who can comfortably interact with the business elite and the community's powerbrokers. But for every chamber exec that fits that description, there is a successful exception. Is there a set of common personal attributes that characterize a chamber executive? Is it possible to create a personality profile of a successful chamber leader?

Common Attributes

A professional survey of a broad cohort of chamber execs was conducted for ACCE in 2010 by TalentQuest, an Atlanta-based human resources firm. Using the firm's TQ Personality Assessment to compare and correlate selected personality traits among chamber CEOs, TalentQuest drew a set of interesting conclusions about common traits among the

313 participating chamber execs. The nationwide study drew from a broad sample with respondents from small chambers (less than $400,000 budgets), medium chambers ($400,000 to $1 million budgets) and large chambers (more than $1 million budgets).

The ACCE-sponsored survey's most notable finding was that, indeed, many chamber CEOs share common personality attributes and leadership styles.

The survey's most notable finding was that, indeed, many chamber CEOs share common personality attributes and leadership styles. As an overall population, chamber CEOs:

- Demonstrate great flexibility, with an ability to apply situational leadership and to be dominating or accommodating, depending on the circumstances

- Display remarkable social sensitivity

- Structure their organizations methodically and effectively

- Display good balance and flexibility, embodying a leadership style for all seasons

- Embrace an accepting, rather than a tough-minded, leadership style

- Apply a calm, even-keeled approach to problem solving

- Demonstrate a style that is politically skillful and tactful

- Act in a highly conscientious manner

The study also found, on a 1 to 10 scale and with 5.5 representing the midpoint, chamber CEOs are:

- More people-oriented (connecting, comforting) than solitary (cool, detached), with the average CEO being a 6 on the 10 scale, with 10 being completely people-oriented.

- More even-keeled (predictable, resilient) than emotional (uneven, varying mood), with the average almost a 7, with 10 being completely even-keeled.

- More controlling (opinionated, in charge) than passive (submissive, conciliatory), with the average just above a 6, with 10 being completely controlling.

- More gregarious (enthusiastic, exuberant) than subdued (reserved, solemn), with the average approximately a 6, with 10 being highly gregarious.

- More conscientious (follows rules, respects authority) than unconventional (ignores rules, resists authority), with an average of 7, with 10 being completely conscientious. This, by the way, was the personality trait on which the chamber executives scored the "highest" (toward one extreme of the scale), revealing a relatively strong trait.

- More fearless (friendly, talkative, outgoing) than cautious (quiet, socially uncomfortable), with the average almost a 7, with 10 being completely fearless.

- Evenly balanced between feeling-oriented (empathetic, intuitive, artistic) and thinking-oriented (logical, solution-focused), with the average slightly higher than a 5, with 10 being completely feeling-oriented.

- Slightly more accepting (positive view of others) than distrustful (negative view of others), with the average about a 5, leaning slightly toward accepting.

- Slightly more pragmatic (bottom-line, fact-oriented) than conceptual (theoretical, internal focus), with the average a 5, leaning slightly toward pragmatic.

- Evenly balanced between unrevealing (hard to get to know) and self-disclosing (open, easy to read), with the average about a 5.5.

- Slightly more self-confident (self-secure, comfortable) than unsure (prone to worry, insecure), with the average just above 5, leaning toward self-confident.

- Evenly balanced between conservative (prefers established patterns) and change-oriented (open to new ideas), with the average just above a 5.

- More team-oriented (enjoys being part of a group) than independent (prefers to work alone), with the average of about 4.5, with 1 being completely team-oriented.

- More detail-oriented (planful, exacting, precise) than unorganized (procrastinates, cuts corners), with the average a solid 6, and 10 being completely detail-oriented.

- Slightly more easy-going (forgiving, tolerant of others) than restless (easily oriented, quick to judge), with the average about 5, with 1 being very easy-going.

Keep in mind that more than 300 CEOs participated in the survey, and the 1-to-10 scale represented a continuum of extremes with a bell-shaped curve in the middle. Few individuals would register completely at one extreme or the other in these categories. Therefore, an average that is as pronounced as a 7 (more conscientious than unconventional) or nearly a 7 (more even-keeled than emotional) suggests a relatively definitive characteristic of the diverse population of chamber CEOs.

Variances Between Executives of Large and Small Chambers

TalentQuest found several differences in traits between CEOs of larger chambers and CEOs of smaller chambers. "As chamber size increases, CEOs impart highly effective systems and processes to provide organizational stability and efficiency," the report noted. "To increase their scope, they demonstrate an admirable ability to work through other people. Due to the larger size of their organizations, on a practical basis they are limited in their ability to extend a personal touch as frequently as they would like, but rather do so as a 'domino effect' by leveraging their executive team down through the organization. CEOs of smaller chambers prioritize individual relationships and interactions and flourish within one-on-one relationships. With a tighter organizational structure, they are allowed greater opportunity to interact frequently and personally with their constituencies and to approach problems and achieve solutions collectively. The CEOs of smaller chambers are also typically immersed in their community and have a demonstrated passion towards community impact."

Passive vs. Aggressive Personalities

Another, albeit less scientific, way to look at chamber personalities is one I've developed after observing hundreds of chamber executives and their leadership styles. I tend to see chamber leadership styles on a 1-to-10 continuum with 1 being an overly cautious, passive caretaker who is the ever-pleasant steward of the chamber, and 10 being at the other extreme – an aggressive, take-no-prisoners, "my way or the highway" change agent.

In my experience, I did not observe a pure 1 or a pure 10 (they likely would have been fired before I got to know them!), but I saw chamber execs who clearly leaned heavily toward the passive or the aggressive. People who lean heavily toward one extreme or the other are probably the most vulnerable in their positions. A passive, congenial caretaker might last years in a chamber leadership position because he or she is well-liked and because volunteer leaders are often reluctant to invite controversy by challenging the employment of a popular figure in the community. However, over time, and especially if the community goes through an economic downturn, business leaders can become restless and impatient, wondering whether the chamber exec is presiding over a set of feel-good community rituals or providing leadership for an aggressive agenda of economic improvement. I observed more than one capable chamber exec fall victim to a growing tide of dissatisfaction because of an economic slump accompanied by a relatively abrupt change of direction led by local business leaders who were influential enough to cause a chamber board to acquiesce, even if they themselves were not members of the board. A perceived caretaker at the helm of the chamber can quickly become the scapegoat for a community's underperformance.

As an illustration of my 1-to-10 passive-to-aggressive measure of chamber leadership, I remember being told of a very popular and politically dexterous chamber exec who retired after a successful, two-decade career as CEO. During a retirement reception in his honor, an influential corporate leader toasted the retiring exec with a commendation which was subsequently reported in the local newspaper: "Well, he kept us in the black." While the comment was probably a tribute to the faithful stewardship of the CEO and was perhaps offered as a somewhat humorous compliment, I wondered if my career would someday be summarized (and in my mind, demeaned) as merely having kept my chamber "in the black."

Expectations of chamber executives vary as do expectations of chambers. I have found that chambers exist somewhere on a "satisfied vs. hungry" continuum. Some communities don't expect their chambers to be change agents and are satisfied with a steady, relatively passive organization that presents awards each year, provides a favorable spotlight for key business leaders in the community and generally makes the community feel good about itself. On the other hand, some communities hunger for economic improvement and general advancement and look to the

Some communities want a chamber CEO with an ambitious vision, an aggressive set of strategies and leadership skills that can make the right things happen. And they expect results.

chamber as the vehicle for achieving those goals. They want a chamber CEO with an ambitious vision, an aggressive set of strategies and leadership skills that can make the right things happen. And they expect results.

A chamber having an aggressive agenda and a chamber CEO having an aggressive personality can be very different things. I observed more than one chamber CEO with an aggressive personality fall victim to local political forces that resisted unilateral assertiveness by the chamber exec. There are former chamber CEOs who assumed their new positions and prospered during an early honeymoon, only to be terminated within the first year because of clumsy missteps that ran afoul of cultural norms or local influence structures such as "old money" or entrenched political bosses.

An overly aggressive chamber executive who doesn't understand political boundaries, doesn't have the finesse to navigate political complexities, or presumes to have the authority to act unilaterally can run into an influential business leader, a powerful mayor or some other immovable force that causes a train wreck for the CEO and for the organization. On the other hand, a more passive chamber exec who merely enjoys the title, basking in the limelight, being in the know about community affairs, and receiving a comfortable paycheck robs the organization and the community of countless opportunities.

A Win-Win Disposition

Successful chamber execs are leaders that favor win-win outcomes rather than a zero-sum, "somebody's gotta lose for somebody else to win" competition. An effective chamber leader must be able to make order out of chaos without being dictatorial. For example, a capable chamber leader who facilitates a board retreat or a town hall meeting where random ideas are thrown out like candy at a Christmas parade will work to accommodate the wide variety of ideas that are put forward and develop a workable plan from the input or place the ideas aside delicately. Such an exec is careful to express the value of all the ideas while shaping, trimming, combining or restating them in a way that ensures the next steps become apparent and gain consensus.

Successful chamber execs are leaders that favor win-win outcomes rather than a zero-sum, "somebody's gotta lose for somebody else to win" competition.

Certainly not every idea is worth pursuing. However, if a chamber leader can identify a valuable kernel within the idea, perhaps that kernel can be embraced. More than anything, the chamber leader must be confident in his/her own position and inclined toward finding ways for everyone in a process to win instead of one group or one individual winning over the others.

I remember participating in an intriguing simulation game during an AT&T executive leadership training program. A facilitator described the rules of the game. Each participant was assigned to a team and given a specific role to play on the team. Each team, representing a different wholesale egg broker, was trying to sell its commodity – its eggs – at the Chicago Board of Trade. The entire setup of the game implied that it was a competitive exercise, with each team seemingly encouraged to outsmart the other teams to get the maximum price for its inventory of eggs. Suspicion and secrecy ruled the group dynamic, but we were instructed that our teams were allowed to privately pose written questions to the facilitator. After an extended period of strategizing within our team but with little progress toward our goal, one of our team members decided to ask the facilitator if our team could communicate with another team. Surprisingly, the facilitator said, "Sure!" No one else had thought of that possibility. It took someone thinking outside the box, considering options other than those explicitly prescribed or subtly implied by the facilitator, to break through the assumed paradigm of the game. Soon after communicating with the other teams, a plan emerged whereby everyone could win the game by cooperating and staging the timing of the sales in a way that allowed everyone to profit more as a group than if one team won and the others lost. We ended up creating an egg cartel so we could all win!

The egg broker exercise had a profound effect on me; I still remember the basic concept and the fundamental lesson of the exercise more than twenty years later. Often collaboration with other self-interested parties can produce a win-win result that is greater than the sum of the parts. In other words, collaboration can often produce dramatically better results than competition or a solo performance.

I've known individuals whose basic personality seemed to dictate that others around them had to lose in order for them to win. They were competitive to a fault and weren't self-confident enough to drop their turf-protecting instincts long enough to imagine an entire group winning. This seems especially true with some partisan politicians; their success seems predicated on the setbacks of the other team (the opposing party). A chamber exec oriented toward getting results is often in an excellent position to bring together conflicting interests and find ways for everyone to win – or at least achieve a satisfactory outcome. Having a bone-deep inclination, disposition and reputation for producing win-win solutions is an effective trait of many successful chamber executives.

■ ■ ■

There appear to be common personality traits that characterize successful chamber executives, and most chamber execs demonstrate relatively moderate personalities. People with personalities that are considered more extreme are unlikely to fit well in a chamber culture. Even if someone with a personality that has sharp edges makes it through a hiring process, that person is unlikely to survive very long as they begin to clash with strong personalities in the community or within their own organizations. Having the self-confidence to let others win and share in success allows chamber execs to gather input from many sources and channel it toward win-win outcomes.

CHAPTER 3
THE SKILL SET OF A CHAMBER LEADER

Can anyone run a chamber? Or are there certain skills that are required of or associated with successful chamber leaders? What is the skill set that chamber board members look for when hiring a chamber executive?

Can Anyone Run a Chamber?

I have occasionally noticed a casual, seemingly dismissive attitude of some civic volunteers toward the special demands of managing a chamber – an incorrect assumption that anyone can run a chamber of commerce. This often comes into vivid focus during a search for a new executive director or president of a chamber. Business people, who if serving on a search committee for their local congregation wouldn't think of hiring a pastor without a theological education and a minimum set of public-speaking skills, sometimes fail to recognize the unique set of leadership skills that will be required to lead their chamber – and more important – help lead their community. Sometimes these volunteer leaders who make highly calculated decisions about matching talented leaders with specialized openings in their own companies seem to approach the chamber search with a more casual attitude of, "Who can we get to take this job?" Rather than considering their choice to be a critical decision about the future of their community and weighing how they can invest in their community by attracting the greatest amount of leadership talent – the horsepower – they can afford, they mentally scan the community for enthusiastic civic boosters who are available on the job market. Perhaps they enlist a recent retiree who accepts the chamber position as a transition to full retirement, or they select a political crony or family member they want to reward with the position. Instead of trying to purchase the maximum amount of horsepower available in the marketplace of leadership talent, they settle for someone they think can hold down the job, provide basic administrative functions and not sink the ship.

Sometimes volunteer leaders who make highly calculated decisions about matching talented leaders with specialized openings in their own companies seem to approach the chamber search with a more casual attitude of, "Who can we get to take this job?"

Sadly, some chambers go for years without noticing that they have been in caretaker mode instead of insisting on vision, goals, hard work and success. I observed communities that were ostensibly hungry for economic and social progress but apparently failed to translate that desire into insistence on a high-functioning chamber of commerce. How can a community that complains about not getting its share of success and prosperity go for years with a passive, go-along-get-along chamber of commerce? How can a community whose leaders openly campaign for economic progress be satisfied that their chamber is primarily known for its annual awards dinner?

This disconnect between the relatively high caliber of business talent typically represented on chamber boards of directors and the sometimes low expectations for their chamber executive is puzzling and, to those of us in the chamber profession and the organizations we serve, troubling. As chamber leaders and leaders within our profession, we have to ask ourselves: How do we strengthen the reputation of our work in the eyes of the business leaders who serve on our boards and have ownership of our organizations?

If a chamber nominating committee for selecting officers and directors is the most important committee for defining the next year or two of the organization, a chamber search committee selecting a new CEO is probably the most important committee for defining the next decade or two. Naturally, a search committee is going to collect and compare applications and go through the process of elimination, but it should also make a focused effort to look beyond the stack of applicants. Who can they identify that is not looking to make a professional move but who might have the unique leadership traits that could benefit the chamber and the community?

A search committee should ask, "Can we get lucky?" In other words, is there a scenario where we could attract more talent and horsepower than we could normally afford? Is there a chamber executive in another community who is originally from the area and would personally benefit by relocating closer to home – to be near children, grandchildren or aging parents? Perhaps we could find a trailing spouse who has just moved to our community and who is uniquely talented and experienced. Perhaps a highly qualified local school superintendent is ready for a different professional challenge and has a pension that a chamber salary will supplement comfortably. There is a vast amount of retired talent on the market across the country. Baby boomers are retiring in droves – to the tune of more than 10,000 per day in the U.S. Perhaps a native son or daughter who has built a substantial career and comfortable financial base elsewhere takes early retirement and wants to return home. Maybe, due to timing and circumstance, the chamber search committee can get lucky and recruit an outstanding new exec.

There are pros and cons to hiring someone from outside the chamber profession, and there seem to be as many success stories as there are disappointments for communities that do so. While it can be tempting to recruit from outside the chamber ranks, there are significant downside risks. There exist widely different cultures in various workplaces (universities, corporations, family-owned businesses, the military, government agencies) and just because someone has been a successful bank officer or a business professor at the local university doesn't necessarily make him/her a good fit for a chamber. I've seen people from the broader business and civic worlds take a chamber position and quickly become completely overwhelmed with the pace and the volunteer-led culture of a chamber of commerce.

Reporting to a set of volunteers who expect you to lead but are not bashful about stating their expectations and latest ideas for the community can present a difficult and sometimes insurmountable challenge for someone who has been in a more formal chain-of-command corporate, military or bureaucratic structure. The level of transparency required of chambers can be difficult to navigate. It can be an alarming cultural shift for someone who has never encountered a reporter determined to get a juicy story or who has not been the subject of a front-page newspaper article or social media barrage. It can be embarrassing for chamber board leaders if a high-profile executive search process results in hiring someone from outside the chamber business, only to find a few months later that things aren't working out and a distasteful separation becomes necessary.

Unique Characteristics of Chamber Leaders

The requirements of being a leader certainly change with time and with circumstances. Having spent more than forty years observing leaders and specifically chamber leaders in different situations, I have a general philosophy about leadership in a chamber context. I subscribe to the notion that leaders are the products of both *nature* (born with certain innate capabilities that allow them to navigate the complexities of personalities, issues, complex tasks, etc.) and *nurture* (acquiring certain skills through formal education, professional development and accumulated experience).

In addition to the influences of nature and nurture, I subscribe to the zeitgeist theory of leadership which is based on 18th-century German philosophy and which generally refers to "the spirit (geist) of the times (die zeit)". In other words, external circumstances create a vacuum in which uniquely qualified leaders emerge and to some extent, are made. Think of Abraham Lincoln – a president considered by many to be a lanky and awkward buffoon (terms used by some in his own party) during his first two years in the White House. However, the Civil War created an environment in which his unique traits of morality, stubbornness and compassion were called to the test and through which the unfolding exigencies created a leader who now holds a central position in the American pantheon of political leaders. Or, in a second instance, consider the extent to which the 20th century racist culture of America and various social forces such as Black soldiers returning from WWII created the seismic cultural disruption to which the Rev. Martin Luther King, Jr. gave voice. Both Lincoln and King were talented, educated and brilliant men who became truly great leaders because of the convergence of the cultural currents of their times.

A perceptive and astute chamber leader who is capable of reading the needs of his/her community as

Leaders are the products of nature, nurture and zeitgeist.

they evolve and through unfolding circumstances is better positioned to adapt and serve the community in profound ways. The election of a new mayor, the announcement of a major new employer, the loss of a major employer, a local scandal that emerges in full public view, the sudden death of the community's most respected leader, the unexpected bequest of millions of dollars to the local community foundation – all are events that shape a community and form the zeitgeist in which leaders adapt and emerge.

Traits and Skills Chamber Boards Expect

Chamber execs feel the day-to-day pressure to live up to board members' expectations and often wonder if those expectations are sometimes out of sync with the reality of managing the organization. It's important to have a realistic understanding of what board members expect in order to meet or at least manage those expectations.

Ali Crain, IOM, CCE, a former executive director of Kentucky's association of local chambers, explored the issue of a possible disconnect between volunteer chamber leaders and chamber execs as part of her master's thesis at Northern Kentucky University in 2015. She surveyed 138 board members and nearly 100 chamber execs in an effort to identify how the two groups differed in their perceptions of the executive position. Her laudable research produced some interesting and valuable results for chamber execs.

As she reported in an article for ACCE's Spring 2016 "Chamber Executive" magazine, one of the starkest differences was that most chamber executives (77%) believe it is important for the chamber leader to be a change agent, while less than half of board members (42%) think being a change agent is an important characteristic. Does that imply that board members want their execs to focus on minding the shop rather than shaking things up?

Most chamber executives believe it is important for the chamber leader to be a change agent, while less than half of board members think that is important.

While some attributes, such as being approachable and having the ability "to empower and engage," received nearly unanimous ratings from both groups, there were also remarkable differences. Just 62% of board members think it's important for the exec to be influential, compared to 84% of execs. Only 56% of board members think it's important for the exec to be a trend watcher, while 77% of execs think that is important. On the other hand, 71% of board members thought the ability to manage the advocacy process was important while fewer execs, 57%, considered that an important skill.

Predictably, there are major differences in expectations between chambers that differ in size, scope and mission. For example, a state or metro chamber board is probably going to put a much greater emphasis on advocacy skills than a small town chamber with a staff of one, while the ability to sell memberships (to generate revenue and keep the doors open) might be considered critical for a smaller chamber.

These differing expectations pose an important challenge for chamber executives: Do we need to educate our board members about what it takes to effectively manage a chamber, or do we need to listen more closely to our leaders and adapt to their expectations? I suggest it's both. If we are over-confident that we possess the right mix of leadership skills needed for the job, and we're waiting for our board members to come to that realization, we risk resistance from our volunteer leaders. If, on the other hand, our volunteer leaders hold unrealistic expectations for our performance (e.g. in recruiting new members), we risk coming up short and causing ourselves headaches or worse. Listening to our board – REALLY listening (as discussed more fully in Chapter 5) – is critical for bringing those differences into sync and for attaining long-term success.

As I privately discussed my retirement plans with my board chairman months before we decided to make the plans public, he asked me to compile a list of the traits I consider necessary for a chamber executive (in this case, a state chamber executive) to be successful. The list of traits I offered him and eventually passed on to the executive search firm that was chosen to help identify my successor is included here.

Consider whether you agree with these and if not, to what extent you would suggest other traits.

1. **Social Intelligence/Political Instincts.** The ability to read situations, interact comfortably with people, forge authentic relationships and motivate other people (partners, policymakers, staff) to accomplish goals.

2. **Administrative Ability.** Sufficient attention to detail to run the shop, including overseeing finance, developing a high-performing team, etc.

3. **Aptitude to Manage Policy Work.** The basic intellectual capacity to comprehend and communicate policy solutions, both internal to the chamber and external for the state.

4. **Work Ethic/Horsepower.** The basic drive to work hard and to achieve exceptional results on multiple fronts. A strong motivation to strive to go to the next level while managing the day-to-day necessities of running a small business (a chamber of commerce).

5. **Communication.** A keen sense of translating "state government talk" (in policy, politics, bureaucracy) for Main Street audiences.

   a. Written. The ability to produce finished documents for publication and other distribution.

   b. Oral. The ability to communicate ideas in various settings such as legislative testimony, speeches to local chambers, television interviews, chamber board meetings and other situations.

6. **Executive Presence.** The ability to represent the chamber as a credible spokesperson in a variety of formal and informal settings.

7. **Appetite for the Political Arena.** The personal eagerness to follow on a daily basis the personalities and events that shape

state and national politics and which create the reality in which the chamber operates.

8. **Catalytic Leadership.** The ability to position the chamber as a respected catalyst for building positive momentum.

9. **Ability to Lead from Behind.** The ability to combine the ideas, personalities and distinct agendas of chamber members, board members and other constituents into a coherent strategy for progress. The willingness to serve in both a subservient role of reporting to a large board while also providing leadership for that board and the organization.

10. **Backbone.** The ability to stand up, when required, to intense pressure from elected officials, other trade groups or demanding chamber investors who attempt to influence the chamber for their own purposes.

11. **Vision.** The ability to facilitate the processes of planning and articulating a coherent, collective vision for the chamber, for the broader business community and for the state.

I would certainly alter this list to some extent for a local or regional chamber exec. And since creating my list, I would add:

12. **Fundraising Ability.** If a chamber expects to grow in the foreseeable future, this skill is essential. The trends associated with fundraising – distinct from selling memberships and soliciting sponsorships – became very clear to me in the last few years at the Kentucky Chamber (see Chapter 8 regarding chamber foundations). I wish I had seen them earlier.

Also, I would add the ability to manage:

13. **Governance.** Matters of governance include board and committee affairs, the nominating process, the bylaws and internal policies relating to how the organization governs itself.

In the volunteer-led world of nonprofit management, governance issues are absolutely critical, and if not carefully executed can quickly lead to organizational chaos and professional jeopardy for the exec.

In the volunteer-led world of nonprofit management, governance issues are absolutely critical, and if not carefully executed can quickly lead to organizational chaos and professional jeopardy for the exec.

While each of us would probably offer a different version of critical or important traits, I think we would agree that there are some traits that are important for navigating the daily challenges of managing a chamber of commerce.

The Top Functions of a Chamber CEO

Another way to view the skills required of a chamber CEO is to consider the basic job functions expected of that person. Former ACCE President Mick Fleming offers the following list and challenges CEOs as well as volunteer board members to rank them for their relative importance to their chamber at their particular time:

_____ Attracting, organizing and leading a motivated staff

_____ Finance and administration

_____ Fundraising of all kinds (including membership)

_____ Communications (writing, marketing, PR & presence)

_____ Formulation and articulation of policies and ideas

_____ Governance (board & committee relations)

_____ Relationship and partnership management (allies)

_____ Member relations, casework (problem-solving)

_____ Attraction and retention of employers & talent

_____ Identifying and understanding regional priorities

Good Judgment – the Essence of Sound Decision-making

Good judgment is perhaps the most important skill for success in a chamber leadership role – the ability to make sound decisions on a daily basis and in a variety of circumstances. A chamber exec is usually rewarded (employed, compensated, recognized, promoted, recruited for higher positions) because of a successful track record that includes but goes beyond dependable management of the organization. Building such a track record involves making dozens of decisions each day, from the mundane to the pivotal, and most of those decisions need to be good ones. From how you greet the spouse of a board member at the mall, to how you balance the chamber's budget, to how you articulate a future for your community when speaking to the city council, your board and your community expect sound judgment. It's the ability to demonstrate good judgment in a public setting as well as making sound internal management decisions. The greater your responsibilities and the more senior you are in your career, the more professionalism is expected in terms of solid decision-making, public presentations, personal appearance, and even private conversations.

How does one develop sound judgment? The ability to see a challenge from multiple angles is essential. The inability to see those angles is dangerous and could eventually be career-threatening. If, for example, you face the challenge of purchasing a new piece of expensive software for your organization, and you only evaluate the issue from a financial point of view – preparing specs, putting out a request for proposals and accepting the lowest bid – you have ignored several important angles: the technology angle (is the software at the end of its lifecycle and won't be supported by the vendor after another year?), the political angle (your incoming board chair owns a software company that submitted a competing bid), the human resources angle (your office manager doesn't want to change software, was left out of the decision process and is probably going to balk at having to implement the changes to the system), and an organizational angle (you are within six months of deciding whether to sign a management contract with your convention bureau, an organization which has not invested in software for more than five years). In other words, any of these additional issues could destroy your otherwise good financial decision. A chamber executive has to be able to see a challenge from multiple angles, not just the one that initially necessitates a decision.

The ability to see a challenge from multiple angles is essential. The inability to see those angles is dangerous and could eventually be career-threatening.

This requirement to consider various perspectives is sometimes what makes it difficult for someone to successfully adapt to the CEO role after being promoted from a specialized position such as CFO, director of membership sales or vice president of governmental affairs. After spending several years thinking of the organization from a specific viewpoint and being rewarded for success in that silo of the organization, taking a broader view of the implications of decisions doesn't always come naturally. It will have to be consciously developed.

I had the pleasure of working with young staffers – some of whom I now proudly consider protégés – who had great potential and solid political instincts for doing great things as chamber execs but who needed a few years of experience, taking the slings and arrows that would hone their judgment and their ability to navigate the political minefield of chamber life. This can be especially critical for someone taking a career step from being the number two person to the CEO spot or coming from outside the chamber arena. That person may have observed the minefield but not faced the challenge of making decisions in real-time to avoid the landmines and having to live with the consequences and the resulting stress.

The "80/95 Rule" for Making Sound Decisions

To attempt to make sound decisions at my chamber, I employed and encouraged my senior team to use what I called my "80/95" rule. It goes something like this: If I'm good at making the day-to-day decisions required of my position by myself – and I mean *really* good – I may achieve 80% good decisions out of the dozens of big and small decisions I have to make every day. If, however, I collaborate on major decisions with trusted people around me (fellow staff, peers in the business, personal confidants, trusted officers of my chamber board), I can lift my percentage for making sound decisions to 95% because those people can smooth the rough edges of my ideas, help polish my decision-making and help me avoid my blind spots.

An example: When I was in my mid-twenties and still relatively new to Chamber World, I attended an international food festival in Louisville and came back to my hometown with the idea of creating an annual food festival. We had a two-century tradition of annual barbecue picnics at Catholic parishes that featured a unique delicacy – barbecued mutton – and which had given birth to about a dozen barbecue restaurants in our relatively small city. From that set of circumstances, we came up with the idea that we should create a barbecue festival. With a lot of hard work and persistence, that's what we did. Now more than 40 years later, the International Bar-B-Q Festival, created by a chamber task force and later spun off as a separate nonprofit, draws tens of thousands of people to the riverfront each spring and is solidly established as the community's signature annual festival. Brilliant idea, right?

If I collaborate on major decisions with trusted people around me (fellow staff, peers in the business, personal confidants, trusted officers of my chamber board), I can lift my percentage for making sound decisions to 95%.

Actually, no, not really. While the basic idea of a barbecue festival that capitalized on a strong community tradition was apparently a good one, I had naively assumed that the dozen barbecue restaurants in town could be convinced to construct temporary barbecue pits on the riverfront and compete against each other for annual cooking honors and bragging rights in several categories (chicken, mutton, pork and a regional stew called burgoo). Fortunately, the first person other than my wife who I approached with the idea was a friend whose family owned the famously successful Moonlite Bar-B-Q Inn. He knew from his experience that the other restaurants would not be eager – or willing – to put their reputations and their competitive positions in the local restaurant market on the line with one annual, outdoor cooking frenzy. There would be too much reputational risk for their businesses. My friend had a better idea: have the dozen or more Catholic parishes from across our county build temporary pits downtown, compete for honors, sell their barbecue from their pits and raise money for their parish schools. The restaurants, meanwhile, would set up booths and sell barbecue sandwiches to the crowd while the parishes were cooking their open-pit barbecue – a process that requires slowly cooking meat throughout the night and most of the following day.

My friend's better idea actually turned my idea – which would have been a non-starter – into a fabulously successful idea and birthed a colorful tradition for my home community – one that we hope our children and their children will carry on for the next century. He helped me get from less than 80% to 95% in terms of sound judgment. As I made many other decisions that involved any level of complexity throughout my career, I routinely involved my senior staff or an appropriate chamber working group to improve my odds for success from below 80% to 95%.

A few years ago, tax reform was a politically hot topic in our state. When the governor released his tax reform package, the newspapers immediately wanted the reaction of the business community and a few advocacy groups. Our chamber's public reaction would be important because it would help frame the debate, our members would be curious about the chamber's stance, the radical left and radical right would probably attack our relatively mainstream position and, because we were addressing the sensitive topic of taxes, we risked alienating some of our constituencies and even losing some of our members. I was out of state at a chamber conference but drafted a two-paragraph response and emailed it to three people (two public affairs staff and one of our policy consultants) who were involved in the issue. One of them offered a substantially altered version (which initially irritated me), another of them slightly revised the first one's statement and I finally tweaked it a little to finalize our media response. Looking back on it, the final statement was substantially better and served us better during the ensuing debates than my off-the-cuff response would have been. We went from less than 80% to 95%.

I feel very fortunate that I had people around me whose collective judgment I usually trusted more than my own. There were some occasions when, as CEO I had to make the final decision, sometimes overriding the collective input I had received from my team. But having a collaborative support system is essential to making sound decisions day after day and issue after issue and frankly, for surviving – certainly for thriving – in the chamber business.

Ethical Leadership

Debating matters of morality is as old as civilization. Attempts to define ethical standards certainly predate the day Moses descended from Mount Sinai with his stone tablets and the ten basic do's and don'ts. Questions of ethics, once the province of philosophers, preachers and parents, now line the bookshelves of business school libraries and help frame decision-making in fields ranging from medical science to the development of genetically

Questions of ethics, once the province of philosophers, preachers and parents, now line the bookshelves of business school libraries and help frame decision-making in a wide variety of fields – including chambers.

modified seed corn and from the use of artificial intelligence to the privacy issues swirling around social media conglomerates.

So, what can we add to the discussion that distinguishes the ethical dilemmas of chamber professionals from any other set of moral principles? Is there anything unique that defines proper conduct in Chamber World compared to other professional fields? Having spent several years of my undergraduate and graduate studies immersed in this particular field of study and more than forty years in and around chambers of commerce, I'll simply offer the following set of possible pitfalls that can be dangerous for a chamber exec – in other words, a few don'ts.

- Self-dealing. Using the advantages of one's chamber position to benefit oneself, one's family or one's close associates can be inherently unethical and problematic, can create the appearance of questionable behavior and sow seeds of doubt about one's professionalism. While some obvious examples such as renting space in your family's downtown building for the chamber office or fudging an expense report might be ethical no-brainers, it's often easy to justify a self-interested action with "Hey, my family's old building downtown was cheaper than anything else available." It is often the gray areas, not the obvious black-and-white infractions that escape our notice. Filing inflated expense reports, accepting gifts or favors, hiring a relative or subtlety working to bring friends onto your board who won't challenge your position, can become problems if they create questions, stir rumors, cast doubt or otherwise injure your reputation for fairness, objectivity and personal commitment to the chamber.

- Self-aggrandizement. Using your position to increase your profile, gain notoriety, grab the spotlight, improve your social status in the community or see yourself on TV are not egregious acts of criminal behavior. But if they are perceived by your multiple audiences (board, staff, members, local elected officials) to reflect a self-serving motivation or appear to be the way you generally operate, they will breed resentment and undercut your personal credibility and professional standing.

- Moonlighting. Whether it is running a company on the side, playing in a jazz combo that hires out for weddings, serving on the board of a local enterprise that has competitors in your chamber membership or serving on the town council, extra-curricular situations can create direct conflicts or send signals that you are distracted and less than totally committed to your chamber. Even if such arrangements are approved by a chairman or a full board, perceptions can take hold over time and problems can emerge unexpectedly because of the perception of split loyalties or biased decisions. Being perceived as a neutral party whose only interest is advancing the chamber and the community builds trust and respect among those around you.

- Confidentiality. A chamber professional doing serious work to advance the community will likely be exposed to privileged information that will be of interest to others in the community. It is important to be professional in holding and processing information that could create advantages or disadvantages for certain chamber members. Whether it's an economic development deal or a private conversation with a city council member or legislator about how an issue is evolving, being able to protect private information is essential in the chamber arena. Just like a banker who doesn't discuss a customer's financial dealings or a doctor who by law must protect personal health information, there is often privileged information that accompanies advocacy efforts, economic development projects and other chamber initiatives.

- The Blind Spots. I'm convinced that even the most fastidious adherent to professional standards often develops blind spots – areas of self-interest that we don't or can't detect. It might be our children, our financial situation, our spouse or a dear high school friend to whom we show favor in ways that are seemingly innocent but might be conspicuous and appear ethically challenged to those around us. How do we notice what we don't notice? If our judgment is clouded by our affiliations and relationships, how do we detect those sensitivities and avoid pitfalls? We all need outside feedback from trusted allies and friends who will be honest with us and to whom we will listen.

- Lacking a Feedback Loop. For those of us who are married or have a significant other, having these people in our lives is critical. Likewise, having a close working relationship with our top chamber officers – a relationship in which we actively solicit candid input on key decisions – is also essential for feedback on work-related issues. For example, when the lease on my chamber-provided SUV came up and I was selecting a new vehicle, a wise board chairman helped me see the negative optics of selecting a luxury-brand replacement (which happened to be priced below my previous vehicle's direct replacement) at a time when the CEOs of four other nearby nonprofit and governmental agencies were making front page news over questionable details of their expense accounts, use of credit cards at high-end restaurants and bonuses they had received. Now was not the time, my friend and board chairman suggested, to draw attention to what might appear to be excessive spending, even though our chamber was financially solid and enjoying conspicuous success.

Perhaps no one would have complained or said a word, but unspoken perceptions can turn dangerous if they snowball into a perfect storm of criticism that suddenly engulfs the chamber exec. Honest, objective and candid feedback from family or close associates can help expose our blind spots and allow us to avoid them.

Responsiveness

Responsiveness is a basic requirement for chamber professionals. If it is not a genetically embedded personality trait, it will need to be developed as a skill and habit. If it isn't, the deficiency can become job-threatening. Responsiveness to a variety of constituencies – board members, the media and political leaders, to name a few – is a fundamental component for building trust and confidence in one's professionalism.

Responsiveness is not the same as subservience and certainly not synonymous with obedience, but listening to people – especially to your multiple bosses – and getting back to them promptly with a respectful response is expected by chamber volunteers, reporters, elected officials, chamber members and your staff.

> Responsiveness to a variety of constituencies – board members, the media and political leaders, to name a few – is a fundamental component for building trust and confidence in one's professionalism.

I told my staff that if one of our key leaders asked me a question or made a suggestion and I failed to follow up, the volunteer probably made an unconscious mental note that "Dave didn't get back to me." It probably wasn't a big deal. The second time I dropped the ball with that person, she/he probably detected a trend and made a more conscious mental note that "Dave is preoccupied in his own world and doesn't consider me important enough to get back to me." If it happened a third time, the leader was probably irritated enough to mention it to another chamber volunteer. That's how negative chatter starts to spread. If that person happens to be one of your key officers or on your performance review committee, you've just cost yourself part of an annual bonus or triggered an admonition in your review. At some point, that negative vibe can snowball and become a significant problem.

After giving a pep talk about responsiveness at a monthly lunch, our senior vice president for administration sent a very constructive follow-up memo to the entire staff and noted that, in a fast-paced organization like ours, we all need reminders occasionally on workplace etiquette. She offered these seven well-stated points about expectations for follow-up and follow-through at our chamber:

1. When a request is made by a co-worker at any level, make a note of the request and don't let it fall off your list. Use whatever system works for you. Task Manager in Outlook or marking emails for follow-up is a great way to keep track. Your goal should be that the person requesting something from you doesn't have to wonder whatever happened to the request or have to ask a second time.

2. If a deadline was not given, ask for one.

3. If you need clarification, ask for it.

4. If you need help prioritizing, ask your supervisor for help.

5. If you cannot meet the deadline at any point, let the requestor know and ask if another deadline will meet that person's need.

6. If the task requires you assigning it to someone else or requesting information from a third party, you should make a note to follow-up with the third party. It's your responsibility to get a response so you can complete the task assigned. Don't ever let "they didn't get back to me" be your excuse for not getting something done.

7. We have a written personnel policy that any request or email be answered within 24 hours, but research shows that especially with e-communications, people expect answers much sooner (same day). Bottom line: Don't leave the other person guessing about the status of his/her request.

My own method of keeping up with requests was to make a note. With some staff members who had earned my trust with crisp follow-through, I knew I could cross the to-do item off my list when I handed it off to them. With others, I left it on my list to remind me to ask them about follow-through. As I bluntly stated to my senior team, when I had to ask them or their team members a second time for a response, my conscious or unconscious impression meant that person's professional reputation had gone down a notch or two. That wasn't meant to be punitive; it's just human nature to notice others' patterns of behavior and draw conclusions about dependability.

Knowing you can't get back to all requests immediately, prioritizing your responses becomes a necessity. Everyone has to develop his/her own hierarchy for responding to requests – a process that requires a fairly cold, dispassionate approach. Your board chairman's phone call gets priority over a general member, the CEO of a top investor company gets priority over a salesperson who is calling about website design, and the mayor takes priority over a staff member wanting to discuss his/her parking space. In my various chambers and while in public office, I always prioritized reporters' calls because they are generally asking questions for an audience of thousands of readers, it's an opportunity to get our message out, and reporters are generally on deadline. I embraced the news media – even when I was irritated with an individual reporter for pressing a preconceived angle on a story – and those positive relationships, over time, served my chambers and me relatively well.

Spinning Plates

Time management for a chamber executive involves unique challenges and deserves special attention. I use the term "spinning plates" by recalling the classic stunt on old TV variety shows in which a performer spins plates that are balanced on top of metal rods, constantly rushing from one to the other to give them another spin and to avoid having any of the plates crash to the floor. Chamber life involves a lot of plates.

If you can imagine an occupation that involves doing one monotonous job for an entire eight-hour shift, day after day and think of it as 1 on a scale of 1-to-10 – with 10 being a job in which no task is ever repeated and every day is different – chamber management would probably land at 7 or 8. Sure, there are repetitive chamber tasks such as preparing agendas for board meetings, but there is also a reality to chamber life that no two days are the same. Different projects, personalities and external demands constantly rewrite the to-do lists of a chamber exec, creating never-ending variety and special challenges to keep spinning plates.

On a scale of 1-to-10 – with 10 being a job in which no task is ever repeated and every day is different – chamber management would probably land at 7 or 8.

It doesn't matter whether you carry a pocket calendar or use the customized ringtones on your smartphone as reminders as long as you have a system that works for you. The swirl of activities and responsibilities in chamber life is so intense, everyone needs a system to remember the tasks that require attention and to be consistently dependable, punctual and able to sift through the noise of time-consuming chamber responsibilities and distractions. We have to be able to focus on the most urgent and follow up on even the mundane items that have a deadline. Chamber execs have to be comfortable spinning many plates or the demands will eventually exhaust even the best of managers.

The 50/50 Reality of Keeping the Doors Open

Based on my experience at several chambers, I estimate that it takes roughly 50% of a chamber exec's time to keep the doors of the chamber open – to do the necessary tasks just to keep the organization running.

If that rough estimate is truly the case, it theoretically frees up the other 50% of your time and mental energy for moving the community forward.

Occasionally during my career, I tracked my time, by project and by task. I kept such notes as: Attended a City Council meeting – 90 minutes. Met with board chair – 60 minutes. Drafted board meeting agenda – 30 minutes. Talked to governor's staff about upcoming news conference at our chamber – 30 minutes. Breakfast with key investor to solicit sponsorship – 75 minutes. Met with downtown design team to consider City Hall presentation – 90 minutes. Conducted annual performance evaluation of governmental affairs director – 60 minutes. Phone call with prospective new employer about workforce availability – 30 minutes.

After I tracked my time for a month or so, I assigned each task and the time involved to either an administrative column labeled "internal" (the time it takes to run the chamber and keep the doors open) or to a column labeled "external" (the work designed to move the community forward). Of course, the tasks didn't all fit neatly in one column or the other. However, in broad terms, I came to the conclusion that as much as I tried to minimize the routine and sometimes tedious internal chores of running a chamber, I struggled to keep those duties from consuming more than 50% of my time. Conversely, I had to work diligently and mindfully to free up the other 50% of my time to do what I really enjoyed doing – and what I think my chamber really wanted me to do: Focus on trying to create progress for the community.

I was once asked to serve as the president/CEO of my hometown chamber and simultaneously as president of our economic development agency while keeping in place the two separate organizations, their boards of directors, their budgets and so forth. The leaders of both groups and I agreed to their goal that I would spend 80% of my time on economic development (primarily business recruitment) and 20% on chamber duties. Fortunately, I was able to hire a highly motivated, retired school principal to manage the chamber side of things very efficiently and with very little involvement on my part. After several months of tracking of my time, I was only able to achieve a 70/30 split, with chamber-related expectations consuming the 30%. And that was with a conscious effort on my part to minimize those duties and delegating most of chamber administration to a highly capable manager.

In my assignments at larger chambers, I found the general 50/50 rule applied, even with a staff of several dozen specialized, talented professionals to whom I could delegate. Board meetings, the annual meeting, investor relations, speaking engagements, internal meetings, expense accounts reviews, performance evaluations, inquiries from chamber members and elected officials, occasional interviews of nieces or nephews of board members who are looking for career opportunities (you can't dodge all those requests), budget and financial oversight, a seemingly infinite number of tasks – together can quickly consume 50% or more of your working hours.

The more you can minimize the primarily internal tasks and comfortably delegate many of them to others, the more you can maximize your ability to expand your external role and focus on moving the community forward.

Big Vision vs. Attention to Detail

Countless executive coaches have written about CEOs, their ability to articulate a bold vision for their organizations and their corresponding pre-occupation (or lack thereof) with minutia. Ronald Reagan was criticized for his lack of command of details but is remembered for his bold, optimistic vision of America that made him one of our most popular presidents. Jimmy Carter on the other hand, was labeled by many as a micromanager who was unable to rally the country behind a vision of greatness. Fortunately, the two traits are not mutually exclusive and, like it or not, chamber leaders need to manage both or find ways to compensate.

One of the lighthearted slogans I occasionally tossed out to my senior staff was, "Micromanagement is way underrated!" I only said it half facetiously. After all, I'd been known to pose questions about why the frayed American flag hadn't been replaced in the front of our building, why the wilted plant in the front lobby hadn't been watered, or why the front row of tables was set too far from the podium at a board meeting. My staff probably wondered about the severity of my obsessive-compulsive disorder and whether I should take an extended vacation.

I've observed a lot of CEOs with a variety of leadership styles and concluded that most of them care deeply about details – for example, the image of their organization, the quality of their product, the efficiency of their processes or, more likely, all of the above. Consider Steve Jobs and his manic interest in the design details of his iPhone. He would abruptly interrupt his own production schedule when he noticed that the glass on his iPhone prototype would scratch too easily when he carried it in his pocket with his car keys.

I knew a CEO who would arrive at work, decide that the newly planted flowers by the company sign were the wrong color and have them replaced later that day. Of course, everything can be carried to an extreme, but CEOs who are passionate about their work and often think about their work long before and after the standard workday, usually care about the details as well as the strategic direction of their organization. I had a decades-long habit of writing down on index cards almost every detail I needed to remember. My staff enjoyed dissing my index cards, but to make order out of the chaos in my brain, I had to commit dozens of details to those lists and manage those details. (The fact that I color-coded the priority items was perhaps a little over the top!)

While it's possible to get mired in the details that consume our workdays, we have to maintain the discipline to set aside time, to pull away from the desk and to focus on the big picture. I found that getting away from the office and attending a professional conference was often the best time for me to take a fresh look, distract myself from endless details, gather new ideas, generate more creative thought and refine my big picture strategies for moving forward. Another valuable time for big picture thinking was during informal planning sessions with my fellow staff members, when we allowed time for an open exchange of ideas about our direction and the new opportunities we could see on the horizon.

Getting away from the office and attending a professional conference was often the best time for me to take a fresh look, distract myself from endless details, gather new ideas, generate more creative thought and refine my big picture strategies.

Navigating Interpersonal Dynamics

Leading a chamber of commerce requires a certain navigational skill – a sixth sense that is a combination of political awareness and social intelligence required to provide leadership and to survive. Being able to read a situation, to size up other people in a given context and to calibrate one's own role in that context are critical for a chamber leader. A chamber exec who can't accurately assess those situations and respond accordingly could face major obstacles to his/her effectiveness, and the lack of that intuition could become job-threatening.

A chamber exec who talks too much in a particular setting; openly or surreptitiously challenges the ideas of volunteers who have more standing in the community; assumes too much about his/her social status in the community; expresses opinions on religion, politics or personal issues too freely; makes off-the-cuff remarks that appear less than dignified at the podium of the annual meeting or makes risqué comments in a business setting can quickly be relegated to a lesser standing and perceived to be incapable of interacting as a peer with top leaders of the community.

This notion of a sixth sense isn't about chamber leaders who engage in an illicit romance with a subordinate, get a DUI on the way home from the Business After Hours reception, take unacceptable liberties with their expense accounts, or commit other conspicuous or egregious offenses. It's more about the subtle, interpersonal day-to-day interactions that collectively define the personality, the maturity and professionalism of the chamber executive. I observed chamber leaders who paid a steep price for overestimating their role in the community or failing to establish an acceptable role for themselves in certain settings. I watched situations build over time and culminate in an action that prompts a special called meeting of the executive committee where the members decide they have had enough.

Is that sixth sense a born trait or something honed through education and experience? It would take a team of social scientists to answer that question, but I'm convinced that education and experience are critical for improving one's ability to navigate complex social relationships. Experience generally helps sharpen one's instincts and ability for sound judgment. I trace some of my imperfect instincts to lessons I learned, sometimes painfully, while participating in student government at my small college. Running for public office or managing a political campaign can be baptism by fire but also worth more than a graduate degree in terms of honing interpersonal skills. Attending leadership development courses throughout my career provided practical methods for understanding myself and others' perceptions of me while sharpening my ability to assess in real-time the motivations, personalities and aspirations of board members, co-workers, and others with whom I interacted.

None of us ever perfects the art of personal interaction. I've seen gifted orators stumble and say things that should have been left unsaid. I've made improvised comments during an after-dinner speech in an attempt to engage the audience and to be humorous, only to later second-guess whether the audience heard me differently than I intended. I've occasionally wondered if I should abandon spontaneity and stick to the script, even if that meant appearing more robotic.

As a practical matter, one way to gauge and refine one's executive presence is to imagine your circle of professional acquaintances and select one of those whose leadership abilities you truly admire and would like to emulate. Then, from time to time, ask yourself how that person would handle certain situations. Would he/she tell a particular joke? Would he/she go the extra mile in listening by asking a question about someone's family? Would he/she avoid offering an opinion when the group is discussing the mayor's personal problems?

The interpersonal skills of an effective chamber leader are exceptionally complex and demanding. Not too many occupations require such an intricate set of interpersonal skills: playing the role of the boss in office settings, assuming the role of the hired help in board settings, providing center-stage leadership in various public settings while refraining from hogging the limelight from your volunteer leaders.

The interpersonal skills of an effective chamber leader are exceptionally complex and demanding. Not too many occupations require such an intricate set of interpersonal skills.

As noted earlier, chamber execs must demonstrate great flexibility, with an ability to apply situational leadership and to be dominating or accommodating, depending on the circumstances. Part IV discusses "You and Your Career" and contains practical guidance for professional development and honing one's interpersonal skills.

Managing Your Political Profile

There is a difference between being opinionated and being dogmatic. Someone who boasts, "I would never make it in politics because I always speak my mind" and "I don't *want* to be politically correct" is probably not someone who would do well in politics – or in Chamber World. It is a mistake for chamber execs to think that a chamber is paying them for personal opinions on political, social or religious issues. On operational issues for the organization, sure. And on policy issues, the knowledge and perspective a chamber exec brings to the table should be extremely valuable.

Naturally, chamber execs hold strong personal convictions on countless issues – some of which can be at odds with our own organizations. I recall a chamber exec whose chamber had taken a position in favor of public universities being able to extend healthcare benefits to the same-sex partners of their employees. He was torn between the chamber position he was required to advocate and the more conservative doctrine of his church and the counsel of his pastor.

> *It is a mistake for chamber execs to think that a chamber is paying them for personal opinions on political, social or religious issues. On operational issues for the organization and policy issues, sure.*

Did I always agree with a public stand taken by my chamber? No. There are times when conscientious human beings are going to differ with the organizations they represent. Our chambers have policy positions on countless public issues, and I believe that no independently thinking person is going to always agree with whatever an employer advocates. But just as a skillful and ethical lawyer represents a client's best interests regardless of personal feelings, we are duty-bound to provide our organization and its members the most professional, effective representation we can give and which they deserve. If my personal opinions differ with my chamber in such a way that I'm uncomfortable or my effectiveness or the effectiveness of the organization is compromised, I have a duty to move on. After all, I don't own the chamber.

Working for a state chamber in a relatively contentious partisan environment, I found it best to be conspicuously non-partisan. I preferred to be viewed as an honest broker who worked toward solutions through consensus rather than as a political operative who sought to chalk up tactical points with the governor or the party in control of the legislature.

Chambers of commerce are by the nature of the business leaders they represent, typically conservative when it comes to national politics and generally right-of-center, especially on fiscal policy, employment and regulatory issues. However, I found chambers and chamber volunteer leaders to be very diverse in their individual politics. I live in a border state, and my relatively diverse board of directors encompassed corporate executives who remained steadfastly supportive of President Obama during his tenure and other board members who were prominent in conservative strongholds such as the Club for Growth and the super PAC American Crossroads.

A chamber exec must be able to navigate the unique political culture of his/her community. If, for example, you are the president of the San Francisco Chamber and your local congressional delegation leans way to the left in its politics, it's probably in your community's best interest for your chamber to project a relatively moderate tone in your policy positions – not to please your elected representatives or to compromise the substance of your business-based policies but because of the political character of the constituencies in your area that re-elect those representatives every two years. One of your chamber's top priorities might be the expansion of the airport or locating a research arm of a federal agency in your metro area. One of your congresspersons could very well be your community's means to get those projects accomplished. And many on your board of directors, drawn from the business community in those districts, could have a strong left-of-center if not outright liberal orientation, especially on social issues. That doesn't mean you don't doggedly represent your member businesses, but your members are probably more interested in your chamber producing results for the community than for you to alienate your most valuable allies over national policy issues.

If, on the other hand, your chamber lies in a strong red state or a Tea Party stronghold, your chamber can find itself at odds with that culture if, for example, it endorses an extension of the library tax or a school construction bond issue.

A chamber executive must have the skill to recognize a distinct political culture for the reality it is and work to advocate the business community's agenda as effectively as possible within that reality. Sometimes, it will require unabashedly marshaling the chamber's political clout in the face of opposition, but many more times it will take finesse and subtlety. Above all, it requires the development of strong relationships with policymakers – relationships built on trust, providing reliable information and persistent interaction.

During most of my tenure at a state chamber, our state was one of only a handful of states with a split legislature with Democrats controlling one house and Republicans the other. To get much of anything significant accomplished legislatively, we had to be particularly adept at pursuing our agenda in that divided, sometimes toxic, atmosphere. Oftentimes, the Democrats would dismiss us as a Republican organization while the Republicans would criticize us at the slightest hint of bipartisan moderation and accuse us of bending over backward to accommodate Democratic leaders. Republican partisans and fundraisers could not imagine a business organization not working in complete lockstep with the Republican Party agenda and we took heat when we sometimes endorsed business-minded Democrats for reelection. The fact that a particular legislator had a 100% voting record with us or introduced business-friendly legislation for us didn't really matter to blindly partisan leaders of the other party.

More recently, our legislature shifted to complete Republican control, allowing much-needed business legislation that had been on the back burner for decades to quickly sweep through the legislative process and become law. Naturally, we took slings and arrows from the new minority party with derisive accusations on the floor of the legislature that, "Now the Kentucky Chamber of Commerce is driving the bus!" In reality, we were working just as diligently in the face of some outspoken members of the new majority party to prevent certain anti-business, socially conservative issues from dominating the legislature and embarrassing our state. Our chamber had to adapt to a radically different political arena, practically overnight.

As I have told our young staff lobbyists when they've had an unpleasant encounter with a legislator, "If you find that you have the Democrats and the Republicans mad at you on the same day, it might be because you're doing your job." When I had a partisan leader or a candidate for office angry with me, I paused and reminded myself that their signatures were not on our paychecks. We worked for the business community.

In defending our policy positions and political endorsements to various partisans who expected me to embrace their policy positions, I reminded them that, 1) It's not my chamber; it's the chamber of commerce and we represent a pretty big tent, and 2) You may be upset with our position on an issue, but you can trust that it represents the carefully developed consensus of the business leaders of our state. And I invited them to challenge us if they ever saw us advocating a position that didn't represent that consensus.

A real-life, highly visible example of the political tightrope chamber execs have to walk was the annual task of selecting a speaker for our annual meeting. Our tradition was to have a national political celebrity (usually a well-known TV commentator) as our featured speaker. Because of the diverse political culture in which our chamber existed, I concluded that we could invite a centrist (we hosted the late Tim Russert), a center-right speaker (George Will), or a balanced left-right team (James Carville with Mary Matalin or Donna Brazile with Tucker Carlson). However, we would get significant fallout if we went far left (Rachel Maddow) or if we went far right (Sarah Palin or Glenn Beck). It wasn't a matter of being timid about stirring up controversy and getting a little criticism; hosting a speaker known for extreme views would represent something outside the bipartisan, voice-of-reason brand our chamber had strategically and methodically cultivated.

Our non-partisan brand was important to our chamber, and we protected it assiduously. Our staff knew that the TV monitors in our lobby and other public areas were set to default to CNBC (a business channel that reinforced our brand for anyone visiting our building), not the left-of-center MSNBC or the right-of-center Fox News. We strove to consistently align ourselves with business issues that had emerged from our membership and had been vetted and refined by our volunteer leaders. We wanted our identity to be business – not Republican or Democrat – and our focus to be on issues, not politics.

The Agnostic Leader

There are certain perils for chamber leaders being openly opinionated on extracurricular issues outside the scope of their chambers. That's why I recommend a certain level of agnosticism on issues that don't lie in the wheelhouse of one's chamber.

The word "agnostic" comes from the Greek word *gnosis*, meaning knowledge, and with the "a" indicating "no" or "the opposite of." In other words, no knowledge. In everyday language, agnostic generally refers to someone without belief or without certainty, as in, "when it comes to the death penalty, I'm agnostic." Either I am ambivalent or I lack the knowledge to have an iron-clad opinion. While most chamber executives surely have deeply held values about partisan politics, family, religious faith and morality, it generally pays to be publicly agnostic and nonsectarian on "extracurricular" topics.

While most chamber executives surely have deeply held values about partisan politics, family, religious faith and morality, it generally pays to be publicly agnostic and nonsectarian on "extracurricular" topics.

It's important for us to realize that even the language we use in public settings can create barriers between us and our constituencies. To illustrate the sensitivity that a chamber exec can encounter when operating in the public arena, I offer the following personal experience:

I'll never forget the first week on the job at a large, metro chamber (Birmingham, AL) and my first public event – a huge luncheon with several hundred members of the chamber's very successful Venture Club for entrepreneurs, venture capitalists and various business services firms. The group's leaders had placed me at the head table where I was to be introduced as the new president of the chamber. At the last minute, the master of ceremonies was ready to start the program and asked me who would deliver the invocation (which I soon learned is often the practice at public gatherings in the deeper South). I had no idea that arranging a prayer was expected of the chamber staff, but having come from a Baptist, anybody-can-be-called-to-pray culture, I said, "Uh, okay, I will." Mustering up all the appropriate thoughts I could in less than 30 seconds, I offered a brief, seemingly appropriate prayer for our gathering. But as anyone who's ever given a public speech knows, the toughest part is figuring out how to end it. So, in a moment of heightened anxiety, I ended with, "and in the name of your son, Jesus Christ, we pray." Period. Done. A sigh of relief later, the luncheon continued without a hitch.

The next day I received a kind letter delivered to my office from a Jewish lawyer, welcoming me to town, expressing his pleasure at meeting me at the Venture Club luncheon, politely taking issue with the Christo-centric prayer I had offered and providing me an enclosed "Guide to Public Prayer." It offered model prayers for mixed-faith audiences. I have since noticed that many religious leaders offer such non-denominational or religiously pluralistic prayers at major public gatherings.

On reflection, the letter of gentle admonition was a huge favor. As a young chamber leader coming from a relatively small, homogeneous city to a very ethnically and religiously diverse metropolitan area, I needed to up my game to be more inclusive and effective in my role. I realized that if I truly respected my relatively high-profile position, the quasi-public organization I represented and the diversity of people and businesses that supported it, I hurt my professional effectiveness when I unconsciously created unnecessary barriers between myself and my chamber's constituents.

So, in many cases, remaining publicly agnostic and as nonsectarian as possible on issues outside our chambers is good. A chamber leader has been provided an important and potentially powerful podium – a so-called bully pulpit – from which to speak for the business community. He/she doesn't own the pulpit; it is provided temporarily. To have the opportunity to provide meaningful leadership for our communities is a unique privilege, but to confuse that privilege with carte blanche license to express ourselves with any opinion we happen to hold is to ignore the reality – specifically the restraints – which are informally associated with our positions.

■ ■ ■

There is no cookie-cutter set of skills required for a chamber exec to be successful, but clearly there are born traits and learned skills that are generally valuable if not absolutely necessary to navigate the special, complex realities of life in Chamber World. The casually dismissive notion that anyone can run a chamber of commerce doesn't recognize those specialized traits and skills and can profoundly handicap a chamber and its community. One of the necessary skills for leading a chamber of commerce is managing one's personal and professional profile within the broader community and avoiding extracurricular issues that distract from one's effectiveness.

PART II
IT'S ABOUT YOU AND YOUR CHAMBER

To provide leadership in a volunteer-led organization, we must first address some basic questions: What is the reason our chamber exists? What is the most valuable role it can play in our community? To effectively manage a chamber of commerce, we have to discover practical ways in which a chamber executive can develop the chamber into a relevant, high-performance organization that can help shape the broader community.

CHAPTER 4
THE DISTINCT ROLE OF YOUR CHAMBER

A friend of mine was selected from outside the chamber business to be the new CEO of a troubled chamber. He was chosen because of his solid reputation as a serial entrepreneur and because he was local (business leaders having grown skeptical of hiring a professional chamber exec from outside the community after a disappointing and costly experience of having to terminate their previous exec and buy out his contract). The new CEO took a clean-slate approach to rebuilding a chamber that had imploded financially and in terms of its reputation. Early in his tenure, while seeking advice on the challenges he faced, he asked me a blunt question: "What is the fundamental purpose of a chamber of commerce?" This back-to-basics question is loaded with relevance for all of us. Why do chambers exist? What defines a chamber's highest value to its community? What distinguishes one chamber from another?

The Distinct Functions Your Chamber Owns

We need to first understand our chamber's current role in the community in objective, dispassionate terms, approaching it as though we were out-of-town consultants hired to conduct an evaluation that identifies our chamber's strengths, weaknesses, opportunities and threats. How can we conduct such an assessment?

Engaging an independent third party is a great way to evaluate a chamber, using anonymous surveys and focus groups of members, non-members, community influencers and others to obtain objective information. But short of spending that kind of money, a simple brainstorming exercise with a board of directors and/or staff can yield some valuable insights. That assessment can begin by simply listing and evaluating the distinct functions the chamber provides to its community – either as the exclusive provider or as the premier provider of specific services.

In a relaxed, informal setting, pose these questions to a group of board members and/or your staff: What does our organization do that no one else does or that we do better than anyone else in our community? What events do we host that are unique in our community? What services do we provide to members or the public that no one else provides? What leaders or groups of leaders do we convene for action in this community? Is our chamber a catalyst for certain projects to be developed or issues to be considered by our community? In sum, what does our chamber "own"? Forcing ourselves and our organizations to answer these types of questions is like looking in a mirror and documenting what we see.

Examples of such characteristics might include:

- Our chamber board is the most prestigious group of business leaders in our community.

- The past chairs of our chamber are a "Who's Who" of our community's leaders.

- Our chamber is the go-to organization for recruiting new businesses to our region.

- Our chamber is the most consistent voice for business when addressing government agencies.

- Our chamber's monthly membership meeting is the most prominent forum for highlighting key issues before the public.

- Our annual meeting is the largest gathering of business and community leaders of the year.

- Our annual small business conference is the only one offered in the community.

- The magazine we publish is the only livability piece routinely used by local Realtors for attracting new residents.

- Our annual farm-city breakfast is the only celebration of agribusiness in the region.

- Our chamber is the only organization in our community that produces a legislative agenda.

- Our discount program for local merchants is the only one of its type in the region.

- Our chamber is the most recognized source of community information in the region.

- Our headquarters is the most popular meeting place for business groups.

Of course, the "ownership" list of a local chamber will differ from that of a regional or state chamber, but such an exercise provides a glimpse of what a chamber's primary stakeholders consider their chamber's role by enumerating its distinct value-adding functions. It helps answer the question: "Why do we open our doors in the morning?" Such an introspective exercise enables you to define your chamber's core competencies, its current role in its community and, by extension, your professional role as the chamber CEO. It also establishes a critical benchmark for evaluating the relative merit of those functions in relation to each other and in comparison to other functions the chamber may consider undertaking.

Answering the question, "Why do we open our doors in the morning?" is an introspective exercise that enables you to define your chamber's core competencies.

Chambers differ widely from each other because they reflect the heritage and aspirations of such different communities. Unlike top-down national organizations that function through local chapters or licensed affiliates, a local or state chamber can be whatever its board of directors wants it to be. One would expect the chamber of Las Vegas to focus attention on conventions and tourism. One would expect a chamber in Huntsville, Alabama, to care about federal funding of the space program and sponsor a huge annual Washington Fly-In for its members who are government contractors. One would expect the chamber in Rochester, Minnesota, to have a health care focus that embraces its world-class brand as home of the Mayo Clinic and the chamber in Boston, Massachusetts, to closely align itself with its world-class universities as the economic engines of that region. Chambers near large military bases typically place a strong emphasis on military and veterans affairs. Some small chambers are primarily focused on a particular community function – perhaps to manage a signature heritage festival or as the primary information hub for thousands of seasonal tourists who fuel the local economy.

A chamber and its unique set of functions can go through various organizational phases depending on the needs of the community and the transition of leadership in public office and in the business community. For example, the chamber in my hometown helped create a separate industrial foundation in the 1960s to recruit industries, but over the years the chamber has transitioned through at least four different organizational models to manage that marketing and recruitment function – forming a three-way chamber/foundation/riverport partnership, later creating and spinning off a separate economic development corporation (EDC), then putting the chamber and EDC together under a management agreement and one CEO, and still later separating from the EDC but co-locating in a new Commerce Center. Meanwhile, the chamber itself gradually took on other functions such as downtown development, leadership training, educational programming, advocacy, regionalism and workforce development. While those organizational changes might be viewed from outside as aimless and incoherent, the metamorphosis was actually a chamber continuing to respond to the perceived needs and priorities of its community leaders. There is a lot to be said for a chamber remaining flexible, entrepreneurial and opportunistic as it responds to the needs of its community.

Establishing the Vision, Mission and Values

While identifying a chamber's current functions helps define what a chamber is, it doesn't necessarily define what that chamber should be. And while we've noted the advantages for a chamber to remain flexible and responsive to its community, a chamber should avoid the tendency to drift aimlessly and allow itself to be manipulated by the latest whim of its most vocal participants. It's important for a chamber to anchor itself to a precise statement of its vision (a broad statement of what the chamber aspires to be), its mission (the fundamental purposes for which it exists) and its values (those attributes that describe how it conducts itself). Because

It's important for a chamber to anchor itself to a precise statement of its vision (a broad statement of what the chamber aspires to be), its mission (the fundamental purposes for which it exists) and its values (those attributes that describe how it conducts itself).

conditions in a community constantly change, it's also important to periodically re-visit those guiding principles, both to remind the chamber's leaders of its previous understanding of the chamber's stated purpose but also to tweak the statement in light of new circumstances.

There are a variety of ways to create a vision, mission and values statement, but I would encourage using an experienced facilitator to lead your board through the exercise. With a group of people offering a variety of opinions about their priorities for the chamber and about precise wording of those priorities, it's critical that the facilitator be able to contain the conversation and direct it toward consensus, perhaps with an additional phase of wordsmithing by the facilitator and a few key officers after the larger group completes its exercise but before final adoption by the board. The vision/mission/values statement becomes the anchor that helps a chamber avoid drifting in a sea of swirling priorities and ad hoc projects.

Chambers have a lot in common, but no one vision, mission and values statement will fit all chambers. For example, because our state chamber operated in an environment of several hundred interest groups that converge on the state capital, we considered the building of coalitions with like-minded associations to be essential to having success with our legislative efforts. Therefore, our vision statement said that we viewed ourselves as a catalyst and convener; our mission statement prioritized advocacy, providing information and delivering membership services; and our values statement included the words consensus-building, entrepreneurial, flexible and non-partisan. A chamber in a large metro area, on the other hand, might prioritize regionalism, diversity and entrepreneurial innovation in its mission statement. The words that business leaders choose to describe their understanding of the core purposes of their chambers are vitally important for attaining a common understanding among your leadership, to avoid distractions and to stay focused on the specific goals that those leaders periodically set for their chamber and which, it is hoped, remain aligned with the agreed-upon vision, mission and values.

Combating a Reputation for "Fluff"

Let's face it: chambers have a reputation for pursuing feel-good projects and blindly engaging in civic boosterism. After all, we all live in the greatest town on earth, don't we? We want our communities to have a positive self-image, and we promote their attributes daily.

Chambers often spend a lot of time working on civic projects their communities have come to expect – legacy programs linked closely with the chamber, for good or bad. And we are constantly being asked to take on something else for the community. Chambers are known as the folks who promote positive things about our communities, we sometimes exaggerate the unique characteristics of our town/city/state, and we are sometimes even blamed or credited with controlling the weather! (Hence, the ubiquitous phrase that is perhaps most commonly associated with our organizations: "Wow, this is chamber of commerce weather!") While that reputation embodies the idyllic landscape we all want to create, it also reveals a less positive side of our reputation – one of cheery optimism and feel-good promotions – fluff. It and the feel-good, civic pride projects chambers are often expected to manage can diminish any sense of gravitas they are attempting to build through serious work in their communities.

I've heard community leaders discuss local economic development issues with great seriousness and in the same breath, either say or imply that traditional chamber activities are less significant. Hosting zany promotions, performing a traditional function for the downtown merchants or managing the local festival can be time-consuming expectations of a chamber and shape a reputation of pursuing superfluous activities. Sponsoring a local contest may raise a few thousand dollars for the chamber and get its board chair's picture in the paper, but does

> *The feel-good, civic pride projects chambers are often expected to manage can diminish any sense of gravitas they are attempting to build through serious work in their communities.*

it also create an image of less-than-serious priorities? Of course, not all such activities should be dismissed as fluff; they can demonstrate engagement and cultivate a strong sense of civic pride. However, a key question for chamber leaders is whether those activities distract from more urgent and mission-driven work that the business community should be pursuing. Should some of those civic projects be discontinued or perhaps spun off to a more appropriate group?

Having a reputation as the community's leading civic booster organization can also make it challenging for a chamber to speak out candidly on problems such as poverty, lagging educational attainment or economic difficulties. I've found we have to be careful when addressing community groups or the media about such challenges because many in our communities expect a positive, forward-looking message from the always-sunny chamber of commerce. They don't expect a message of gloom and doom, and an objective assessment of community problems can be perceived as a negative indictment unless it is accompanied by a positive, balanced, way-forward message.

This challenge is especially difficult when local and regional chambers have formal economic development and/or tourism promotion roles. Can a chamber on the one hand promote the positive attributes of its region to outsiders while at the same time holding up a mirror for the community to examine its weaknesses?

Avoiding Feel-Good Distractions

It's often said that chambers have a tendency to be a mile wide and an inch deep, feverishly taking on project after project without making tough strategic choices about priorities. Perhaps they fail to ask: How does our chamber focus on making meaningful change? How do we avoid getting mired in pursuing limited impact, feel-good projects while leaving significant community issues to City Hall, developers or other powers that be? A personal story illustrates the dichotomy of chasing feel-good projects versus shaping meaningful progress. It's a tale of time and effort misspent on a frivolous feel-good project without reflecting on the rationale behind it.

The first indoor shopping mall opened in my community a year or two after I was hired by the local chamber as project manager. There was a lot of hand wringing in the community and on the editorial pages about the dismal future of downtown as long-time retail establishments closed or moved to the dazzling new mall with its tropical plants, fountains, bright lights, piped-in music and acres of free parking.

Chambers have a tendency to be a mile wide and an inch deep, feverishly taking on project after project without making tough strategic choices about priorities.

At that time, many downtowns across America were nervously reacting and trying to imitate the atmosphere of a comfortable indoor shopping mall by closing off downtown streets and converting them to pedestrian malls with trees, flowers, bike racks, fountains, up-beat music, vintage lamp posts and so on. Ironically, many downtown pedestrian malls from that era have since been torn out and the streets reopened to vehicular traffic, but at the time, suburban malls represented the future of retail in most mid-sized and large communities, and downtowns were attempting to play catch-up.

Our downtown exodus occurred a few years before our chamber created a downtown development corporation so to a great extent the chamber filled the role of advocating for downtown redevelopment. Being a young, enthusiastic chamber staffer, I proposed to my boss that we attempt to improve the atmosphere of downtown and make it more pedestrian-friendly. We first proposed a pedestrian mall, but City Hall vetoed the idea of closing any city streets to vehicles. I then proposed that we raise money from downtown property owners, install speakers on the utility poles that lined Main Street and broadcast upbeat music along four or five blocks of what was left of the retail district.

My chamber boss gave me an incredible amount of latitude to do my work, create projects and generally define my job, and he gave me a green light for this particular downtown project. I recall spending days working on the project as I managed a variety of other chamber duties. I eventually succeeded, and nice music was broadcast on Main Street. The newspaper reported the new feature of downtown, and we were quite pleased that we had done something positive for downtown.

In retrospect, I wish my boss had reined me in. I wish he had asked the question, "Is that the best use of your time and the chamber's resources?" Of course, we didn't realize then that the suburban shopping trends sweeping across America were basically irreversible – at least for the next few decades. Playing nice music, planting a few trees and removing parking meters to compete with the free parking of shopping malls were essentially wasted efforts, and it would take decades for a true urban renaissance to begin bringing people in meaningful numbers back to America's downtowns.

To our chamber's credit, we eventually created a separate downtown development corporation, spun it off with its own dedicated board of directors and helped raise money to hire consultants to offer more substantive solutions for downtown. And, to our partial defense, some of the ideas (albeit, not the music idea) we advocated in those years had a positive and lasting influence on the downtown renaissance that eventually came to that city and continues to this day.

My point is about short-sighted chambers pursuing well-intentioned projects for their communities without pausing to identify meaningful, strategic solutions. Time would have been better spent working to form the downtown development group earlier and preserving the downtown's historical character than chasing the trendy notions of pedestrian malls and piped-in elevator music. A chamber having the ability and maturity to back up from a pressing issue and to ask what is the most consequential approach we can take to addressing the issue is paramount for achieving its best and highest purpose in its community.

"Pancakes and Parades" vs. Public Policy

Since this point about feel-good projects vs. meaningful progress is critical to the distinction between a chamber that is merely busy with activities and one that shapes its community's future, I offer a second illustration best described as "pancakes and parades" – a phrase frequently and effectively used to characterize the tendency of many chambers to take on smaller, feel-good projects. Sometimes a community project or program becomes enshrined as a tradition the chamber is expected to manage for years to come and becomes a labor-intensive distraction that annually consumes the chamber staff and volunteers. Examples might include Fourth of July parades, beauty pageants, the local heritage festival, and fundraising for a few scholarships. And larger chambers are not immune; most chamber execs can probably point to a feel-good legacy program or two that they inherited when taking on their new positions as chamber presidents.

There will probably always be opportunities for a chamber to be the catalyst for creating and sustaining a community project, and some of those efforts can be truly transformational. For example, the critical role the Atlanta Chamber played in organizing its business community to bid on and eventually host the 1996 Olympics would be hard to overstate in terms of historic and lasting impact on that major metropolis that wanted to join the ranks of the most prestigious cities in the world. Communities will probably always look to their chambers to play a leading role with civic initiatives, especially if the chamber is highly regarded as a go-to organization for getting things done. There is great value in many of the suggestions that land on a chamber's doorstep, but we have to filter through them to find the ones that fit with our strategic priorities and deserve our time and effort. Otherwise, we may simply be selling more pancakes and sponsoring more parades.

I've come to believe that the ability of a chamber to positively affect the future of its community is much greater in the policy arena than in the pancakes and parades arena. By policy arena, I am referring to a broad sense of policy – well beyond a chamber's government affairs activities at City Hall and the state capital. While that advocacy function is vitally important and deserves diligent engagement by our chambers, consider also the long-range planning function of a community in terms of improving education, expanding the arts, promoting wellness, training the workforce, embracing technology, nurturing entrepreneurism and generally helping our communities imagine their futures and shape their destinies. This broad notion of policy development is fertile ground for chambers that wish to play a leadership role.

The ability of a chamber to positively affect the future of its community is much greater in the policy arena than in the pancakes and parades arena.

When we consider the countless opportunities for a chamber to initiate programs that require an investment of its time, money, volunteer talent and its brand, I would err on the side of investing more time in public policy and less time on pancakes and parades. As a chamber matures and its role in the policy arena becomes more central to its function, it will be perceived as more relevant and consequential in its community. And it can probably monetize that role, gaining financial support for serious initiatives to address major opportunities and issues in the community.

Your Chamber's Brand

Chambers in general have a positive reputation. ACCE conducted a nationwide study called the Shapiro Study in 2007, updated it 2012 and found that the vast majority of people routinely attribute positive value to the name "chamber of commerce." Products, issues and political candidates are viewed in more positive terms when associated with, or explicitly endorsed by, a chamber of commerce.

In 2016, the Council of State Chambers (COSC) commissioned a survey by Luntz Global (Frank Luntz being the guru of political wordsmithing and the author of *Words That Work: It's Not What You Say, It's What People Hear*). They surveyed 1000 C-level executives nationwide – 73% being business owners and/or CEOs – about their opinions on various issues and their impressions of state chambers. On the question of favorable vs. unfavorable impressions of state chambers, 22% had an extremely favorable view, 37% very favorable view and 23% a somewhat favorable view, for an overall favorability rating of 82%. That's a very positive brand for state chambers, and I suspect many local chambers are regarded even more favorably.

Chambers don't suffer from lack of name recognition. The name chamber of commerce is well known, having been in common use in this country for more than two centuries, and it generally implies a standard of quality and integrity when associated with an organization, product or political candidate. The challenge for chambers is to build a brand that carries something more specific than a vaguely positive, generic connotation.

When I first arrived at the Kentucky Chamber in 2005 and undertook a branding campaign with surveys, polling and focus groups of members and non-members, I found that many non-members had very little knowledge of our state chamber. While they recognized the term chamber of commerce, they had very little understanding of what a state chamber does, and they often confused the state chamber with local chambers and the U.S. Chamber. Some even thought that the state chamber was an arm of state government, a common misconception I often heard from friends and neighbors who asked, "Oh, you work for the governor?"

> *Chambers don't suffer from lack of name recognition. The challenge is to build a brand that carries something more specific than a vaguely positive, generic connotation.*

I realize that state chambers have a special identity problem, if not a name recognition problem. State chambers operate at a second level of abstraction from the Main Street reality of local chambers. Not only are they more geographically distant from most of their constituent businesses, they generally operate more in the realm of public policy than in the realm of programs and projects that often provide a local chamber a relatively high-profile in its community. Local chambers are in a better position to define themselves by offering hands-on services to their members, sponsoring in-person networking events and attracting local news coverage.

Many businesspeople and political leaders assume that if a business belongs to a local chamber, that business is also a member of the state chamber and the U.S. Chamber. The distinction between the various chambers is lost on most of the public and even many in the business community. This can be particularly troublesome when one chamber takes a controversial stance on a public issue or political candidate and other chambers are linked by association. We had to be careful at my state chamber when we endorsed legislative candidates because often local chambers would get angry phone calls about why they (we) endorsed one local candidate over another.

The positive brand of an individual chamber is something that must be built over time. It's much more than a new logo or tagline. It's well worth the time to do a brand analysis, even if it only means conducting an exercise with your board to determine what words they think describe your chamber and what words they think should describe your chamber. Although I've never had the opportunity, I'd love to pose those questions to a few hundred random citizens in my community or randomly selected members of my chamber and create a word cloud that gives a visual display of the most common words they associate with our chamber. Coming to a consensus with your chamber leadership about how the chamber sees itself and wants to position itself is important and carries practical benefit. It may help the organization decide whether it wants to invest its time in sponsoring an annual golf outing or taking on an in-depth research project about a key issue in the community.

The personal brand of the CEO is very much part of the chamber's brand, especially if the CEO has been in his/her position for several years or brings a relatively high-profile from a previous role in the community. Just as the image and reputation of a college or university is closely linked to the president's visibility and reputation, a chamber's brand is closely linked to the CEO. Is the CEO generally regarded as a forceful, talented leader? Or as a bull in the china shop? Is he/she considered a politically astute, behind-the-scenes operative? Or, is there an image of an empty suit who survives by glad-handing the powerbrokers of the community? Is the CEO known as an entertaining speaker on the civic club circuit? Or as an inclusive, progressive community leader who is capable of tackling the tough issues faced by the community?

Your chamber headquarters can be an important part of your brand – whether you occupy a downtown storefront, a stand-alone building with high visibility on the busiest highway or an anonymous floor in an office tower. How people visualize your headquarters creates an impression. Does the headquarters reflect success and sophistication? Or does it bombard the senses of your visitors with a clutter of brochures and maps displayed in the lobby? Do the donated, outdated furnishings reflect a struggling organization living on a shoestring? Those features convey to the public and to chamber members the role the chamber plays in the community.

In some cases, the building itself is considered less important to the organization's overall image than its programs. When the Birmingham Chamber was considering selling its historic fourteen-story building and moving to two floors of an office tower in the heart of downtown, the board decided the physical building was not critical to the chamber's reputation; its programs and its role in the metro area would shape its brand. However, when designing the interior, we were very careful to convey an image of modern sophistication and seriousness for visitors who came for important meetings and conferences. The chamber made a conscious decision that it wasn't in the business of serving the walk-in visitor; it was in the business of convening serious meetings to address the region's most important challenges. That was our chamber's decision, but other chambers select their headquarters' locations with the decided purpose of being highly visible and serving walk-in clients.

When we expanded our state chamber headquarters in Frankfort, Kentucky in 2010, I suggested to the architects that I wanted visitors to our building to have a Kentucky experience. I suggested we design a building with an equestrian flavor to emphasize our claim as The Thoroughbred Capital of the World or something that mimicked the rustic architecture of a bourbon distillery or a building that reflected our growing automotive manufacturing industry, even imagining a Kentucky-made Corvette on display in the lobby. The architects convinced me otherwise, suggesting that a contemporary building with a strong Kentucky-inspired interior was the better way to go. They suggested that a prominent, high-profile façade would take advantage of our prime, high-traffic location on I-64 between Louisville and Lexington. Therefore, we designed an addition that extended and accentuated the facade of our building and included an attractive public conference space. To provide visitors a Kentucky experience, we designed the public spaces with custom lighting to serve as an art gallery featuring the works of carefully selected Kentucky artists (paid for by a Louisville-based corporation with a track record of supporting Kentucky artists).

Other decisions about the headquarters focused on making the desired impression: televisions in the lobby and public restrooms were set on CNBC to convey the sense of business being conducted in our building and to avoid the political polarization associated with other cable channels. No promotional items were allowed in the public spaces. The one brochure we allowed was a booklet that featured the "Kentucky

Chamber Gallery" with beautiful photos of our Kentucky-crafted works of art. Coffee table books on display in the lobby celebrated the heritage of Kentucky, and we worked to avoid the messy items often found in a meeting space (disposable cups, napkins, etc.). A few board members wondered if we were creating an excessively opulent headquarters that would alienate our dues-paying members or the general public. That was a risk, but we felt it was a risk worth taking. Was it excessive? No. Once it was completed, I never heard a word of criticism that we splurged on the building or furnishings. More common were glowing comments from members and visitors who came for meetings or simply to admire the building's interior and the artwork.

We wanted our space to reflect the success and sophistication of the leaders of our business community who are the owners of our chamber. I justified our decision to invest in Class A office space by suggesting that rarely are people offended by the elegant surroundings in other professional settings. For example, in the lobby of a top law firm, a chandelier, granite countertops and thick carpets imply professionalism and success whereas worn-out furniture and outdated wood paneling leave you to wonder if the attorneys are barely scraping by. I suggest that chambers want their surroundings to reflect professional success and sophistication.

After a couple of years in the new space, my executive assistant and I estimated that with the hundreds of committee, task force and coalition meetings we hosted, we were serving more than 5,000 lunches each year. I hosted luncheons for the state's university presidents, meetings of top business executives, receptions for government officials and foreign dignitaries, and news conferences with governors and other officials. We often had to decline requests for meetings by outside groups, even wedding receptions. And as I told our board, "We're not trying to be the Marriott".

I've seen chambers suffer financially when they try to operate a conference center as a profit center. Managing a conference center was not a core function for our chamber, but bringing people together definitely was. By building what is arguably the most attractive meeting space in our capital city (except perhaps the Governor's Mansion), we enhanced our brand as an organization that is open, hospitable and successful that brings people together to conduct serious business.

Your Chamber's Communications

The ways chambers communicate have changed more during my career than probably any other aspect of chamber management. A few decades ago, communicating with your members involved a monthly newsletter and reaching the outside world meant holding a news conference and hoping the local newspaper, radio stations and area television stations covered it. That all changed dramatically with technology and, especially, with social media. While I was fortunate to have coworkers who were usually ahead of me in adopting new methods, I learned that I had to become comfortable on multiple platforms and establish my particular social media profile and distinct voice in those spaces.

It wasn't just a matter of becoming adept on those platforms; it was a continuing exercise of fine-tuning the content and tone of our communications. Did we want to be known for promoting our programs and events or for our commentary on community issues? Did we want to bombard our members with organizational details such as recognizing new members or did we want to reserve our messaging for more substantive news bulletins? Did we want to exude the friendly, folksy style of a community cheerleader or reflect the gravitas of a chamber engaged in the serious issues of the community? How did we bridge the generational divide between our youthful, tech-savvy staffers who tweeted on behalf of the chamber and the older demographic of our members, key investors and policymakers? As I reminded our staff during an internal discussion of our social media voice, "Remember, this isn't summer camp. We're talking to chamber members and community leaders who are, on average, a generation older than our communications team."

Navigating the ever-shifting social media landscape holds great potential for chambers, but it is not without peril. There are horror stories of former chamber professionals (emphasis on former) who inadvertently posted a risqué photo or unleashed a snarky political comment in the heat of the moment, only to be called on the carpet by board members or even lose their jobs. I know of situations in which capable individuals were passed over for job openings and promotions because of their overheated rhetoric on social media.

I once innocently backed into a social media firestorm involving an elected official who got caught up in a personal controversy. He was an important friend of our chamber and a personal friend of mine so I was naturally tuned into the social media onslaught that ensued. As I casually glanced at my Twitter feed while walking down a street, I noticed a particularly strident comment by a state legislator who called on the accused official to immediately resign from office over the accusations. When I continued scrolling down the feed with my thumb, I unknowingly hit the heart icon on my screen, accidentally indicating that I agreed with the call for the official's resignation.

It was a couple of hours later when the official texted me his profound disappointment that our supposed friendship would not have afforded him the benefit of the doubt during his gut-wrenching personal crisis. At first, I didn't know what he meant. As I put two and two together, I realized my error. In a panic, I had to nervously figure out how to withdraw my "like" and had some serious digging out to do as I tried to explain my clumsy mistake. It took a couple of months and a few personal encounters with him before I eventually convinced myself that he believed my explanation and accepted my apology. Meanwhile, I saw a personal friendship and a valuable chamber relationship go up in smoke over a social media faux pas. And I learned a painful lesson about the explosive nature of a social media mishap.

In spite of these risks and challenges, a chamber's voice can be amplified exponentially by skillfully using social media and constantly monitoring and adjusting strategies for breaking through the onslaught of digitized information. Chambers hold a distinct advantage as organizations that thrive on providing interpersonal connectivity and human relationships. Enhancing that role through electronic channels can build on a chamber's strengths and help it adapt to the ever-changing communications environment.

Chambers as Think Tanks

As I reflect on a career full of pancakes, parades and public policy, I am increasingly drawn to the notion that a chamber can best serve its community by functioning almost as a think tank – not exclusively in that role (realistically, there are too many other demands on a chamber as noted above) – but embracing that potential and growing into it.

A standard definition of a think tank is a body of experts providing advice and ideas on specific political and economic problems. But a think tank doesn't have to be a team of PhDs publishing a steady stream of white papers on esoteric topics. Nor does it have to be a separate thing; it can simply describe a philosophy by which the chamber views itself and operates in the community. Whether we realize it or not, chambers have an incredible wealth of expertise at hand. For example, who knows more about environmental regulations and hazardous chemicals in your community than the safety engineer working for your largest manufacturer – i.e. one of your chamber members? Multiply that by all of the talent and expertise your chamber represents in your community. A chamber can play a profound role in shaping its community by advising it on public

A chamber can play a profound role in shaping its community by advising it on public policy from the experts within its membership.

policy from the experts within its membership, providing original economic information, processing information on behalf of its members and community policymakers, and leaning into the future to articulate a vision for growth. In that sense, a chamber can create and sustain an essential place for itself in the life of its community.

■　■　■

How does a chamber leader stand back from the rush of daily activity to reflect on his/her chamber's best and highest function and lead the chamber to focus its time, energy and money on more important work? It starts with defining its basic purpose, minimizing the superfluous fluff of chamber work and delving deeper into the issues that will shape the future of the community.

CHAPTER 5
WORKING WITH A BOARD OF DIRECTORS

Reporting to a board of directors is very different from having a single boss. It can be exhilarating and inspiring, yet sometimes challenging to the point of overwhelming. What are the unique challenges of answering to a board? How does a chamber executive interact with multiple bosses and maintain a steady sense of direction?

Answering to a Group

Friends of mine outside the chamber have asked, "How on earth can you work for a board of 75 people?" They can't imagine having to report to such a large group of people, especially to prominent people who are generally successful in their own fields and often have strong personalities. Whether a chamber board is fifteen or 115, working for a group of independent business and community leaders is certainly challenging.

Despite those challenges, I found the experience generally enjoyable and stimulating. I count all of my former board chairs as friends and maintain contact with dozens of former board members. I truly hated to see most of them leave the chamber board as their terms expired. Sure, there were occasional brush fires to put out, egos to soothe, malcontents to placate and bullies to avoid or confront. But I found that if I earned the volunteers' trust and they received whatever benefit they wanted from their chamber involvement, my work environment seemed nearly as free and liberating as being self-employed.

I considered it my goal to find a unique way for each board member to make a distinct contribution to our chamber. It might have been by providing financial support, playing the role of go-between with the mayor on a sensitive topic, using personal contacts to secure a marquee speaker for our annual meeting, using political connections to arrange an important meeting, or donating a company's marketing department for a membership survey or the graphic artwork needed for a publication. It might have meant writing the first check for a particular cause and challenging other business leaders to do the same.

Generally, boards of directors expect a certain element of leadership from their chief executive; they certainly expect a self-motivated professional with a sense of direction and intention. They want a conscientious exec who looks to board leaders for objective feedback, strategic direction and personal affirmation and who can take input from a variety of sources, aggregate it and suggest practical ways to move forward.

Working with a board of directors is like walking a tightrope, balancing between asserting yourself too aggressively as an overly confident leader and retreating to a passive, subservient role, possibly allowing the organization to swallow you up. That balance is not something you negotiate in an employment contract or settle by drafting a job description – although those formalities help parties reach a basic mutual understanding of roles and responsibilities. It is a daily exercise that requires artful navigation and finesse during each meeting, phone call and social interaction that chamber professionals experience. With each encounter, we are either accumulating or spending our professional capital with our volunteer leaders. We're either enhancing or diminishing our reputations with our boards.

Some personalities fit well in the volunteer-led culture in which the CEO reports to a board; others don't. Sometimes, a capable professional without the background or personality to work for a group of people as the boss is overwhelmed with the complexity, the subtlety and the occasionally unavoidable confusion inherent in working for a board.

> *Some personalities fit well in the volunteer-led culture in which the CEO reports to a board; others don't.*

A New Boss Every Year

Working for a volunteer board of directors gives most chamber executives the opportunity and challenge of adapting to a new boss every year. Although board chairs are rarely given the formal authority to single-handedly hire or fire the chamber CEO, a board chair usually has a substantial amount of informal influence throughout the year. Other officers and board members tend to defer to the chair because that person usually interacts with the CEO more than any other volunteer and is perceived to be the volunteer leader with the most at stake in the success of the chamber. At a personal level, the chair typically plays a prominent role in the life of the chamber exec that can make the year very pleasant or the year from hell.

A well-oiled chamber has a lot of planning, history and momentum behind its programs – enough that a particular board member or board chair with a personal agenda will find it difficult to disrupt the direction of the organization without paying a pretty steep reputational price among his/her peers. I encouraged incoming board chairs to seek guidance by privately posing questions to previous board chairs about the chamber's priorities, about how much time is involved in holding the office, what it's like to work with the exec and the staff, and what are the possible pitfalls. If they received candid, constructive advice, as I hope they did, they came away believing that there was a solid body of work in terms of chamber goals and programs on which to build.

I was always included on the nominating committees of my chambers and participated in a supportive role in the process of selecting officers and directors. I was occasionally asked by the committees if one candidate for board chair would be better than another for me to work with. I was very reluctant to give direct answers, instead deferring to their judgment. I provided information that might affect their decisions, such as, "Tom says he's only two years from retirement," or "Marilyn is taking over the company from her father next year," or "We haven't had a female board chair in six years" or "There's really bad blood between Fred and the mayor," but I avoided trying to manipulate the process toward an outcome. As naive and potentially perilous as that might sound to some seasoned chamber executives who want a greater say in who ascends to the chairmanship of their chambers, a hands-off approach worked well for me and gave me safe distance from the decision-making when a board member felt slighted by not being tapped for a higher position.

Admittedly, there were times when the anticipation of an incoming chairman caused me anxiety. Even though I would usually get to know a rising board chair pretty well before he/she took office, approaching a new chamber year and a new chair with a different personality and management style could cause apprehension. Will he be overbearing? Will she attempt to flex her new-found profile in the community and assert her political muscle? Will the fact that he was upset with last year's chairman cause a schism within the board? Will the fact that her accounting firm lost the bid to audit the chamber's books cause her to hold a grudge against me or the finance director who oversaw the bid process? Will his inordinate desire to see his name in the newspaper cause him to seek the spotlight and speak for the chamber in inappropriate ways?

Board chairs differ widely in their appetite for engagement. I had board chairs who had intense demands in their corporate jobs and could only allocate a minimal amount of time to the chamber – presiding at board meetings, wanting succinct memos on key issues and seldom interacting except for necessary phone conversations to stay on top of the requirements of their office. At the other end of a spectrum, I knew a board chair who temporarily shifted his duties within his company to have a maximum impact during his year as chair of the chamber and asked if he should have a dedicated office in the chamber building.

I have found that former board chairs are very proud of their affiliation with the chamber and their respective years in that role. We found ways to engage them with an occasional dinner, and each year we invited them to serve on the board of our political action committee. Other chamber CEOs take it a step further and occasionally convene former chairs who are still active in the community as a sounding board on sensitive issues. They are certainly a resource for the chamber that can be tapped for support in a variety of ways.

One of my board chairs, the CEO of one of the state's largest and most prestigious employers, was busy hiring another 700 employees during his year as board chair, and he made a fantastic spokesperson for our chamber's top priority – workforce development. Local chambers across the state wanted him as their annual dinner speaker, and he accommodated several because he enjoyed speaking about the future of his industry. We couldn't have had a better spokesperson for our No. 1 priority for that year. In contrast, another of my board chairs from early in my career was so nervous about his speaking part at our annual dinner, he excused himself from the event altogether. A chamber executive must be able to adapt to these different personalities and changing circumstances. Being able to accommodate board chairs with such extreme differences in leadership styles can be challenging for a chamber executive who is working to provide consistency and predictability to an organizational culture.

Being able to accommodate board chairs with extreme differences in leadership styles can be challenging for a chamber executive who is working to provide consistency and predictability to an organizational culture.

I was fortunate in my career that my occasional anxiety about working with a new board chair always proved to be misplaced. While there were occasional rough spots as a new chair and I started working more closely, I am fortunate that I can now count every chair I worked with in more than thirty years as a friend and respected colleague. The number of times I had a direct, somewhat intense encounter with a board chair I can count on one hand. The one that comes most vividly to mind involved a chair who was a construction executive and took a special interest in the design of our building expansion. After several months of planning, I worried that he was micromanaging the project, and he probably felt I was pushing for a building that was extravagant by chamber standards. In retrospect, however, his questioning and perspective turned out to be pivotal in creating an amazingly attractive new conference center that was much better than I had imagined.

Being able to read your board chair is critical to adapting, surviving, being effective and enjoying being a chamber executive. One board chair might rely on you to prepare talking points for board meetings and will stick very closely to the printed word, while the next might be initially offended that you would even suggest what he/she might say in a board meeting. Some board chairs are eager to hear about the political maneuvering at City Hall or the state Capitol and want regular, insider updates. They will eagerly spend thirty minutes or more on the phone discussing political matters but don't want to spend more than two minutes discussing the chamber's budget. Others, just the opposite. Some board chairs prefer working behind the scenes while the next chair sees his/her time at the podium as a profound, once-in-a-lifetime opportunity to share his/her opinions about the community and to wake up an apathetic civic establishment.

Trying to ascertain a volunteer's basic motivations is a challenge that must be addressed. It's helpful to have a small set of trusted advisors either in the community, on the board or at the senior staff level – or some combination thereof – who can confidentially but candidly help the chamber exec understand what makes key volunteers – not just the board chair – tick. Is it a desire to advance the community, a directive from their employers, an opportunity to increase social status or enhance the profile of their own companies?

After analyzing the key motivations in an objective, non-judgmental way, a chamber exec can attempt to address those needs. Arranging speaking engagements, having the chair featured on a public affairs television show on a comfortable topic, or arranging a series of private lunches with local elected officials and corporate leaders may prove beneficial for gaining the chair's personal buy-in for the chamber, the CEO and the staff. One of my incoming board chairs confided to me that he felt bad that had never traveled in the other end of our state. We decided to arrange a three-day visit to that region with tours of major industries, lunches with local officials and receptions with local chamber leaders. He was delighted and said the itinerary made him feel like he was running for governor. Meanwhile, it was one of the best goodwill tours we ever orchestrated for our state chamber.

One thing I found that I had to keep at the center of my interactions with my board chairs and other top officers was the thought that "It's not about me; it's about their chamber." That can be hard to do when you constantly find yourself in the middle of chamber decisions and are frequently expected to step into the limelight as the chamber's spokesperson. But losing perspective and asserting yourself inappropriately can severely damage your reputation with your volunteer leaders.

I liked to think in terms of a chair's time in office as his/her year. While there is a significant amount of momentum that carries a chamber's strategic plans, priorities and programs forward from one year to the next, I wanted my board chair to look back and think of one or more key accomplishments that were initiated or completed during that time. For example, "That was the year we created the local leadership program," or "We created the downtown development corporation that year," or "We got a tax levy passed for the new high school." I like to think in terms of specific accomplishments my chamber made during my tenure as the exec, and I found that board chairs who typically held the position for only one year also enjoyed focusing on one or two signature accomplishments during their year. To commemorate their leadership, we usually gave our outgoing chairs a photo book of highlights to serve as a personal reminder of the chamber's distinct accomplishments during their respective years.

The No Surprises Rule

I worked for at least thirty different board chairs during my chamber career. Were there ever any tensions? Occasionally. But one tenet that was central to my relationship with board chairs can be best summed up as the no-surprises rule. If I knew of something that might catch a board chair off guard at an upcoming board meeting, I would shoot him/her a heads up email or text. I tried to anticipate questions from the chair and answer them before they were asked. For example, at the beginning of each chamber year, I gave my incoming chair and my treasurer an updated list of all of our legally binding financial obligations, our maintenance contracts, our special employment arrangements, the contracts we have with various consultants, the agreements we had for employee benefits and retirement programs and so forth. I just gave them a list – not the volumes of documents unless they asked. (They never did.) It was a detailed, three-page list but after the first time it was created, it took very little time to update once a year.

Why bother my board chair with such minutia? After all, I never had a board chair ask me about our HVAC maintenance contract. First, I wanted my board chair to have that list on file in case a question ever arose from a board member. I wanted my board chair to have complete confidence that I was open and ethical with our business dealings and was not, for example, paying my brother-in-law to pave the chamber's parking lot. More important than the details on the list was the relationship I wanted to have with my key leaders. I wanted to offer a level of transparency that minimized surprises and built maximum trust.

I avoided many surprises by asking my board chairs at the beginning of their terms about how they wanted to be briefed before board meetings. When I was at my smaller, hometown chamber, we prepared a printed agenda, and I discussed it with my board chair before the monthly meetings. However, I did not prepare a set of talking points or a script. My board chairs presided informally over the meeting, and I covered the agenda items I was supposed to cover, answering questions that were posed directly to me.

I wanted my board chair to have complete confidence that I was open and ethical with our business dealings and was not, for example, paying my brother-in-law to pave the chamber's parking lot.

When I arrived at a larger, metro chamber (Birmingham, AL), several things were different from my hometown chamber. They had quarterly meetings, the board was larger, the meetings were generally longer and more formal, the executive committee handled more of the routine chamber business, the committee structure played a greater role and, perhaps most important, the level of corporate leaders leading the chamber were some of the most prominent and influential leaders of Alabama. Many of my board chairs were accustomed to being prepped for meetings and public appearances by their staffs, in some cases with their public affairs or communications staff involved. From that point on, and later at my state chamber, I prepared talking points (in essence, an annotated agenda) for my board chair before each executive committee and board meeting.

About two weeks before each of those board meetings, I sent my board chair a rough list of the topics I suggested we include on the agenda and indicated which ones might be the dominant, more time-consuming topics. I also shared the outline with my senior staff and invited their input on topics they felt needed board attention. About a week in advance, we (staff) finalized the agenda and assigned suggested times to agenda items, indicating the anticipated pace of the three-to-four hour meeting. For example, we may have handled six or eight administrative items (the minutes, financial report, etc.) with a consent agenda that was approved with a single vote in less than five minutes. A topic that deserved some discussion might be assigned 15 minutes. If a university president, a consultant, the governor or some other special guest was going to address the board, we assigned 30-45 minutes, plus time for questions/answers. A panel of guests may have been allotted an hour for their topic. At some meetings, we allocated time for a discussion on a pressing issue, and we usually had a designated person (an officer, facilitator or myself) lead those sessions.

With the agenda finalized, we put together the executive committee and board notebooks, delivering the executive committee books by overnight mail a week early and the board notebooks handed to board members as they arrived at the meeting. Key materials for the board meeting had been posted about a week in advance on a protected website that board members could access. Increasingly during board meetings, board members worked from laptops where they accessed the electronic agenda and supporting documents. The annotated agenda for the chair contained notes that reminded him/her, for example, to recognize a board member who just received a significant honor, to present a gift to the guest speaker, or to invite the board to attend an upcoming chamber event. Of course my suggestions were simply prompts and could be used or discarded as the chair saw fit. I had some chairs who, even though they were very comfortable and confident at public speaking within their own companies or industry settings, would stick very closely to my suggested talking points. Others simply used the notes to remind them to comment on various items but otherwise ad libbed their parts in the meetings.

Board Meetings Worth Attending

If a chamber is going to attract the highest level of talent and prestige to its board, the meetings have to be worth attending. Board members should learn something they wouldn't have learned by reading the morning newspaper, meet other key leaders that they don't interact with on a regular basis, hear from a prominent speaker or have the opportunity to voice opinions on important issues. We often piggybacked a social event (usually a reception, dinner and light entertainment the night before) that added value and made it worthwhile for an executive who had to drive four or five hours across the state to sacrifice time at work to attend our meetings. Of course, the situation with local or regional chambers is different, but the principles are the same: Board members need to feel a distinct benefit and sense of privilege and prestige from serving on the chamber board.

A large part of that privilege comes from being in the same room with other business leaders who are peers in the community. Occasionally a board member would call and ask my executive assistant if he/she could send a surrogate. We routinely declined their offer, and we even started mentioning in our board meeting notices that proxies were not permitted. If a board member sent a representative from his/her company to the meeting, that immediately sent the remaining board members a signal that in-person attendance wasn't all that important and they could send one of their lieutenants. Allowing proxies affects the chemistry of board meetings and makes the remaining board members wonder why they bother to attend if junior members of other companies are allowed to attend. Is that elitist? Perhaps, but I found that the key members of my boards eagerly supported that approach, even when they occasionally had to miss a meeting.

I've often said that as a rule of thumb, the effectiveness of a nonprofit organization is inversely proportional to the amount of time the board spends discussing the bylaws. If a chamber board – or any nonprofit board – spends half its board meeting reviewing the treasurer's report, amending the by-laws or reviewing a list of members who have not renewed their memberships, a strong community leader will exit the board at the first opportunity or decline to participate in the first place. He/she will have very little patience for spending time processing that level of organizational trivia. Unless the chamber is in financial trouble and board members are forced to concentrate on keeping the chamber's doors open, routine business needs to be expedited so the board can focus on more meaningful community issues.

As a rule of thumb, the effectiveness of a nonprofit organization is inversely proportional to the amount of time the board spends discussing the bylaws.

Countless nonprofit organizations aspire to have a stronger board, a more prestigious board, a more resource-rich board, a board of C-suite decision-makers. What many of these organizations fail to realize is that an organization and the organization's CEO must first gain the respect of those top leaders, and that involves a multi-year process. If a prospective board member or a current board member has the impression that the organization is dealing in fluff – feel-good programs and less-than-critical community activities – he/she will quickly dismiss the chamber and look to invest time in more meaningful or higher-profile roles in the community. I told new board members that I would work to provide them a meaningful and enjoyable experience. I wanted them to look forward to each meeting and to enjoy getting to know the other board members, socially and professionally. To borrow a line from the Broadway musical, "Hamilton", I wanted them to feel good about "being in the room where it happens."

I served on numerous nonprofit boards during my career – some by virtue of my chamber position and some because of my personal interest in an organization's work. Once when attending my first board meeting of a particular nonprofit organization, I was only able to stay for the first hour of a meeting that was scheduled to last two and a half hours. The president decided to postpone the start of the meeting because one board member was caught in traffic and would be arriving 20 minutes late. Since the meeting was scheduled to begin with lunch, the president was in no particular rush to get the meeting started. So the lunch hour basically consisted of an hour of casual conversation. In the same meeting, the president mentioned that we (the board) really needed to work to get some top people on the board. I had to ask myself, "What's wrong with this picture?" You can't expect to recruit top talent to a board when the organization doesn't operate efficiently or – to use a term I prefer – crisply.

So, rule No. 1 for engaging top-level leaders with the chamber is to use their time wisely and efficiently. They have many demands on their schedules and opportunities at their businesses, many of which will actually make them money or gain them points within their own companies. Yes, time is money. In a very real sense, their spending valuable time at the chamber is either costing or making them money. At a basic level, if a board member makes $200,000, $500,000 or $1 million a year, their professional time is worth $100, $250 or $500 an hour, respectively. I once calculated that if our chamber had to pay our 75 board members to attend our four-hour board meeting, it would be tens of thousands of dollars. And that dollar figure didn't account for the opportunity cost of what they could produce for their own companies in an hour's time.

As I planned quarterly board meetings for my state chamber, I not only had to orchestrate a three- to four-hour board meeting that was worth their time, I also had to consider the fact that our board meetings typically involved a board reception and dinner the night before and, for many, a long drive across the state and back. I had to plan a board meeting that was sufficiently compelling and valuable to warrant their attendance.

How did we do that? I tried various formulas. The main elements of a board meeting usually included necessary chamber business (kept at a minimum), facilitated discussions and decisions on pertinent policy issues, guest speakers and structured briefings on key issues. The relative emphasis and time commitment for one of these elements versus the others depended largely on timing and circumstance but one thing became a constant for me: Try to minimize the time spent on the chamber's internal business operations.

I adjusted my thinking about the dynamics of board meetings after serving six years on the board of the U.S. Chamber. I found those three-hour, quarterly board meetings with more than 100 board members present to be relatively formal and scripted, but very worthwhile. Most of the U.S. Chamber's internal and policy materials were contained in a three-ring director's notebook with about 30 tabs subdividing the material. The committee recommendations and actions were combined into a consent agenda and were typically approved on a single voice vote. Most of the meeting was dedicated to presentations by major elected officials (the Speaker of the U.S. House, the Majority Leader of the U.S. Senate, even the President of the United States), presentations from a wide range of other interest groups (even, for example, labor leader Richard Trumka of the AFL-CIO) and presentations on key issues such as immigration reform, the economy and other timely topics.

While board members and committee members of my chamber were usually very capable and strategic-minded professionals in their own fields, I noticed that those same leaders would sometimes fall into a black hole of needless conversation on such pedestrian matters as the dues structure, membership renewals, bylaws and budgets if we allowed it to happen. If a board meeting veered into those areas and the conversation dragged out, I wondered if members might later question if the meeting had been worth their time.

Volunteer Leaders Who Operate at a Higher Level

I had the pleasure of serving with top-level executives who took time from their professional lives to serve as our board chair for a year. Sometimes they were executives with access to corporate aircraft, communication teams and hundreds or even thousands of employees reporting to them. One board member had 25,000 team members reporting up through channels to her. Many of her employees would have coveted an hour of her attention, and I knew I needed to function efficiently and bring my "A game" when interacting with her. The same holds true with other volunteer chamber leaders.

When I needed to brief my chairs or to seek their counsel on significant decisions, I usually made an appointment with their secretaries, suggested the length of the meeting and arrived with two copies of a printed agenda. After some friendly conversation, I asked whether they needed to share anything with me before I turned to my agenda.

That scenario wasn't always the case, of course. I had board chairs who budgeted a significant amount of time for their year as chair and who frankly, had more time than I did for a casual conversation. Channeling that level of commitment into opportunities for meaningful leadership was a challenge I gladly accepted. Having high-caliber leaders committed to our chamber was a major asset for our organization, and I felt it was up to me to find ways for our chamber to benefit from it.

"Paying" Your Volunteer Leaders

Certainly not every volunteer leader is motivated by getting his/her picture in the newspaper, but providing recognition for board members and especially your board chair is one of the best ways to compensate them for their time, effort and commitment. Moreover, if your board chair is the caliber and prominence your chamber wants and needs, you want your chamber to benefit from being associated with your volunteer leader's prestige in the community.

Providing recognition for board members and especially your board chair is one of the best ways to compensate them for their time, effort and commitment.

Throughout most of my career, we used paid advertising to display the photos of our board members and top investors in newspapers, business publications and promotional brochures. We displayed a prominent, framed copy of a photo spread of our board members and key investors in our lobby and in the offices of our senior staff members. The posters got an amazing amount of attention from visitors. Because we had a large board that only met quarterly, we included a copy of the board spread in the front pocket of every meeting notebook. From where I sat at the head table, I frequently saw board members studying the two-page spread. With a large, statewide board, this photo display of Who's Who proved very useful and popular.

I was amazed at the number of people in coffee shops and barber shops who mentioned the display ads and the caliber of people pictured. And, of course, the board members, investors and their families enjoyed hearing their neighbors mention the pictures. It served as an extremely valuable advertisement for our chamber, a compelling recruiting tool for new investors and a conspicuous thank you to our board members and investors.

I realize some chamber CEOs shy away from putting their board leaders in the limelight because of controversy that might accompany a chamber position on an issue, but in my experience, and with our chamber being bold on some tough issues, I rarely had board members get nervous or gun shy about being associated with the chamber. I had board members who were threatened with boycotts of their businesses over controversial chamber positions but instead of cowering, they stood tall for the chamber and let the chips fall wherever they might fall. Strong, relatively independent board members are often in a position to do that.

Listening – Really Listening – to Your Board

Every three years, we conducted a survey of our board members, using an independent third party such as the marketing department of a board member's firm or a private marketing consultant. The survey provided our seventy-five board members a confidential outlet for expressing their opinions about our governance processes, organizational culture, communications methods and political tone, asking whether we were speaking too stridently or too timidly on important issues. Not only did we offer the survey as an outlet for board members, we reported the aggregate results to the board.

It wasn't a policy survey about specific issues. It was more about the way the chamber conducted its operations and carried itself. It's one thing for board members to offer casual compliments about the annual dinner or the latest newsletter; it's another for board members to have an outlet for candid, confidential feedback about the performance of the chamber, the professionalism of its operations and their overall satisfaction with the organization. The responses helped us stay aligned with our mission and strategic plan and helped us gauge how aggressively we might pursue our issues. If a chamber exec chooses to publicly weigh in on an issue and perhaps disagree with a mayor or governor on the front page of the newspaper, it's very important to know the intentions and sensitivities of the board beforehand. Obviously, the board surveys didn't address every situation that came along, but they helped our leadership and me better understand the collective thinking of the board and its appetite for the chamber to assert itself.

It's important for board members to have an outlet for candid, confidential feedback about the performance of the chamber, the professionalism of its operations and their overall satisfaction with the organization.

The Power of Match-Making

As I reflect on a career in nonprofit management, I wonder if I could have been more effective if I had put the word matchmaker at the top of my job description and perhaps scrawled it across my shaving mirror as a daily reminder. I am referring to being a matchmaker in the sense of connecting the right community issue or chamber project with the right, highly motivated volunteer leader. As almost every chamber exec knows, getting the wrong volunteer behind an important task leads to intense frustration and the hopeless feeling that you are pushing a rope up a hill. You have to nag the volunteer to call meetings, stay on task and make progress toward a goal. Conversely, getting the right leader who takes ownership of a cause can lead to results that far exceed your expectations.

Getting the wrong volunteer behind an important task leads to intense frustration and the hopeless feeling that you are pushing a rope up a hill.

A case in point: After I arrived at the Kentucky Chamber, I immediately noticed that the headquarters building was relatively dated and nondescript. Plus, we were out of space. It was barely adequate for the existing functions and could not accommodate any additional staff unless we asked a couple of partner organizations that leased space from the chamber to leave. We didn't want to jettison those groups or to weaken our strategic partnerships with them.

I came up with a relatively modest plan that involved expanding the back of the building and refinancing our mortgage to cover the costs. A substantial amount of discussion and even a full set of expensive architectural drawings went into the plan before my board chairman said, "If we're going to do this, let's do it right!" His bold challenge and his pledge of the first $100,000 to get the board involved in supporting the project led to a complete rethinking of the plan. After a mid-course correction, the project evolved into a $3 million expansion on the front of our headquarters – an expansion that literally redefined the image and reputation of the organization. It even caused a dramatic shift in our function as a convener of like-minded business and trade associations to address state issues. With the most modern, most accessible meeting space in the state's capital, we were able to expand our mission as a convener and collaborate with dozens of organizations to achieve our chamber's goals. The highly successful project reminded me, once again, that matching the right volunteers with the right individual tasks can multiply the chamber's effectiveness exponentially.

Board members may serve for the prestige of the position, for recognition, to protect their business interests, to be in the know or from a sense of civic duty. Regardless of the reason, most community volunteers are motivated by a cause they believe in. Sometimes, you can point to existing chamber programs or projects that are compelling enough for a prospective board member to want to engage. Other times, it's a matter of suggesting a future initiative or task that you can use to motivate a particular board member. I was often surprised at the energy and time a board member was willing to invest when a particular initiative hit his/her hot button. Ask the right board member to conduct a branding study, commission a survey, design a new logo, host a meeting, turn loose an employee on a specialized issue, call the mayor or take on some other task, and he/she will turn loose and usually bring a very professional approach that your organization could not afford to purchase on its own. Ask the right board member to chair the membership drive or the building campaign and you might have the luxury of standing back and watching it unfold in ways you couldn't have accomplished on your own or even imagined.

Confrontation with Volunteers and Community Leaders

There are a multitude of books and articles on conflict management, some of which deal specifically with nonprofit, volunteer-led organizations. But what does conflict management mean when it comes to managing a chamber, specifically in terms of conflict with your chamber board members, other community leaders and chamber volunteers?

I was fortunate to have consistently positive relationships with board members and especially board chairs during my career. I have heard other chamber veterans comment on troublesome, overbearing board chairs, and I have sympathized with them. I realize circumstances can produce a board leader with whom your personality or skill set simply doesn't match. I have to wonder, however, about chamber execs if they have continuing issues with board leaders. Either the system of identifying and recruiting volunteer leaders is flawed, the chamber exec is not performing at the level the chamber's volunteer leadership expects or the chamber exec is just extraordinarily unlucky in having a string of troublesome volunteers.

With the strong business leaders most chambers want on their boards, one can expect strong opinions and impulses. But if the organization is moving forward with an adopted set of goals established through its multi-year strategic plan and its annual business plans, and if there is positive cohesion among board members, those individual impulses can be held in check or properly channeled. The chamber exec doesn't have to be the referee of all the capricious impulses of the volunteers. A volunteer who goes rogue and decides to pursue an independent course can be brought back into the fold through peer pressure from the broader group of board members or a strong board chair willing to corral individual members.

I was advised to always have a volunteer between myself and any controversy. In other words, if a board member insisted that I do X, I could respond, "Actually, the board decided earlier this year that we should do Y," "You probably need to talk to the board chair," or "That's an interesting idea, but Frank chairs that committee, and you probably need to take it up with him before we pursue it."

I found that some of my most contentious interactions were actually with individuals who were second or third-level lieutenants operating as surrogates for their bosses who were on my board. They would sometimes take liberties with their demands and could be more confrontational than their bosses would be. I countered those impulses by trying to talk firmly but respectfully about our chamber's position on the issue at hand and deflect their demands with, "I'll need to consult my board leadership about that," or by calling the person's bluff with, "Is that something you could put in an email to me, with a copy to (your boss)?"

I was advised to always have a volunteer between myself and any controversy.

My experience over several decades suggested that firm but respectful responses generally established a relationship whereby the chamber exec avoided becoming a punching bag for heavy-handed political players and instead was positioned as a constructive force who had to be acknowledged, if not appreciated, by outside stakeholders. That doesn't mean all conflicts were resolved with absolute harmony. There were some situations with persons who seemed to consistently deal in bad faith and with self-interested agendas that could not be satisfied. I admit there were a few people – fortunately less than a handful – I encountered in my career who were generally intolerable and who I avoided as much as possible. I couldn't trust them and worried that they would use any statement of mine against me or my chamber, so my conversations were stiff and guarded. In some of those circumstances, I even wanted to protect myself by having a third person in the room who could make contemporaneous notes of the encounter. In one extreme case, after a contentious conversation that had the potential to blow up and even be job-threatening to me, I followed with a certified letter to the person (a corporate lobbyist of a major chamber member), summarizing my thoughts on the issue at hand and requesting a written confirmation. I wanted a paper trail.

No profession is free of conflict but in some, confrontation is more inherent. During the 12-year portion of my career I spent in politics – both on the staff of a U.S. Senator and later as mayor of my home-town – I found there were more occasions when people operated with fairly sharp elbows, aggressively pursuing their political agendas at the expense of others. I considered some of those individuals blatantly self-interested, others quietly manipulative and still others diabolical to the point of sociopathic. They certainly weren't the norm – many good, well-intentioned people serve in government and politics – but in general, the sharp elbows were more prevalent in the political realm than in the chamber arena. I found that the vast majority of my interpersonal relationships in Chamber World were with people who rose through the ranks of their companies and professions by learning basic professional skills, practicing ethical behavior, channeling their ambition in constructive ways and being rewarded and/or promoted during their careers for demonstrating good faith toward others. Chambers and chamber volunteers with those successful backgrounds in business usually bring with them an aura of positive energy, good will and optimism.

■ ■ ■

The ability to work with a board of directors, continually adapt to new board chairs, navigate different personalities and manage sensitive situations as a chamber executive comes with the accumulated experience of surviving difficult situations in the past, confidence in what you are doing and who you represent, and knowing that your volunteer leadership has your back. Earning the trust of a board of directors can give a chamber executive considerable professional freedom, a positive environment in which to manage a chamber and the opportunity to provide dynamic leadership for the organization.

CHAPTER 6
DEVELOPING YOUR BOARD

Most nonprofit organizations – including chambers – aspire to strengthen their boards by recruiting more horsepower in terms of prestige, political wherewithal and access to financial resources. How does a chamber exec strengthen a chamber's board of directors and attract the leadership needed to grow the chamber? How does the chamber exec build up a board of directors that can effectively address the community's toughest challenges and most promising opportunities?

The Size and Make-up of Your Board

There are countless books about board dynamics, many of which address the proper size of boards. During my career, I worked comfortably with boards ranging from 25 to 75 members, and I don't believe there is one correct answer for board size, nor do I believe that a smaller board is necessarily more efficient than a large one. Chambers of all sizes need to reflect the broader business community, to be the face of a diverse business community, to avoid the impression of cliquishness and to consistently gather input from multiple constituencies. It is also important for a board to represent various industry sectors, the major investors in the chamber, the demographics of the chamber's service area and, in the case of metro and state chambers, the geographic regions of the chamber's service area. Those many factors require a delicate balance.

Chambers of all sizes need to reflect the broader business community, to be the face of a diverse business community, to avoid the impression of cliquishness and to consistently gather input from multiple constituencies.

When a chamber has a relatively large board, a smaller executive committee can operate efficiently on behalf of the board, diving deeper into organizational details such as budgets, financial reports, performance reviews and internal policy oversight. It can provide the more thoughtful deliberation and collective judgment that helps steer the ship and provide guidance to the CEO, the staff and the full board. Processing certain governance decisions through an executive committee requires a healthy level of transparency and trust between that smaller group and the full board to avoid turf issues and resentment. A larger board that sees value in the content of a well-planned board meeting and trusts the executive committee to process more complex, sensitive and internal decisions on its behalf – thereby saving board members' valuable time – will appreciate the role of the executive committee.

A critical way to establish that trust is to ensure transparency, allowing the board to monitor and understand the workings of the executive committee. At each of my board meetings, the minutes of recent executive committee meetings were included in the materials so board members could maintain a sense of what the executive committee was processing on its behalf. We also offered the opportunity for board members to pose questions about the workings of the committee structure – not only the executive committee's actions but also important committees such as our public policy councils. Utilizing a highly engaged executive committee allowed us to structure our board meetings to be more substantive and interesting.

Some organizational experts encourage separating the formal governance and fiduciary duties of an organization from the larger board of directors and vesting those matters in a much smaller group. This is meant to provide greater efficiency but also to reduce liability for board members who attend just a few meetings a year and don't want to see themselves drawn into a liability issue such as an employee grievance, an insurance claim or a lawsuit. Our chamber did not adopt that level of separation during my tenure, but with board members' time constraints a constant challenge, we gradually moved toward more governance at the executive committee level and less at the board level. In some cases, the executive committee might have spent an hour or two, spread over a couple of meetings, navigating an important issue for the chamber before formally recommending a solution to the full board with a brief summary leading to a voice vote to ratify the executive committee's actions. Other times, the executive committee actually made a decision during the interim between board meetings and then reported the decision and the rationale behind it in a memorandum to the board or at the next full board meeting. Technically, the board could override any decision of the executive committee unless the decision had legally obligated the chamber, but that never happened.

A question about board makeup that many chambers have to address is whether to include elected officials on the board. The upside is that you actively engage those officials in the workings of your chamber and you can build productive partnerships with government leaders. On the other hand, having elected officials on the board can sometimes stifle discussion among business leaders about sensitive policy issues and subject some of your correspondence and your board documents to open records inquiries (assuming the elected officials have the documents in their possession). There is also a risk that having, for example, the mayor and the county executive invited onto the board, only to have those officials decide later they are too busy to serve and end up appointing a city or county council person or a municipal staff member as their surrogate. When that happens, the chamber loses the direct line of communication with the top government decision-makers and may end up with placeholders who ostensibly represent the local government but are actually more motivated by the prestige and privilege of being on a board with prominent business people. There is no right answer to the question of government representatives on the board but having your business leaders make those decisions after a serious weighing of the pros and cons (addressed in greater detail in the following section on accepting public funding) and building protections into your bylaws, such as limiting ex officio slots to only the mayor and county executive, can be important.

Competing for Volunteer Talent

Certainly chambers don't have a monopoly on the volunteer talent in their communities; they have to compete for the attention, respect, time and resources of top leaders. Generally, building a stronger chamber board involves a multi-year, strategic effort to gradually nurture the strength, profile and prestige of the board.

Building a stronger, chamber board involves a multi-year, strategic effort to gradually nurture the strength, profile and prestige of the board.

Usually chambers are interested in attracting blue chip business leaders who are decision makers in their own companies and whose companies are already committed to the chamber's mission. The nominating committee discusses how it can get the bank president, the industrialist, the philanthropist and the healthcare CEO on the board. While members of the Who's Who of a community's business community are appropriate prospects, there are other factors that contribute to developing a strong board. Sometimes chambers find it advantageous to recruit board members with specific expertise such as fundraising, legal, accounting or marketing, and they consciously work to diversify their boards by adding members from sectors of the community that have been under-represented in the past.

As you work to build a stronger, more diverse board, it's not only a matter of choosing what prospects to recruit, it's also important to select the right person to do the recruiting. It's easy to underestimate the value of having your top volunteer leaders recruit their peers to the chamber board. It's often easy and efficient (and occasionally self-serving) for the chamber exec to volunteer to make the recruiting calls on behalf of the nominating committee. But having a bank president call another community leader who is a business or social peer can be extremely valuable. If your incumbent board member truly believes in the chamber, he/she can make a more convincing argument for getting involved than you can as the paid staff person. Using your best and most influential leaders can give you a competitive advantage. They can often use the won't-take-no-for-an-answer method with their peers, something the chamber exec might not be brash enough to attempt or able to pull off. The exec might simply not have the asking rights to successfully recruit a targeted board prospect, but the prospect's banker....or the prospect's former college roommate...... or his next-door neighbor might.

I had past chairs who took pride in the members they recruited to the chamber board, and I observed one situation in which a top CEO called another and left him a voicemail, telling him (not asking him) that it was his time to step up and serve on the chamber board. The recipient of that impersonal, unilateral directive was a prominent CEO who would have been coveted as a board member for any organization in our state and who, a few short years later, emerged as a very effective board chair for our chamber. And it all traced back to a voice message left by someone who had the standing, the asking rights and the nerve to pull it off.

Whom should you target? If you have, for example, a local leader from a national bank that has a branch in your community, you might gain prestige from that person's profile, but you might also have a board member who can't approve an expenditure of more than $1,000 without going up the corporate ladder in the bank's regional headquarters in another city. Those factors need to be weighed. There is also a risk in asking a CEO to serve, only to have him/her decline and offer you an assistant marketing manager as a substitute. It's important to have a back-up plan for who is next on your list of prospective board members so you can politely decline the offer to accept a substitute, and you're able to say that the nominating committee has instructed you to extend invitations to a specific list of targeted nominees who have already been vetted by the committee.

Needs vary, but generally you should strive for decision-makers and strong civic-minded leaders. At a very basic level, it's important to encourage your nominating committee to consciously answer the following questions about each prospect:

- What, specifically, does this prospect bring to the table for our organization?

- How will his/her joining the board make the board stronger?

- Does the candidate have access to key influencers? To money? To talent they can mobilize for the chamber's priorities?

- Who among our pool of prospects might make a strong candidate for the executive committee and perhaps for the chairmanship two or three years down the road?

Diversity and the Face of Your Chamber

Minorities will be the majority population in the U.S. by 2045 and chambers, traditionally older, whiter and often predominantly male, must adapt. Heaven forbid that we reduce that imperative to an issue of appearances. We need to embrace the more compelling economic case for diversity: Businesses and communities that practice diversity, equity and inclusion are better prepared to recruit and retain talent and are more effective at navigating the diverse, competitive marketplace with their products and services.

Chambers are becoming increasingly aware of the value of diversity and inclusion in their organizations, on their boards, in their programming and within their staffs. Culturally, we are becoming more aware – thankfully – to think in terms of racial diversity, gender, sexual orientation and gender identification. But diversity in a chamber context has even more dimensions as leaders work consciously to engage representatives from across various business sectors and work to balance large businesses with small businesses. Do we have any young entrepreneurs on our board? Do we have more lawyers than manufacturers? Are Black and Hispanic business leaders properly represented?

Striving for greater board diversity poses a question for chambers: Should the diversity of the board reflect the collective leadership of the business community, its primary investors, or the broader community which is probably very different from the business community in age, gender, race and socio-economic standing? I don't suggest that any one of these three approaches is perfect. However, if your board reflects only the established business leadership, your chamber will probably be viewed suspiciously in the broader community, e.g. by neighborhood activists and city council members when you go to City Hall to represent the business community. On the other hand, members who invest in your organization and who are genuinely interested in participating have a right and often an expectation to be represented on the board. The right answer is probably somewhere in between these alternatives, with an eye toward building a diverse board based on the distinct contribution that individual board members can bring to the table.

The image of an exclusive group of older white men sitting around a board table behind closed doors and making decisions for your chamber and community is not the brand you want to convey to a modern audience – certainly not to a younger, more diverse audience. But striving for greater board diversity shouldn't be treated as merely an issue of optics; being an inclusive organization is a major factor for the effectiveness of chambers. Diverse board members bring diverse perspectives that are essential for developing and executing strategies that lead to an organization's success and a community's economic prosperity.

As the new president of the Birmingham Chamber of Commerce in 1999, I quickly learned that racial diversity was a top priority of the chamber, and the African-American Business Council within our chamber had more active programming and more members than the local African-American Chamber of Commerce. Our Hispanic Business Council had more energy and enthusiasm than any of our other business councils or committees. Leaders of those communities sought connections to the major companies in town, and the chamber offered the best platform for building important business-to-business and personal relationships. The councils offered employment programs, diversity training, seminars on procurement and even cultural festivals. They also taught me that there was lucrative sponsorship potential for their activities, and many small, minority-owned businesses joined the chamber just to be part of those councils.

Diversity was a priority within the Chamber's governance structure, specifically during the deliberations of our nominating committee. I sensed that part of that inclination was "to do the right thing" and part was a more pragmatic cultural sensitivity honed from years of the racial experience in that community. Local business leaders had developed, in my view, a progressive recognition of the organizational and economic value of diversity, and racial inclusion was top-of-mind with many of Birmingham's business leaders.

At the Kentucky Chamber, I learned that geographic diversity was a sensitive issue in the areas of the state that are more remote and feel neglected by urban elites and state government. And as virtually every chamber exec can attest, small businesses always feel left out when corporate leaders are provided a high profile within a chamber. On the other side of that coin, I find that small business leaders also want very much to be involved with an organization where corporate leaders from the larger companies are engaged. A chamber's air of exclusive privilege can make a board seat more coveted by those who are outside the inner circle of an organization.

As I prepared for our annual nominating process, I gave our board development committee a wealth of data and a statistical profile of our relative diversity – or lack thereof – in terms of ethnicity, gender, business sectors (e.g. hospitals vs. law firms vs. manufacturing vs. finance, etc.), small businesses vs. large businesses, regional representation and investor levels. To a lesser extent, being a state chamber in a partisan political environment also caused us to sometimes consider the partisan political profile of our individual board members, hoping that even if we didn't have numerical balance, we had a defensible mix of political donors and operatives with partisan credentials and connections to key policymakers.

> Diversity doesn't just happen; it requires intentionality. A chamber leader has to consciously decide that his/her chamber must be more inclusive and then work to attain the right mix.

Diversity doesn't just happen; it requires intentionality and attention to details. A chamber leader has to consciously decide that his/her chamber must be more inclusive, gain the support of key board leaders who are part of the nominating process and then work to attain the right mix that will make the organization more effective.

Building the Financial Strength of Your Board

Chamber leaders naturally want to attract board members who can access resources and make decisions to commit those resources. You also want board members who are comfortable making business decisions that are larger than the scale of your organization. I was privileged to work for boards where many of the members led larger organizations, had huge responsibilities and were paid several times what I was paid. They were generally more accustomed to the role of a board member (policy) versus the role of the CEO (operations). I found that if they respected me and trusted the job I was doing, they were not going to quibble when it came time for raises or bonuses.

When I was still in my early 20s and invited to attend my first chamber nominating committee meeting, my boss at my hometown chamber told me privately and bluntly, "If you get members on the board who make less than you do, you can expect problems." He went on to explain that a person who is perhaps on a second or third rung of the ladder at his company and is assigned by his/her employer to serve on the chamber board, has difficulty understanding why a chamber exec should be paid a professional salary, especially if it's more than that board member makes. After all, how difficult is it to run a chamber, go to ribbon-cuttings, attend civic meetings and say nice things about the community?

Having board members who are accustomed to making financial and management decisions larger than the chamber routinely makes helps avoid the micromanagement that can bog down a chamber board's more important planning and decision-making role.

While that admonition was not universally true, I found it to ring true time and again – not just on matters of compensation but on a variety of issues relating to who should manage the chamber and how involved a board member ought to be in the day-to-day decision-making of the organization. Having board members who are accustomed to making financial and management decisions larger than the chamber routinely makes helps avoid the micromanagement and obsession with minutiae that can bog down a chamber board's more important planning and decision-making role. Those higher-level business leaders are also better positioned to access financial support for the chamber from their own companies, from foundations and from their peers in the community.

Onboarding New Directors

Developing a stronger and more diverse board is more than identifying and recruiting key business leaders; orienting new board members is also an essential step for onboarding. At the suggestion of a former board chair who wanted to offer a welcoming environment for new board members who were coming from across the state to a meeting of 75 people, the majority of whom they didn't know, we recruited incumbent board members to reach out as mentors to first-time members, telling them what to expect and answering their questions about serving on the chamber board.

We offered an orientation session for our new directors – usually a breakfast hosted by our board chair immediately before their first board meeting. They were introduced to each other and to the staff and given an orientation notebook with materials about chamber programs, expectations of board members and the role of volunteer board members (setting policy) vs. paid staff (managing operations). They were briefed on the structure of the chamber, their fiduciary responsibilities for the organization, the current strategic plan, the current year's business plan, the budget and the chamber's public policy priorities. Each of our key staff members described the products and services offered in their respective areas of responsibility.

It's very easy for those of us at the staff level to forget that board members – even those who have served on other nonprofit and corporate boards – often lack a basic awareness of a chamber's distinct mission, the wide variety of services it offers and the organizational culture of a volunteer led, professionally managed organization.

Creating a Cohesive Social Group

It's very important to create a strong sense of camaraderie within the ranks of your chamber board – an esprit de corps founded on a shared sense of mission, sufficient opportunities for social interaction, meaningful conversations at chamber meetings and a certain pride in being included in the decision-making of the group. In a real sense, you are creating a strong, cohesive social unit of acceptance and mutual support. I felt a sense of accomplishment when I heard that a chamber board member made a meaningful new business relationship or friendship by serving on the chamber board. That told me we were creating the right chemistry.

Our chamber staff was very intentional in how we structured events, the unique venues we selected for board receptions and dinners, how we structured the agendas, how we arranged the seating. We wanted their experience on our board to be of higher quality, more enjoyable, more prestigious and more exclusive than they would expect from their other civic engagements. Some of our leaders served on or even chaired the boards of their state and national trade associations. Many had seen how top-notch professional associations functioned and conducted their meetings, so we knew the bar was very high if we were going to retain their participation and loyalty.

Something I would have never anticipated is that many of our board members liked to travel together. We backed into that realization. In 2014, we hosted an invitation-only trip to Dubai with board members and spouses paying their own way. Kentucky had a unique relationship with Sheikh Mohammed bin Rashid Al Maktoum, the ruler of Dubai, through the thoroughbred horse industry and the international equestrian federation. He owns three large horse farms near Lexington, Kentucky. Seizing the opportunity to create stronger links, I invited our governor and first lady to lead our delegation, and we took approximately thirty in our first chamber delegation. While it was billed as a trade mission, it was actually about 80% tourism (tours, cultural experiences, shopping, dining, etc.) and 20% business (formal receptions, business meetings, etc.).

Many of the board members would not have ventured to the Middle East on their own, and even if they had, they probably would have not experienced such exclusive events as a tour of the Burj Khalifa, the world's tallest building, and a lavish reception hosted by Princess Haya on the plaza of the Armani Hotel. The participants on our first trip had such a good time together that on the flight home, they lightheartedly pressed our incoming chair, the president of Toyota Motor Manufacturing Kentucky, about where he was going to take them during his year as chairman. That led to our next delegation visiting Japan the following year and sponsoring a reception at U.S. Ambassador Caroline Kennedy's residence in honor of more than 150 Japanese companies that have operations in Kentucky. A Japanese conglomerate with bourbon distillery operations in Kentucky was delighted to sponsor the event. The next year: Great Britain, where the U.S. Ambassador was from Kentucky. The next year it was Ireland, the ancestral home of one of our board members who along with her husband, restored and converted an abandoned church near his boyhood home into an Irish whiskey distillery and popular tourist attraction. In 2018, our delegation of 60 went to Canada, where the U.S. Ambassador was from Kentucky and happened to be married to our board chair. In 2019, the destination was New York City, where the now former Ambassador to Canada served in her new position as the U.S. Ambassador to the U.N.

The common theme for these excursions was selecting a destination with a unique connection to our state. We weren't trying to run a travel agency, but we created a tradition that board members wanted to continue. The chamber broke even on the trip while covering the travel costs of several senior staff members who accompanied the group and managed logistics. It wasn't meant to be a moneymaker for the chamber; the real benefit was the camaraderie and overall team building that such experiences generate. Just as colleges and universities commonly offer alumni travel opportunities, the point is not the revenue; it's building a base of loyalty among alumni who happen to be among the most likely donors to the schools' (and in our case, the chamber's) subsequent fundraising campaigns.

I'm not suggesting that all chambers need to get into the travel business. At my smaller, hometown chamber, it was an annual board retreat. For others, it might be an annual dinner cruise or a bus trip to the state capital. The point is that social cohesion is an integral part of strong organizational dynamics; all of the relationships and good will created on our trade missions accrued to the benefit of the chamber as an organization. They helped foster a healthy, cohesive organization that can take on tough issues, work as a team and generally function at a higher level. The travel component at our state chamber also created a social group that others wanted to join.

Balancing exclusivity with inclusivity requires an ongoing effort and great finesse. A strong chamber needs both. Having a diverse and inclusive board and offering unique board experiences that create personal bonds among members help achieve and sustain that important balance.

Balancing exclusivity with inclusivity requires an ongoing effort and great finesse. A strong chamber needs both.

■ ■ ■

Developing a strong board of directors is essential for increasing the effectiveness and the overall standing of a chamber within its community. It requires an ongoing, multi-year effort of recruitment, training, gaining respect, building camaraderie among board members and offering opportunities for meaningful engagement for those members. Strategic recruitment can't be an afterthought on the chamber exec's to-do list; it has to be among the highest priorities, or the chamber will never raise the bar of its reputation and impact in the community.

CHAPTER 7
DEVELOPING YOUR STAFF

Whether your chamber staff is one or one hundred, getting the right people on the bus as *Good to Great* author Jim Collins succinctly stated, is critical for success. Creating a professional team that understands and truly feels part of the larger mission not only multiplies your effectiveness as a chamber leader but strengthens the chamber's organizational capacity to shape the community's future. How do we build and sustain buy-in from our staff regardless of size?

Hiring People Smarter Than You

We've all heard successful CEOs say that one of their keys to success is that they have surrounded themselves with people smarter than themselves. Whether that claim is feigned humility or a sincere management philosophy is hard to determine unless you look deep inside their organizations. In one sense, hiring people smarter than you is automatic. After all, unless you know accounting, hiring an accountant or even a competent bookkeeper puts you in the category of hiring people smarter than you are. Multiply that times the number of other people around you who have a specialized role and, assuming they have a relatively high level of competence, you are now surrounded by people smarter – or at least more capable in their roles – than you are.

Raising that notion to a higher level, let's add specialized motivations to the mix. It's important to surround yourself with people who can truly do a better job because they also possess distinct motivations that drive them to excel in their particular roles. Finding and grooming individuals with the drive to consistently perform at exceptional levels should be a CEO's continuing priority.

To illustrate this point, I point to a few members of the team I had in place when I retired. Our senior VP of membership and development (our chief rainmaker) not only enjoyed asking people for money for a cause she believed in, she was a numbers person, and keeping track of the metrics of our sales team was how she kept score of her success. She couldn't wait to make another pitch for one of our fundraising causes, and she was bolder in asking than I was. Our senior VP of public affairs had relationships with elected officials that far exceeded mine, and she loved nothing more than asking a wavering senator if he was going to stay true to his word and vote the way he said he would. Our senior VP of business services, who oversaw more than $3 million in events, publications and seminars annually, had the ability to create high-caliber programs and possessed a customer service instinct that I could never sustain over time. He had the patience and tact to juggle peoples' personalities and smooth out conflicts. All three VPs were specialists in their areas, had distinct motivations to excel and did their jobs far better than I could – even if I had the background knowledge they possessed.

When I could recruit and empower that level of talent-plus-motivation down the line with our entire staff, I knew we had created a well-oiled, high-performing team. We had, for example, a team of highly motivated membership sales managers for whom I had profound admiration. I couldn't imagine motivating myself every morning to get out of bed and approach prospect after prospect, enthusiastically offering our chamber's membership proposition and getting several no's before getting a yes. I often wanted to hug our sales reps when I saw them in the hallway; I was amazed at their work ethic and their tenacity – their ability to get a "no thanks" and bounce back.

When we had vacancies in our organization, I generally looked to our staff vice presidents to advertise the open positions in their divisions, screen the applicants, interview their finalists and select their team members. Occasionally I participated in the final interviews of one or two leading candidates. My questions for the vice presidents might have included: Have you run personality profiles on your finalists? Have you checked their references and other background sources? What makes them uniquely qualified for this role? How does a particular candidate explain the multiple moves from job to job earlier in his/her career? What makes you think this candidate is genuinely hungry for success in this position? I might also have suggested factors in the hiring process that an individual manager might overlook, for example: Have you actively recruited minority candidates? How do you think your preferred candidate will interact with a particular staffer in another division who is critical to the success of one of our major programs?

I don't know of anyone who claims to have scored 100% when it comes to hiring successes. There are so many factors to consider, any one of which could lead to a great fit or to a very disappointing mismatch. After several decades of hiring chamber staffers, I continued to revise the factors I considered critical for an employee's success. I admit my list of priorities continued to evolve, usually affected by the last hiring mistake I made. Hiring success or failure is very easy to see six months or a year after you've hired someone; what you know after a few weeks of working with someone is infinitely greater than what you gleaned from a resume and after a couple of hours of an interview process.

My evolving list of key criteria included what I call spark (a special drive), basic intelligence and a track record of striving for success. The key word is striving. All of this adds up to an overarching criterion I call horsepower. Does the candidate bring a high level of horsepower to the organization, regardless of what level position we were filling? If a young candidate didn't have a long work record, was there a college experience that demonstrated a desire to achieve? While I considered a candidate's grade point average a relevant indicator of how someone applied him/herself, I was far more impressed by an extracurricular record that demonstrated leadership or engagement in what was going on. Did he/she participate in a team effort such as sports or writing for the campus paper? Did he/she travel overseas? Was he/she promoted by his/her peers to a position of leadership, perhaps in a Greek organization? Or did the candidate merely go through a few years of attending class and taking the required tests in order to obtain the obligatory degree? Four years of "seat time" wasn't sufficient to assure me of future success.

My evolving list of key criteria for hiring a new employee included what I call spark (a special drive), basic intelligence and a track record of striving for success. The key word is striving. All of this adds up to an overarching criterion I call horsepower.

I recall a job candidate in her 30's who did not have the benefit of a college degree but who – according to one work experience listed on her resume – had worked as a teenager at a fast food restaurant. What really impressed me was that she had been promoted to shift manager while still a teenager. Wow! That indicated to me that she had the spark, the maturity and the horsepower we needed on our marketing team.

My goal when hiring was always to consider myself truly lucky to have recruited the person we hired. Occasionally, I had the good fortune to attract a high-powered professional I couldn't otherwise afford. For example, I benefited from attracting the trailing spouse of a professional recruited by another employer in our region. Another time, I benefited from hiring a very talented woman whose husband was a local surgeon, whose kids were now school age and who wanted to make a significant contribution to our community. She ran our leadership program successfully for several years at a compensation level that by no means corresponded to her competence or time commitment. She was passionate about interacting with emerging leaders and being associated with their continuing career success. I felt I hit a home run in finding her.

I learned that there is also incredible talent available to chambers by engaging experienced individuals on contract instead of through full-time employment (what some have called "renting" talent instead of "buying" talent). At our state chamber, we could attract exceptional talent and experience by bringing retired state government veterans onto our team and offering a relatively modest monthly retainer and an hourly fee for the time they spent working on our projects. We obtained more horsepower for far less than I could have ever afforded with full-time employees producing similar work. We recruited a former chief of staff to a governor, a former legislative analyst and director for the state attorney general with detailed knowledge of government operations, a former legislative budget director, a former chair of a state political party and even a former governor. In all of these cases, we simply could not afford to hire their levels of expertise in a full-time capacity, even if such individuals were available for those positions.

It's also important to find new employees who fit well with the current staff. Because we often spend as much time with our coworkers as we do our family members, it's important to create a convivial atmosphere that allows each staff member the opportunity to be engaged in a cause that is bigger than our individual goals. Nothing is more satisfying than to hear former staff members say that they look back on their time at our chamber as the most enjoyable and fulfilling job they ever had.

Building a Diverse Staff that Reflects the Community

As I matured in my chamber career and my own social consciousness, staff diversity became a greater priority. When I moved to the Birmingham Chamber, I grew in my awareness of issues of racial inequity, and I adopted a philosophy that our chamber staff of about 40 should reflect the diverse region we served. Upon my arrival, there were only four African-American staffers, two were janitors (we owned a historic 14-story building), one was a long-time secretary and one was a staff director over several of our programs. As I left five years later and after consistently advocating the goal of greater diversity, our staff included ten African-Americans including two vice presidents on our executive team of six vice presidents. I created one of those two positions as a VP of Community Development and recruited the public affairs assistant to the Birmingham mayor and former television reporter to join our staff and oversee our outreach efforts in the community.

Racial diversity on our staff didn't just happen. It required deliberate action. When posting an open position at our chamber, African-American job candidates didn't always emerge in the stack of resumes in proportion to their demographic profile in the community. There were multiple reasons for that – too many factors to responsibly address here – but we tried to overcome those cultural challenges by recruiting at nearby colleges and HBCUs, Historically Black Colleges and Universities, in Alabama. While we weren't able to achieve all of the goals we set for staff diversity, we made substantial and noticeable progress. And it made us a better and more effective chamber for that community. Today, I'm proud that my former chamber colleagues include distinguished African-American staffers who have gone on to great professional positions as entrepre-

While we weren't able to achieve all of the goals we set for staff diversity, we made substantial and noticeable progress. And it made us a better and more effective chamber for that community.

neurs, political figures, higher education administrators, chamber execs and, in at least one case, as a gifted metro chamber CEO.

Establishing a Rhythm

It's important to establish a rhythm that your staffs can depend on and by which they can pace themselves. Our weekly staff meetings (which were mandatory for our senior team but were open to all staff members), our monthly all-staff lunches, our monthly senior staff planning sessions, our quarterly board meetings (to which all staff were usually invited), our annual staff outings, our casual dress days, our holiday luncheons, our annual evaluations – all enhanced communication and contributed to a more predictable and structured rhythm that shaped our chamber's internal team culture.

While regular Monday morning staff meetings for comparing our calendars and reporting on our individual projects may have seemed mundane and too detailed for those who were eager to start their week and tackle their to-do lists, I'm convinced that the time spent sharing those details saved us considerable time later by avoiding confusion, clumsiness and scheduling conflicts. Plus, it gave staff members who were working in their own functional silos the opportunity to hear what was happening elsewhere in the organization and to more fully comprehend the breadth of our mission.

Coaching by Delegating

Perhaps the best ways to nurture a strong staff is to invest in professional development (discussed later in Chapter 17) and to assign increasingly challenging tasks to those who demonstrate their abilities and gain your trust. My assistant was hired within a year of my arrival into a relatively traditional secretarial role and as a gatekeeper for my office. But because of her attention to detail, her professionalism and her routine contacts with board members and their executive assistants, she grew into a role that was absolutely crucial not only for managing the logistics of board meetings but to sustaining the cohesive board culture that made our chamber strong. Board members' and their executive assistants' confidence in her professionalism and their dependence on accurate and timely information from our office helped increase trust and respect for the chamber. She had a great appetite for expanding her role and her value to our chamber.

Admittedly, delegating comes hard for some of us who have enjoyed an element of success in our respective roles, have been rewarded for our attention to detail and have high standards for things being handled well. We have to discipline ourselves to stand back from our wide assortment of responsibilities and force ourselves to consciously identify functions we can delegate to others. We have to remember that delegating has at least three distinct benefits: one is for the organization – to efficiently manage an array of routine tasks and new initiatives, another is for the CEO to multiply his/her effectiveness by utilizing other team members and a third, very important purpose is for the individual staff member's professional development. In that third sense, delegating is primarily instructive, allowing someone to learn by doing and hone the skills needed to take on increasingly greater responsibilities in the future.

Managing Turnover

One of the organizational issues that negatively affect chambers is staff turnover. I found it relatively easy to attract talented people to the chamber. They have the opportunity to meet many of the most influential people in the community, be an insider on many community issues and events, and work for a cause that is bigger than self. But soon after new staffers came on board, they got noticed – by chamber board members, by elected officials, by other nonprofits and by community leaders who interact with the chamber. They learned important skills such as managing projects and interacting with volunteers. And they sometimes got stolen. That problem comes with the territory for chambers of commerce. If your chamber has a high profile in the community, your staff members are going to be noticed by the community and offered other job opportunities.

I didn't resent chamber staff members going on to greener pastures, IF they had made a reasonable investment in their own careers while at the chamber. What's reasonable? I often talked to job candidates about what I called my "two-year handshake." I wanted a candidate to look me in the eye and tell me he/she planned to make an investment in our chamber of at least two years. After all, our chamber would make a significant investment in the candidate's training and development. Neither the candidate nor I could foresee the personal and organizational circumstances that would affect their tenure, but I didn't want someone to join our team and then use it as a springboard to float resumes to other organizations a few months later. We (the chamber) and a new employee owed it to each other to make a good-faith commitment of at least a couple of years. I realized I was not offering him/her a guaranteed employment contract for two years and likewise, I realized that if that person's spouse got a professional opportunity in another community, or developed health issues, or won the lottery, their life circumstances would change. But short of extraordinary developments, I wanted the new employee committed to stay at least a couple of years.

While sometimes staff changes are necessary, hiring capable people through the front door but losing years of experience out the back door does not reflect a chamber that is on a trajectory toward excellence.

One of the important elements of developing a stable, high-performing staff is to manage turnover. I've seen chamber staffs decimated in terms of their collective experience and institutional knowledge because of a new CEO cleaning house or because of other organizational disruptions. While sometimes changes are necessary, hiring capable people through the front door but losing years of experience out the back door does not reflect a chamber that is on a trajectory toward excellence.

There are various factors involved in staff turnover: staff morale, compensation and benefit levels, having the right people in the right positions, and having staff leadership that is committed to creating a culture that nurtures talent. There are factors that also increase the likelihood of turnover, such as the common perception that opportunities for upward mobility are limited in small organizations.

I monitored turnover (total years of experience divided by the number of employees) on a quarterly basis because I wanted to increase our average tenure, even as we occasionally lost talented employees to other jobs and gradually expanded our staff (thereby reducing the statistical average of years per employee). As a member of an ACCE task force in the early 2000s with the responsibility of modernizing the ACCE annual benchmarking survey of chambers, I advocated including average staff tenure as an indicator of organizational stability and collective institutional knowledge and as a way chambers could compare their turnover rates with a national average for our industry.

According to the latest ACCE national data, the average tenure of staff members for all participating chambers is 6.5 years. During my tenure at a state chamber, we built our average tenure to nearly nine years (which I thought was very good) but at one point, we experienced a sharp decline to 6.7 years due to the retirement of a single 35-year employee and a dramatic staff expansion of eight new employees in our workforce center. Even though we experienced a temporary statistical decline, we were growing in staff capacity, and my interest in monitoring turnover was not diminished. Gaining more experience, talent and combined institutional knowledge on our staffs should always be the goal of an ambitious chamber.

■ ■ ■

A stable, experienced staff is critical for the performance of a chamber. While larger chambers are more likely to be relatively staff driven, developing your staff – regardless of size – and constantly working to increase its capacity to manage effectively and gain the confidence of your chamber's volunteer leaders is at the top of the list of responsibilities of a chamber executive. Hiring people who perform better than we could ever perform in their respective jobs, establishing an internal rhythm, delegating responsibilities and managing turnover are key elements to success for achieving increasingly higher levels of success.

CHAPTER 8
DEVELOPING RESOURCES

A chamber that is truly aspirational, wanting to accomplish more for its community, will naturally want to grow as an organization. Growth in membership, financial resources, board strength, influence, profile and programming are all parts of wanting to do more and to do it better. How do chamber execs look beyond the status quo to create a new reality, grow their chambers and expand their effectiveness? Traditional means of growing our organizations remain critical, but there are also some exciting new ways that show tremendous promise.

Expanding the Membership Base

We all want more chamber members. Membership growth is the traditional method by which chambers keep their doors open and expand their financial bases. However, expanding the number of members is becoming harder to do. Fewer and fewer businesses join a chamber out of a sense of civic obligation. As discussed in Chapter 12, people don't join organizations the way previous generations did. I find that more and more business people want a distinct ROI, a return on investment for their dues, gauging what's in it for them personally and professionally. "What am I going to get out of it? Increased exposure at the annual meeting? More business contacts? The opportunity to interact with 'the big players' (the more influential business leaders in town)? More clout on my issues at City Hall or at the state capitol?"

Membership growth is the traditional method by which chambers keep their doors open and expand their financial bases. However, expanding the number of members is becoming harder to do.

The concept of tiered membership, with different member benefits linked to different investment levels (as opposed to strict dues formulas based on the number of employees of a firm) has swept Chamber World in the past few decades. At our chamber, we kept a traditional dues formula that we used primarily as an opening talking point with our prospects, but our membership team quickly pivoted to the investment tiers we called our recognition levels. And with most of our chamber programming (annual meetings, conferences, seminars), we typically offered preferential seating, exposure, a speaking part on the program, a booth in the lobby, and other benefits for higher-paying participants and sponsors. I found that although no one enjoys sitting on the back row of a banquet, chamber members generally understood and accepted tiered pricing for participation, for sponsorship and even for stratified membership benefits.

Growing a membership base, especially the <u>number</u> of members, is increasingly difficult and growing the <u>dollars</u> of membership revenue takes a concerted effort. I've had members cut back on their membership investment (often attributing it to corporate belt-tightening) while simultaneously offering to sponsor a key event for greater exposure or donate to our chamber foundation from a different pot of corporate money. That's part of the new reality facing chambers – both as a threat but also as an opportunity. One of the charts I occasionally showed our executive committee was a 20-year trend in our number of dues-paying members, and it wasn't very flattering when viewed by itself. Our chamber experienced a precipitous decline in members – several hundred dropped out – under the previous administration of our state chamber. I'm not throwing stones at the previous president; I actually mention this with admiration. The chamber lobbied for worker's comp insurance reform in Kentucky and was successful in passing sweeping reforms and saving the business community hundreds of millions of dollars. But in doing so, it essentially put the chamber's own workers comp insurance program (with its lucrative revenue stream) out of business. Businesses that had joined the chamber just to get the insurance discounts left when the program ended. Since that exodus, we struggled to even remain flat in our number of members. Many chambers across the country have also experienced a decline in their number of members but not necessarily a drop in membership revenue.

When creating the annual budget for our state chamber, we typically budgeted between 89% and 91% retention of membership dollars. Most recently, ACCE reported a median retention rate of 88% for chambers. During the Great Recession, we dropped to 89%, and some years we enjoyed up to 91%. In other words, each year we expected to receive 89% to 91% of the dollars we received from last year's members, taking into account some member businesses closing during the year. Of course, that meant we had to recruit at least an equal amount of new dollars to cover the churn of members departing our ranks. Chambers in smaller, more cohesive business communities can sometimes achieve higher retention percentages, but all the chambers I know have to peddle pretty hard to keep up with the inevitable attrition that typically characterizes a voluntary membership association.

The good news I gave our executive committee was the other part of my chart of membership trends: During that same 20-year time period, the average investment of our members (dollars per member) grew dramatically, and our overall membership revenue grew at a healthy, albeit incremental, pace. In other words, fewer members – by definition our most loyal members – stayed with us but were willing to pay more – not because they were volunteering to pick up the slack for the drop-outs, but because they perceived real value from their affiliation. I suspect that many chambers that are growing in revenue have experienced the fewer-total-members-paying-more phenomenon.

From my vantage point, I don't foresee a day when chambers completely abandon membership dues, although many have already abandoned their strict membership-based-on-size-of-company formulas. Dues revenue still keeps the doors open and allows a chamber to fulfill its most basic mission in a community. But as I explore in the following sections, I see much more potential for revenue growth in other areas, and I believe chambers will need to adapt to new realities to grow.

Generating Non-dues Revenue

While members paying dues has historically been the core of chambers' business model, the term non-dues revenue gained currency (pun intended) in the latter half of the last century. Chambers grew their organizations by producing fee-for-service revenue from such activities as seminars, training programs, golf outings, publications and awards banquets. Various affinity programs (often called member discount or endorsement programs) also caught favor, offering members preferential discounts for specific chamber-endorsed products and services while producing royalties or commissions for the sponsoring chambers. Long-distance telephone discounts, workers' compensation and health insurance discounts, shop-local incentive programs, 10% off office supplies for small businesses, airline discounts and other such programs were offered. Many affinity programs were tried, only to lose favor a few years later. Some, including insurance programs, typically had a longer shelf life and produced meaningful revenue for many chambers. After disappointments with a few lackluster affinity programs that we ultimately decided to discontinue, I instituted a policy that we required a $15,000 up-front guarantee of first year revenue before we would consider endorsing and lending our name and credibility to someone else's product or service.

The three chambers I served experienced occasional windfalls from such fee-for-service and/or affinity programs. In the case of my state chamber, total non-dues revenue grew to the point of exceeding membership dues, allowing us to offer countless services we couldn't afford to offer if we were dependent solely on dues revenue. We introduced several new programs that were financially successful, but we didn't discover a silver bullet affinity program that would ever substitute for the shoulder-to-the-wheel hard work and determination required to expand a membership base. Non-dues revenue certainly helped us expand our services to our members, and it made us a stronger, more resilient organization because it diversified our revenue streams and made us less dependent on membership dues.

Non-dues revenue certainly helped us expand our services to our members, and it made us a stronger, more resilient organization because it diversified our revenue streams and made us less dependent on membership dues.

Maximizing non-dues revenue involves more than finding a magic new affinity program a chamber can offer; it also requires constantly and aggressively testing the market for pricing your traditional services (seminars, annual meetings, networking events) so you are covering your chamber's true costs (including staff time and overhead costs) and not subsidizing those specialized membership services from dues revenue.

One thing that almost all chambers have in common is the desire to expand their revenue base. ACCE offers copious revenue-generating resources for membership and business services professionals on its website, in various peer groups and at its annual convention.

While I have commented on the two traditional legs of a three-legged revenue model for chambers, I will now go into greater depth on what I consider a promising third leg.

Cause-based Fundraising

A promising opportunity for new revenue lies within a general category I'll label cause-based fundraising. I use this broad term to convey more than soliciting financial sponsorships for the usual membership activities. I am referring to the conscious act of identifying a cause – a new building, a scholarship fund, an issues campaign, an endowment to sustain a chamber program into the future – and setting a goal to raise a certain amount of dollars for that specific cause. The opportunity for a chamber to attract cause-based donations is fertile ground for ambitious chambers to plow.

The source of these resources includes but is not limited to companies with budgets for memberships, marketing and charitable giving. Other sources include an unprecedented amount of individual wealth in our country and, while billions of dollars are concentrated in the hands of well-known national foundations such as the Ford Foundation, the Kellogg Foundation and the Bill and Melinda Gates Foundation, a tremendous amount of private wealth resides in the hands of people who live in our own communities. According to the consulting firm Accenture, the transfer of more than $12 trillion of private wealth from the World War II generation to Baby Boomers continues in North America, and an even greater transfer of assets is beginning as Baby Boomers bequeath their private wealth, estimated at more than $30 trillion, to beneficiaries in the next generation. At its peak between 2031 and 2045, more than 10% of this wealth will change hands every five years.

How does that transfer of wealth affect chambers of commerce? Sure, much of that money will pass to the heirs of the older generation, with a portion being siphoned off by federal and state governments through estate and capital gains taxes. But there is also a substantial amount being designated to charities and charitable foundations that have been established to accomplish specific goals of the donors. As evidence, consider the dramatic growth in the past couple of decades of locally based community foundations. Some of the goals of wealthy private donors and their foundations run parallel to the goals of a chamber of commerce – improving education, improving the quality of life in our communities, expanding economic prosperity to underserved populations and so forth. The overlap between charitable causes and chamber missions is our opportunity zone – our sweet spot – and compels us to consider an active fundraising strategy to identify financial resources and match them with our chamber's goals.

I realize there are many folks in our professional ranks who recoil at the notion of fundraising; many simply don't like asking for money. On a personal level, I found traditional fundraising for a routine civic commitment such as soliciting friends and neighbors for contributions to a PTA fund-raiser or a local charity to sometimes be

The overlap between charitable causes and chamber missions is our opportunity zone – our sweet spot – and compels us to consider an active fundraising strategy to identify financial resources and match them with our chambers' goals.

tedious, time-consuming and distracting, but fundraising for an exciting new chamber initiative was often invigorating and fulfilling. A major ingredient for success is a strong personal belief in what your chamber stands for and what it is trying to accomplish, a clear sense of the opportunities that lie ahead for your chamber if you can raise sufficient resources, and the chamber's (and your) general willingness to undertake serious initiatives in the community which command respect and are worthy of financial support.

The most valuable role of a chamber exec might be in strategizing and facilitating fundraising, more than in direct solicitation. I was once told by a professional fundraiser that the "Four Rs of Fundraising" are to have the Right cause, to ask for the Right amount, to ask at the Right time and to have the Right person making the ask. Therefore, strategizing about how to recruit someone who is in a better position to make "the ask" can be much more effective than the chamber exec feeling personally responsible for countless solicitations.

There are multiple avenues for attracting cause-based resources for your chamber, your established programs and those initiatives you hope your chamber can undertake in the future:

1. Donations to the chamber itself, such as a building campaign or a multi-year economic development campaign

2. Charitable donations to a chamber's 501-c-3 charitable foundation for causes that benefit the general public and for which there are often tax deductions available to donors

3. Issue campaigns the chamber conducts through the chamber itself or through a chamber-affiliated 501-c-4 entity, such as a campaign to get a referendum or tax-levy passed for a new high school or to support a candidate who supports the chamber's agenda

4. Political donations given to a chamber-affiliated federal or state political action committee (PAC) for the purpose of supporting specific political candidates or causes

Of these, the potential for attracting charitable contributions to a chamber foundation is probably the most promising opportunity for accomplishing great things for our communities and substantially increasing the financial resources chambers need to grow.

My experience with our chamber foundation convinced me there is fantastic potential for chambers in the realm of philanthropy, attracting donations from foundations and individuals whose charitable interests overlap with a chamber's mission. Some of those possible areas of common interest include education; workforce; health and wellness; economic development; diversity, equity and inclusion initiatives; visioning projects; historic preservation; justice reform; government efficiency; poverty; programs targeting underserved populations; economic mobility; housing; community appearance and community image.

I believe this great, largely untapped potential not only has profound implications for chambers, it has important implications for chamber professionals. By way of illustration, I'll offer an analogy from higher education – specifically from colleges, universities and their presidents.

Having chaired the board of trustees of my alma mater, a small liberal arts college in Kentucky, during the search process for a new president, I was struck by the strong consensus among my fellow trustees that a new president's track record of successful fundraising was absolutely critical – more so than having a Ph.D. We needed someone with demonstrated success in cultivating the donor base of alumni/ae, foundations and friends of the college. With small colleges facing multiple headwinds in recruiting from a declining pool of traditional college students, rising overhead costs and competition from online learning, hiring a president who was not suited by disposition or professional skills to raising money would literally pose an existential threat to the school.

The college analogy, I believe, sheds light on our profession and tells us that chamber execs of the future are going to have to be more like college and university presidents – constantly matching the needs of their institutions with potential donors, cultivating those donors (what some have called "friend-raising"), and eagerly making the ask or recruiting the right person to make the ask when causes and donors are aligned. To focus on those opportunities, chamber execs are going to have to be skillful in minimizing the time they spend on the operational overhead and the fluff that have long encumbered our roles. To put it bluntly, we cannot afford to spend an hour listening to a Rotary speech or attending countless community events to provide what I call the "warm body treatment" (making sure someone is present to represent the chamber) or serving on extracurricular nonprofit boards and committees when that same amount of time spent with a potential donor could yield thousands of dollars of investment for the important initiatives of our chambers. Chamber professionals will have to be especially selective in deciding how to allocate their time and their mental energies in order to maximize their focus on resource development. Friend-raising and fund-raising will need to be at or near the top of their lists of priorities.

Immense Private Wealth in our Communities

To highlight the potential of strategic fundraising for our chambers, I offer an inspiring story from a small county of 23,000 citizens in Kentucky. It's not typical of all communities, but I believe it makes a relevant point for all chambers about the vast potential for chambers to attract outside money.

The late Felix Martin was a native of Muhlenberg County, a coal-producing county in western Kentucky that has been hard-hit by the decline of the coal market. Early in his career, he held various public relations jobs with the telephone company in Kentucky, but when his father died, he inherited $267,000 – a handsome sum, especially in 1960 – and he moved to Florida and became a full-time investor in the stock market. Thirty years later, he returned to his hometown to care for his mother. She died in 2001 at age 98 and left him an estate of about $8 million. A bachelor, he lived on Main Street in his parents' home, attended the Rotary Club and the United Methodist Church and generally led a quiet, unassuming life. Little did the community know that before he died in 2007, he had amassed an estate of more than $60 million. Even more eye-popping than his wealth was the fact that he had quietly created a private trust, the Felix Martin Jr. Foundation, to be administered by the Community Foundation of Louisville for the exclusive benefit of the citizens of Muhlenberg County. He wisely chose an out-of-town foundation to manage the funds because he wanted his trust administered by professionals who didn't have a conflict of interest with the local community. At the moment of his death, his estate deposited $50 million in his new foundation and his gift was announced posthumously to the community.

The Felix Martin Jr. Foundation's mission is what provides a relevant lesson for chambers of commerce. On its website, the stated purpose is *"to create a charitable foundation … for the benefit of the education, civic, and cultural needs of the residents of Muhlenberg County, Kentucky."* The list of community projects to which the foundation has given more than $25 million since its creation reads much like a digest of traditional chamber initiatives: economic development, education and various quality of life initiatives. Felix Martin wanted to see his beloved community and his fellow citizens grow and prosper. His foundation is advancing a mission not unlike the missions of most chambers of commerce.

Not every community has a mega-wealth benefactor, but there is a startling amount of wealth in most American communities. According to the U.S. Department of Labor, 1.02% of all households in America have a net worth of $10 million or more – making them so-called deca-millionaires. Therefore, a typical community with 100,000 households has 1,020 very high net worth households. Most of that wealth will pass on to heirs, but countless millions will pass to other beneficiaries favored by those households: churches, colleges, the local history museum, the United Way, the Salvation Army. As chamber professionals, we must ask

> According to the U.S. Department of Labor, 1.02% of all households in America have a net worth of $10 million or more – making them so-called deca-millionaires. Therefore, a typical community with 100,000 households has 1,020 very high net worth households.

ourselves: Where are the community-building initiatives of our chambers – for scholarships, for historic preservation, for job-training programs, for economic development and many other programs – on the list of priorities favored by those wealthy individuals? How do we identify those potential donors and determine how their charitable priorities align with the needs of our chambers and communities? How do we approach those potential donors or their foundations and make our case? This is where the skill set of chamber executives will need to adapt to a new, potentially powerful opportunity for our chambers and our communities.

Chamber Foundations: Shaping a New Business Model?

Expanding on the proposition that there is more potential for growing a chamber through strategic fundraising than membership dues, I suggest that this potential could also point to a new business model for chambers – one involving the three-legged stool of revenue streams: membership dues, non-dues revenue and a determined commitment to cause-based fundraising.

With this new approach, chamber members who resist a $100 dues increase will instead invest $10,000 or $100,000 for a cause for which they are passionate. Those causes could include community development initiatives such as a new riverfront project or establishing a scholarship endowment for local high school graduates to attend the community college – the types of quintessential chamber initiatives that can attract substantial support from the business community and from philanthropic sources.

Chamber members who resist a $100 dues increase will instead invest $10,000 or $100,000 for a cause for which they are passionate.

When I explore the fundraising potential of chambers, I focus primarily but not exclusively on raising money through a chamber-based foundation, a charitable arm of a chamber set up under IRS code 501-c-3. I focus on four types of chambers:

1. Chambers without a foundation. For chambers that have not created a separate foundation as a charitable arm of the chamber, I encourage you to contact a local attorney or an accountant and ask for assistance in establishing one. ACCE, which has its own very active foundation, offers resources for creating a separate foundation. It's not difficult or expensive. Obtaining approval from the IRS and registering your foundation in your state – generally with your Secretary of State – require a minimal fee.

   Back in the '70s and '80s when many large and mid-sized chambers were creating their own foundations, the IRS seemed skeptical, questioning why a chamber of commerce would claim to be a charity. Hence, chamber foundations often used names that were more charitable-sounding like the Community Growth and Education Foundation. Today, that's not so much an issue. Hundreds of local and state chambers have their own foundations, and they are often named more explicitly. For example, ours was simply the Kentucky Chamber Foundation. Another, much larger example of a chamber-based foundation is the U.S. Chamber Foundation that raises millions of dollars each year to support specific U.S. Chamber initiatives that fall within the charitable parameters defined by the IRS. While lobbying Congress for tax reforms or offering exclusive product discounts for chamber members are clearly not charitable in nature and can't be supported through a chamber foundation, conducting research into how to improve achievement in public schools clearly is. A chamber-based foundation can raise money and pay for those kinds of chamber activities if they are conducted under the auspices of the foundation.

2. Chambers with dormant foundations. These are chamber foundations that were created in the past for a particular

purpose and still exist on paper but are now dormant; they exist legally but serve as a vehicle only if and when someone wants to make a tax-deductible donation for a specific cause. For chambers with such a foundation, I encourage you to consider the programs your chamber offers or wants to offer and consider what charitable resources in your community or beyond could help your chamber expand. Much of what your chamber does would likely qualify as a charitable endeavor because it is either educational in nature or with a clear public benefit. Perhaps a local bank wants to be recognized in the community for helping disadvantaged kids learn financial literacy, or a local hospital has expressed interest in getting employers involved in improving community health, or a wealthy individual has demonstrated a passionate interest in a particular cause that lies within the mission of your chamber, or an outside foundation on the state or national level is known to favor certain causes that your chamber espouses. Begin cross-referencing your chamber's existing programs and proposed goals with a list of possible sources of charitable contributions and their individual giving histories.

As a practical and immediate step, consider recruiting one of your more dedicated board members to chair your foundation and challenge him/her to take on the task of making the foundation a more active part of your chamber.

3. Chambers with active foundations. These chambers have foundations that regularly solicit contributions to support ongoing chamber programs such as community leadership programs, programs to encourage entrepreneurism, scholarship programs, programs to support beautification projects and so forth. These chambers are experienced at using their foundations as the charitable arms of their chambers and allowing supporters to gain tax advantages by donating through their foundations. They can receive grants from other charitable foundations that share their interests. And chambers with active

foundations have a base of experience from which to advance to the next category of chambers.

4. <u>Chambers with intentional foundations</u>. The key word I use for this category is intentional. These are chambers that consciously and systematically commit to fundraising, soliciting charitable donations to extend the chamber's mission and effectiveness. They make specific organizational adjustments within their chambers to actively identify and pursue local, state and national funding sources. Their leaders have made a decision that is far more deliberate than simply saying, "Let's apply to the Bill and Melinda Gates Foundation and see if we can get some money for our XYZ program," and it involves a much longer-term strategy than soliciting a one-time donation to cover a gap in the annual budget. It needs to be strategic and must be a multi-year effort. It will require some organizational adjustments within the chamber, examples of which are discussed below.

As a practical example of the transition of a chamber from level 3 to level 4 in the categories of foundations, I offer a few lessons we learned with our chamber foundation. I would like to claim that its growth was due to a brilliant master plan hatched in a strategic planning process but, honestly, we backed into a few substantial grant opportunities and pursued them before we realized that we were entering a whole new world – and perhaps developing a new business model for our chamber. At some point it dawned on us that we needed a more thoughtful strategy to position our organization for more active and deliberate fundraising. We needed to incorporate fundraising as an ongoing element of our chamber's role in the community and institutionalize it within our daily operations.

We didn't realize it at the time, but the basic concept was laid out in ACCE's 2015 "Horizon Initiative" and its "Nine Influences" that are predicted to shape the environment for chambers in coming years.

The prescient insight contained in that report didn't register with me during my first reading. Specifically, I didn't fully internalize the point that speaks to the value of aligning a chamber's goals with resources that will support those goals. It took some practical experience for me to connect the dots and gain a better understanding of this new frontier. Because we were expanding our chamber's programs and had naturally explored possibilities for outside funding, our foundation revenue was growing rapidly, and we noticed it now rivaled the revenue we received from membership dues.

> Because we were expanding our chamber's programs and had naturally explored possibilities for outside funding, our foundation revenue was growing rapidly, and we noticed it now rivaled the revenue we received from membership dues.

The sources of our foundation revenue were individual contributions, corporate contributions, corporate foundation grants, private foundations (national, state and local) and public/private partnerships involving government contracts. An example of the latter is a program in which we partnered with our state government. State education and economic development officials approached us because they liked what we were doing in workforce development – specifically engaging employers in workforce solutions. They proposed that we enter into a contract by which we would hire five "talent pipeline managers" to convene industries in regions across our state and develop industry-specific streams of talent for their operations. In similar fashion, many local chambers have often entered into government contracts for programs such as promoting tourism, downtown development and business recruitment. In some cases, these contracts are between a government agency and the chamber itself. In other cases, it has been advantageous for the contract to be with the chamber's foundation – a topic explored in greater detail in Chapter 10.

Our chamber's work in public policy began to attract favorable attention and, eventually, substantial outside support and funding. Some of our work on education standards attracted the attention of the Gates Foundation, and they approached us about how they could support our efforts. They wanted us to ramp up our efforts in ways our limited resources wouldn't allow. We received an initial grant followed by several subsequent grants, and at some point, I realized that we were getting more money from a single foundation than all the money we were bringing in by selling new memberships.

Another example was one of our issue campaigns that was aimed at reforming the state's pension systems. We decided to produce a radio ad for a few targeted radio markets, primarily to encourage a couple of key legislators to support our bill. We put up a modest $5,000 and solicited the Kentucky League of Cities for a matching $5,000 to run a limited number of commercials. When a Texas-based foundation that champions public pension reform heard about our ad, they offered to wire us $100,000 the next day so we could add 200 more radio stations across the state. We couldn't use our charitable foundation for such a lobbying effort and instead channeled the money through the chamber itself, but the opportunity was becoming much clearer to us: There were outside groups with vast resources that would support the types of initiatives that are the meat and potatoes of chambers of commerce. And we started to pay greater attention to the potential for becoming more intentional and strategic with our fundraising.

Here are some practical steps (not necessarily in order of priority) that can help your chamber pursue such a course:

1. Engage a few key board members and make the conscious decision to actively pursue fundraising for your chamber's top priorities, using your foundation, your chamber itself, your 501-c-4 and/or your PAC as appropriate vehicles.

2. Activate your foundation board. We expanded our board, recruited strong leaders, increased its profile within our chamber, created formal bylaws and started having regular

meetings that piggybacked our chamber board's quarterly meetings.

3. Include fundraising as a priority of your day-to-day CEO responsibilities and outline the first practical steps you will take.

4. Develop a strategic plan for your foundation – a plan that is separate from, but aligned with, your chamber's strategic plan.

5. Make necessary internal staff adjustments. We decided to rename our senior vice president of membership and marketing (our chief revenue officer) as "senior vice president of membership and development" and we revised her job description to move toward a 50/50 time commitment between traditional membership sales and fundraising. Because she supervised our membership sales team, we decided to elevate one of our sales managers to director of membership development to relieve our vice president of some of her supervisory and sales duties. This transition didn't happen overnight; with a set-back here and there, we continued to work toward the 50/50 goal so our vice president could commit more time to concentrate on identifying sources of outside money, grant writing, cultivating relationships with foundations and donors (which are critical to eventually making the ask) and fulfilling the reporting requirements of foundations that provide donations.

6. Determine whether you have the staff capacity to raise private dollars or write grants. If you don't, work to recruit a volunteer or engage someone on contract to provide that service.

7. Consider recruiting a consultant who is an experienced fundraiser and who knows foundations and their giving patterns.

8. Attend carefully selected conferences where foundations gather, perhaps in your state. Talk to them about your efforts – without initially soliciting funds. Listen to their priorities and find areas of common interest.

9. Schedule a routine update from your foundation board chair during your chamber board meetings.

10. Work to elevate the profile and prestige of your foundation within your chamber's communications program.

Because we had a tiered dues membership structure with graduated levels of recognition for our investors, we decided to recognize charitable donations to our foundation as part of our investor recognition categories such as Trustees, Chairman's Circle and Commonwealth Partners. We decided to give a 50-cents-on-the-dollar credit for donations to our foundation. In other words, a company investing $5,000 in dues would still get full credit for that investment in the chamber, but if they gave an additional $5,000 to our foundation, they would get 50% credit ($2,500) for that donation and recognition for a combined chamber/foundation investment of $7,500. In some cases, this put an investor into a higher, more prestigious category when we published our investors' photos in advertisements, printed event programs and in a prominent display in our lobby. We chose not to give full credit for donations to our foundation because we didn't want to dis-incentivize dues investments that sustain the core mission and functions of the chamber.

One closing thought about cause-based fundraising: A chamber that becomes intentional in its fundraising has to be careful about a downside that can come with pursuing grants. A foundation that has resources it is willing to dedicate to your chamber's cause probably also has a distinct agenda of its own – an agenda that overlaps with but is not necessarily identical to your chamber's mission. Often those foundations are eager to have the business community as a partner for their cause and they can attempt, consciously or unconsciously, to steer the chamber toward specific goals they have in mind. Case in point: When our state chamber received major financial support for our Kentucky Chamber Workforce Center to engage employers in dealing with the opioid problem in our state, we had to occasionally remind ourselves that we were not an addiction clinic or a placement agency; our interest in the opioid problem was a workforce issue for our employers. We had to carve out our role in the workforce space, stay in that space and not be lured toward many other well-intentioned goals associated with the opioid problem. We had to work to avoid mission creep and gradually moving away from our exclusive mission as a business association.

The Administrative Costs of Managing a Foundation

As a chamber expands its fundraising, it should also recognize that those activities will place added responsibility on the chamber itself in terms of staff time and overhead expenses for accounting, auditing, compliance requirements of private grants and public contracts, sometimes keeping time sheets and other administrative tasks. In addition, the chamber takes on reputational risks by accepting outside money and by lending its name to partnerships with outside groups. Rather than have your chamber subsidize your external fundraising by absorbing the costs of administrative services and the value of the chamber's endorsement, I recommend adopting a policy for capturing for your chamber a certain percentage of the money flowing through your chamber foundation from outside grants and contracts.

> *As a chamber expands its fundraising, it should also recognize that those activities will place added responsibility on the chamber itself in terms of staff time and overhead expenses.*

A few years ago, I advocated that the Council of State Chambers (COSC) adopt a policy that would in effect create an industry standard for state chambers to capture 12% of pass-through dollars (dollars flowing through their foundations, their PACs or their foundations, their PACs or other chamber-affiliated entities) to cover their administrative costs. COSC adopted such a policy and our chamber in turn adopted the

12% as our policy, pointing to the COSC policy as the normative expectation for state chambers.

Admittedly however, our 12% "policy" had no teeth; it was simply a guideline and served as our opening talking point when formalizing a relationship with an outside funding source. If, for example, a private foundation responded by saying it only allowed 10% for administrative overhead, we generally didn't contest the point; we accepted 10% and negotiated any other costs associated with fulfilling the grant. If a partnership with a donor required more than an administrative effort on our part and involved, for example, raising a sizable amount of additional money for a particular campaign or agreeing to staff a particular program (vs. merely serving as a fiscal agent for the grant), considerably more than 12% for overhead might have been warranted. Consideration of being reimbursed for the direct costs of required staff time would be in order. In some cases with funding from national foundations, we captured a percentage for overhead _and_ billed our documented staff time at individual hourly rates for staff members who were directly involved with managing the funded project.

Avoiding Extracurricular Fundraising

I offer a word of caution about forms of fundraising that can be a serious distraction to chamber execs – namely extracurricular fundraising for causes outside your chamber. Being a chamber executive usually involves serving on a variety of job-related boards such as the tourism authority, the airport board or a special task force the mayor has appointed. I once made a list of my board obligations, and realized that I had to serve on more than ten boards, task forces and commissions. Several were required by a statute or ordinance that specifically named the chamber president or a chamber representative. Others were a civic obligation, for example, because the mayor or governor called and asked me to serve on a special task force. Some requests you simply can't turn down.

In addition to required board service associated with your chamber position, execs are often recruited to join other extracurricular boards – at church, in your neighborhood, at your kid's school or a local arts group. Because you are closely associated with the business community, you are often viewed by outside organizations as a valuable connection to local business leaders and more important (at least for those groups), as an immediate fundraising connection to what they often unrealistically perceive as the business community's vast wealth. I've had various worthy groups want to partner with our chamber and ask me to serve on their boards with the fairly obvious objective of wanting me – or our chamber – to tap the business community for money. I declined most of those invitations because, a) it often led to cannibalizing my own set of professional contacts and sources of money for my chamber, and b) my ability (or inability) to tap resources for another organization or cause would almost surely disappoint that group because of the groups' typically unrealistic expectations that businesses will open their wallets and finance that group's latest initiatives.

Not only can serving on job-related and extracurricular boards be a dark hole of distraction, it can also put a chamber exec in a position of competing with his/her own organization for valuable time and financial resources. If you are helping the United Way with its annual campaign or the Boy Scouts with a capital campaign for a new headquarters, you are not raising resources for your own chamber. Frequently when someone suggested having lunch to discuss their cause, I went through a rather cold calculation of how many of my own board members or other stakeholders I needed to have lunch with for a specific

I asked my board leadership to either formally (in my job description) forbid me or informally discourage me from participating in fundraising for outside organizations that weren't directly related to a specific objective of my chamber. It gave me an easy answer when I was asked to participate in some other organization's fundraising campaign.

chamber (fundraising) purpose. Not to sound callous or self-important, but I had to realize that an hour of my time focused on the needs of my chamber could be worth $5,000 or $10,000 or more in new investment in our chamber's mission; likewise, an hour of my time on someone else's latest, albeit worthwhile, priority could involve a comparable loss to my chamber.

In each of the three chambers I served, I asked my board leadership to either formally (in my job description) forbid me or informally discourage me from participating in fundraising for outside organizations that weren't directly related to a specific objective of my chamber. That protected the chamber from its executive (me) being distracted with outside demands, but it also gave me an easy answer when I was asked – sometimes by one of my own chamber board members – to participate in some other organization's fundraising campaign.

■ ■ ■

Raising money for your chamber is not everything, but almost everything a chamber aspires to do involves raising money. As chambers look to the future, being able to strategically match community and chamber goals with the financial resources available to support them will be a necessity for a growing chamber and will require professional skills developed by determined chamber executives. Cause-based fundraising will be the third leg of the revenue stool for ambitious chambers wanting to expand and have a greater impact in their communities. Whether fundraising becomes a substantially new business model for most chambers, only time will tell. Meanwhile, viewing fundraising as an unpleasant necessity of chamber management instead of an avenue to substantially expand our ability to shape our chambers and our communities will risk leaving our chambers on the sidelines of our communities' progress.

Raising money for your chamber is not everything, but almost everything a chamber aspires to do involves raising money.

CHAPTER 9
GOVERNANCE ISSUES

For a chamber executive to be effective as a steward of an organization, as a spokesperson for the business community and as a catalytic community leader, there are certain basic matters of governance that must be mastered. What are the key elements of professionally managing a high-performing chamber that is continually raising the bar of expectations and results?

Bylaws: the Backbone of Chamber Operations

Revising the organization's bylaws can be the bane of a chamber exec's existence, but the bylaws are the central rule book by which the organization operates and sustains trust among its constituents. Although seldom read by chamber volunteers, a chamber's bylaws serve as the primary governance document that allows the organization to function efficiently, predictably and ethically. Managing them and occasionally updating them, however, can be tedious, time-consuming and distracting. That's why I considered revising our chamber's bylaws to be a necessary but infrequent exercise.

The bylaws are the central rule book by which the organization operates and sustains trust.

Throughout the interim period between revisions, I made occasional notes for my bylaws file about possible future revisions, but I didn't rush back to the board with every possible tweak that came to mind. When a comprehensive review was warranted, a small group of board members that included a volunteer attorney and myself was appointed by our board chair to oversee the process. The attorney made sure any revisions complied with the most recent state laws for nonprofits and suggested other ways to update the document. We incorporated updates from the notes I had collected since the previous revision. One or two drafts later, we had a document and a succinct side-by-side summary of the proposed changes ready for quick approval at the next board meeting.

ACCE offers great resources for gathering samples of other chambers' bylaws, and other chambers in your vicinity can offer helpful samples. It's good to compare a few of them to gauge the relative level of formality and the degree of detail other chambers use. Of course, bylaws are not intended to be a complete collection of all internal operating procedures or policies. They articulate the basic governing rules by which the organization operates, processes decisions and perpetuates itself, but other written policies and guidelines such as personnel policies, public policy statements adopted by the board and operating procedures for the chamber's daily functions are also needed.

For chamber execs taking a CEO role at a new chamber, an initial review of the existing bylaws within the first 100 days – assuming the time-crunch of one's early months on the job won't allow an immediate and comprehensive rewriting of the document – should be a high priority. If nothing else, it provides an introduction to the culture and the operational expectations of the organization.

Making Policy

One of the most difficult aspects of governance is managing the process that comes with engaging in public policy deliberations. State chambers deal with that challenge on a daily basis, working to gain what Gene Barr of the Pennsylvania Chamber calls "significant consensus." Local chambers, whether or not they have a robust government affairs function, are routinely called upon by local officials and/or chamber members to take a stand on issues at City Hall. Rarely do chambers have the luxury of unanimous support on one side of an issue. If the issue is one-sided for your membership, say with a 90/10 split in support, it's probably safe to speak out. You may lose a member or two, but that's the price of having a backbone and truly representing your constituent businesses. But having a 60/40 issue is a huge problem. Sometimes you have to sit out an issue because it will rip your organization apart. It's not a matter of being timid; you simply want to live to fight another day and remain effective for your community.

One of the thorniest issues is the endorsement of political candidates – for mayor, for state legislature, for governor. We endorsed state legislative candidates after interviewing them, having them answer our surveys and getting references

> *If the issue is one-sided for your membership, say with a 90/10 split in support, it's probably safe to speak out. But having a 60/40 issue is a huge problem.*

from their local chambers. We did not endorse in statewide races and, while I admire some of my colleagues who do endorse in races such as those for governor, I didn't advocate that with my leadership because of the harm it would do to our long-term effectiveness and our role as a consensus-builder. The same precarious situation exists with mayors' races. They can split chambers apart. Every chamber exists in a different political reality with its own track record of making or avoiding candidate endorsements, and each has to navigate public policy issues carefully and with a defensible process by which it makes those tough decisions. One thing is for sure: Having internal policies on how those public policy decisions are made and having your board leadership standing with you is critical; otherwise, you can find yourself alone, out on a limb. Even with policies in place, a chamber exec often finds that entering the policy minefield is necessary for a chamber wanting to represent its members boldly (see Chapter 4 regarding pancakes vs. policy). But navigating that minefield is frequently more art than science and requires great finesse.

Budgets and Finances

The chamber's budget can be the most important policy document a chamber will adopt in a given year and effectively managing the chamber's finances is critical for avoiding the No. 1 cause of chamber CEO demise – letting the finances get away from you.

Managing the chamber's finances is critical for avoiding the No. 1 cause of chamber CEO demise – letting the finances get away from you.

The annual budget should define the scope and scale of the chamber's operations, its immediate goals and, to some extent, its longer-term aspirations. It reflects whether the chamber's resources are aligned with its strategic priorities. However, the budget and the subsequent reporting of the chamber's finances to a board of directors can become major distractions if not properly managed. Dwelling on the budget and finances at board or executive committee meetings can tempt individual board members to micromanage the organization, distracting them from more meaningful deliberations.

When I hired our finance director (who later advanced to become our CFO) at the Kentucky Chamber, I challenged him to make the finances of our organization a non-issue. By that, I suggested that we develop a high level of trust with our board and thereby minimize the amount of time the board and/or executive committee needed to spend focusing on internal financial matters. With a high level of transparency, an engaged treasurer, a functioning finance committee and the accompanying trust they earned with the broader board, financial reports generally consumed less than five minutes during a three-hour quarterly board meeting. A written financial report was routinely provided in the board materials available online in advance of each meeting, but we reduced the additional reporting at the board meeting to a minimum. Our auditors' annual presentations to the executive committee were limited to 10-15 minutes, and we didn't invite them to make a presentation to the full board. After our finance and executive committees approved the audit, the full board considered it as one of several items on our fast-tracked consent agenda. To foster a spirit of transparency, we occasionally asked our treasurer or CFO to give a two or three minute summary of the audit's highlights. That streamlining of financial reporting and audit approval is only possible if there is considerable trust earned and sustained among the CFO, the CEO and volunteer leaders.

Our annual budgeting process was handled by our CFO with equal transparency and efficiency. As he started the process each year, I typically provided him my general thoughts about what we needed to accomplish financially in the coming year. Because we had capable and experienced vice presidents managing the four operating divisions, the CFO worked with each of them through a phase we called the "wish-list phase" (when they outlined what they hoped to include in their divisions' budgets), through the "reality phase" (when everyone had to trim their wish lists to stay within our anticipated revenue), and through the "adoption phase" that involved gaining consensus within our senior team, review by the board treasurer, approval by the finance and executive committees and ratification by the full board.

I was proud that our budgeting process (with the exception of com-pensation decisions) usually involved only an hour or two of my time each year. I admired our CFO and senior team for having command of their respective duties and the ability to resolve issues without my having to referee the process. This level of trust allowed me to focus on chamber priorities that were external to the organization and had greater potential to move our state forward.

Our CFO knew that I had far less interest in the monthly financial statements than I did in two other sets of documents he routinely provided me:

1. His year-end forecast. It consisted of a list he updated each month of positive and negative financial developments that would impact our budget by more than $5,000 along with his latest prediction of what those factors would mean to our year-end bottom line. Obviously, his predictions became more precise as we moved through the fiscal year, and I often asked him in the closing months, "How are we going to land the plane?"

2. His trend analysis. I preferred to monitor trends in specific financial areas such as personnel costs compared to previous years, how the compensation of individual staffers had grown over a period of time and how efficiently our membership sales team was generating revenue compared to the cost of staffing that sales team.

During my career at three chambers, we almost always budgeted for a relatively tight, break-even budget with expenses matching anticipated revenue. We might have built in a small cushion for contingencies or a small deficit depending on our set of assumptions for the year, but generally we worked toward a break-even budget. Occasionally a board member from a for-profit company would question that philosophy because of the private-sector's focus on producing a profit. However, my rationale for breaking even was built on an assumption that our members wanted us to be as strong as our resources would allow in a given year, that there were expenses built into the budget to responsibly cover most replacement costs (depreciation of property and equipment), that we had adequate operating reserves and that building additional reserves would tempt a future board or administration to spend money on speculative projects that might not generate a responsible return on the investment. Unless there was a stated purpose for generating a surplus such as building a dedicated cash reserve, paying off the chamber's mortgage or increasing a permanent endowment for specific purposes, I was satisfied to maintain an adequate operating balance for stability in daily operations while being as strong, well-staffed and effective as possible for our members in a given year.

Creating a Culture of Transparency

Creating and nurturing a culture of openness is critical for building trust with your board, your fellow staff members and external constituencies. However, transparency means different things for government agencies, corporations that are publicly traded, privately held or family-controlled corporations, churches, colleges and trade associations such as chambers of commerce.

What is transparency? Generally, it means an organization's relative level of openness to scrutiny by internal constituencies (staff, board members and chamber members) and by external parties (the media, governmental agencies, the general public). For the purposes of this discussion, I include in the basic expectation of transparency the minimum legal standards for nonprofits (standards defined by state and federal law along with the explicit or implied standards of the IRS 990 reporting requirements for nonprofits) and beyond those basic formal requirements, the willingness to make available additional information that builds trust with relevant stakeholders.

What level of transparency is appropriate for chambers of commerce? Transparency can mean different things to various chamber constituencies. In our case, there was information we made available to the board of directors that was not readily available to the general membership. There was information available to my executive committee that was not typically provided to the full board. There was information shared with my three-member compensation committee that was not generally provided to the executive committee or the full board. For chambers that are responsible for business recruitment, there may be confidential information about business prospects that is restricted to the economic development director, to the CEO or to the economic development council of the chamber. Not all of these different levels of transparency were formally defined in policy or in the bylaws, but our practices evolved over the years with various levels of disclosure and candor within the organization.

Transparency is more than disclosing information about the organization; it also involves avoiding unnecessary secrecy and suspicion within a chamber's operations. For example, I monitored the relationship between the board and the executive committee very closely, making sure the larger board was comfortable with the level of decisions the smaller executive committee made for the organization. I included the minutes of all executive committee meetings, as noted earlier, on the consent agenda for the following board meeting, to give the board a sense of the executive committee's decisions and the opportunity to question them. Also, with a confidential survey of our board every three years, we asked board members about various governance issues and whether they felt the executive committee was taking on too much or too little of the chamber's decision-making.

Another aspect of transparency lies between the organization and its volunteers and outside parties. A chamber member or outside critic of the chamber might demand to see the salaries of all staff members, and the organization has to make a decision about what, if any, information beyond what is legally required on the IRS 990 form to disclose. A persistent reporter might call about the CEO's compensation or ask whether the chamber provides its exec a country club membership. A CEO's compensation for the past several years is a matter of public record through web sources such as Guidestar, but a nonprofit is under no legal obligation to reveal the specific perks its employees receive except that certain benefits such as an auto allowance are taxable as income and therefore must be reported in aggregate as part of total compensation. Conveying information about personnel issues, including compensation, is inherently sensitive and can be damaging to internal morale.

We had policies about transparency that required all staff members to report credit card and out-of-pocket expenses monthly, to report any gifts from business associates exceeding $100 (for example, tickets to a professional sporting event) and to request pre-approval for out-of-state travel. We had written guidelines about the appropriate cost of a meal when traveling and/or entertaining, and on rare occasions, I asked staff members involved in an expensive meal to reimburse the difference between those guidelines and the actual tab – the same practice I followed with my expenses to maintain the integrity of the guidelines and promote a culture of responsible spending.

I reviewed the expenses of our senior staff and signed off on them for our auditor. Our board treasurer reviewed my expenses and any gifts over $100 on a quarterly basis and briefly reported his review to the executive committee so the meeting minutes could reflect that level of oversight. Our chamber enacted stricter financial controls in the wake of a major scandal in which four other high-profile nonprofit associations and government agencies were investigated for extensive abuse of credit cards, gifts and travel and were subjected to front-page media scrutiny that led to the dismissal of four otherwise successful CEOs. Our finances had not been questioned internally or externally during that controversy, but we decided to formalize several of our practices into policies as safeguards for the future.

Having once lived in the fishbowl of elected office with reporters regularly reviewing my expense reports, my travel to conferences at taxpayer expense, the number of times I paid for a carwash with a city hall credit card and so on, I learned that such expenses would eventually be publicly disclosed, and I understood that everything I spent might have to be justified on the front page of the newspaper. Today, that level of scrutiny can be amplified, manipulated and distorted through social media. Chambers of commerce don't usually face as much close scrutiny as government agencies unless there is an organizational crisis or a controversy that becomes public and prompts the media to publicly scrutinize the chamber's operations. Once when our senior vice president of public affairs testified before a legislative committee about reforming our state's unemployment system, a skeptical reporter included our vice president's salary in his front page story, apparently in an attempt at irony ("lobbyist with executive salary wants to limit benefits for the unemployed"). It was uncomfortable at the time but it was an unavoidable downside of managing a nonprofit organization that is required to report certain basic information about its operations.

Not all internal information needs to be volunteered to a curious member or reporter. For example, I didn't feel obligated to answer a reporter's questions about my compensation or that of my staff, but I did provide context for how compensation was set. Instead of declining comment, I would provide information about how my compensation was reviewed by a formal performance review committee, how data from comparably-sized chambers was used as benchmarks and so forth. I would leave it up to the reporter to find other, more specific compensation information on his own; I didn't feel compelled to do his research for him.

Instead of seeing transparency as a set of rules and regulations that the CEO must tolerate, chambers and their CEOs can embrace a basic level of accountability and transparency as the foundation for building trust and good will within the organization and the community.

Instead of seeing transparency as a set of rules and regulations that the CEO must tolerate, I suggest that chambers and their CEOs embrace a basic level of accountability and transparency as the foundation for building trust and a culture of goodwill within the organization and the community. Maintaining a culture of relative openness and approachability will usually pay handsome dividends down the road.

Metrics

How do you objectively measure the strength and viability of a chamber of commerce? Ultimately, it is up to your board of directors, members and investors to decide the relevance and viability of your chamber and its impact on the community. Often those decisions are based on subjective impressions that can be collected and evaluated, but there are also quantifiable ways to monitor the relative health of your organization and ways to communicate that value.

I like to think of the chamber's viability in two ways: external and internal. External viability involves the impact of the chamber on the environment outside the organization, especially in the community it serves and with various external constituencies such as elected officials, government agencies, the media, private citizens, voters and even visitors to your community. Later in Chapter 15, I address the impact a chamber can have on the broader community. However, this section focuses primarily on the internal workings of a chamber and measuring the organization's relative strength as a nonprofit organization – as an organization that is, in effect, a small business that has to keep its doors open, pay its bills, function as a responsible employer and provide stewardship of its resources.

Being generally interested in observing trends within our chamber, I developed a set of key metrics – my dashboard – that I regularly monitored and used for reporting purposes with my key leaders. Both times when I relocated to a new chamber, I asked the chief financial officer to go back ten years and gather statistical information to create a spreadsheet that became my dashboard. In neither chamber was there an existing collection of the information I was seeking. The closest thing on hand – and a critical one – was the set of annual audits, but in my view, a more comprehensive set of year-over-year data was needed to reveal critical trends showing the long-term viability of the chamber's business model. For example, was membership growing – in numbers of members and in dollars of revenue? Which of the chamber's revenue streams were growing and which were declining? Was revenue from sponsorships or revenue produced through the chamber foundation outpacing traditional membership revenue? What percentage of the chamber's budget was dedicated to compensation? Were the chamber's unrestricted net assets increasing or decreasing?

Most of the data for the thirty-plus indicators were easily gleaned from the previous ten audits of the chamber's finances. Much of the information was financial but some was membership related (the number of paying members and the average dues per member) and some was personnel related (the average tenure of our staff members, total payroll and the average staff salary). With staff continuity and succession planning being relatively important to me, high-level personnel data and the trends they revealed were of great relevance.

I occasionally revised my dashboard as we discovered more about our chamber. As our 501-c-3 foundation became more active and we saw foundation revenue as an important and potentially game-changing opportunity, I started including foundation revenue as a key indicator of our diversified revenue streams and our programmatic activity.

My dashboard could tell a board member or my executive committee more on one piece of paper than I could with a box full of annual reports, financial reports and audits. I usually delivered an updated version to my executive committee once a year – at the first meeting after our audit was complete and after our budget for the coming year had been approved. It probably contained more granular detail than my executive committee needed, but I offered it along with an abbreviated PowerPoint overview to let them know what we were tracking, to illustrate important trends that gave them a better understanding of the general direction of our chamber and to foster a level of transparency that built confidence in the organization.

A very helpful tool for organizational analysis is ACCE's annual Benchmarking Survey. It can be challenging for a participating chamber to collect the information the first year, but it is relatively simple to update by the second year. Using cumulative data from chambers across the country, the survey can increase our understanding of our own chambers and can help inform certain management decisions. For example, when our chamber was considering a relatively expensive building expansion, I was able to point to ACCE data from other chambers of similar size and assure my board officers that even after our expansion, our total occupancy costs would still be below the national average of what chambers pay for their building (whether renting or owning) as a percentage of total operating expenses.

My dashboard could tell a board member or my executive committee more on one piece of paper than I could with a box full of annual reports, financial reports and audits.

Certainly it can be counterproductive to become overly involved in crunching numbers and creating spreadsheets, but creating a dashboard of important organizational metrics can be a relatively simple and enlightening exercise. In an effort to offer answers to my volunteer leaders before they posed questions about our operations and to sustain a culture of transparency with my board, we provided objective information – both the good news and bad news – and created a greater level of trust that served our chamber well over the long haul.

Becoming an Accredited Chamber

There is a widespread misconception that all chambers of commerce are affiliates of a larger chamber of commerce, presumably the U.S. Chamber. Friends of mine outside Chamber World are often surprised to hear that chambers are autonomous and that nearly any group – even proprietary, for-profit enterprises – can use the name chamber of commerce for just about any enterprise they choose. For example, a chamber of commerce in my state was created by a group of immigrants from another country whose primary purpose in establishing their chamber was to sell imports from their home country. Apparently they thought the use of the name chamber of commerce benefited that enterprise. Their purpose wasn't nefarious or fraudulent; they simply chose a name that implied legitimacy and prestige in the United States. Another example is the organization created by the Koch brothers called Freedom Partners Chamber of Commerce, Inc. that raises millions of dollars and supports conservative causes.

One meaningful designation that ties chambers together and defines professionalism within chambers of commerce is the accreditation process that was created and is administered by the U.S. Chamber of Commerce. The initial process of applying to be an accredited chamber involves submitting an application and processing fee followed by an extensive self-study by the applicant chamber of various aspects of its organization including governance, finance, internal policies and procedures. After the self-study, the full application must be submitted along with supporting materials and, assuming they are deemed sufficient, an outside consultant for the U.S. Chamber evaluates the application, reviews the organization and provides written feedback on how it might improve. If the chamber satisfies the accreditation criteria, the U.S. Chamber Board of Directors grants accredited status with a particular level of distinction (three stars, four stars or five stars based on points scored). Accredited status lasts five years, after which the local or state chamber must apply to be re-accredited. If the chamber doesn't re-apply or doesn't meet the standards, the accreditation status is withdrawn.

When I was hired at my hometown chamber and first learned about accreditation while attending the U.S. Chamber's Institute for Organization Management (IOM), I became eager to obtain that distinction for my chamber. Having never applied before, we took the process very seriously, appointed a board committee to oversee the self-study, tightened up various policies and procedures and filed our application. We were successful on the first attempt and proudly proclaimed our victory when the status was granted. All of our publications featured the Accredited Chamber logo, and we bragged about our achievement for a year or two. I doubt that my board was as proud as my staff and I were, but they took notice and considered it a milestone for our energetic and ambitious organization.

Looking back on that process, it was an excellent self-study that greatly benefited our small chamber and especially benefited me because it taught me what reasonable expectations were for a well-managed chamber of commerce. Having observed only one chamber, I had no reference point for what excellence meant. In retrospect, I don't know if our accredited status made a meaningful difference in how our members viewed the chamber. While it probably implied success and organizational stability, I doubt if it sold any memberships or otherwise created any significant monetary advantage. However, the internal benefits to our organization and to me professionally were substantial and well worth the effort.

When I left my hometown chamber for the Birmingham (Alabama) Regional Chamber, I was surprised that it wasn't accredited. I inquired of other metro chamber CEOs and found that most were relatively lackadaisical about accreditation. It wasn't that they were negative toward the U.S. Chamber (quite the opposite) or even toward being an accredited chamber, but most held the opinion that the standards stated or implied in the accreditation process were somewhat irrelevant to a larger chamber. An organization operating with a larger budget and with the level of professional management expected at a metro chamber would consider the criteria for accreditation to be a basic expectation. After all, a larger chamber has bylaws, an annual audit, a personnel manual that addresses things like harassment and whistleblower protections and a formal procedure for nominating board members. In other words, such policies and practices were considered non-issues at the metro chamber level. And the CEOs, most of them not aspiring to move to a larger chamber, probably didn't see any professional or career advantage of accreditation. Therefore, it wasn't considered a significant bragging point for the chamber or for the exec.

I temporarily backed off my ambitious plan to gain accreditation for the Birmingham Chamber, but I decided that when I could identify an up-and-coming manager in our organization who demonstrated a commitment to professional development and seemed inclined toward a chamber career, I would ask that staff person to oversee an application for accreditation for our chamber. Gaining accreditation might benefit our organization in specific ways by reminding us that we needed to update our policies in some particular area, but more than anything, it would be a profound learning opportunity for an aspiring chamber professional. He/she could gain an understanding of what excellence means in Chamber World. We soon had that opportunity with a promising staff member and we achieved accreditation within a few months. Our board of directors took at least a passing notice of the achievement when we announced our new status, but frankly, it was not a big event for the organization. The manager who oversaw the exhaustive process probably added the achievement to his resume; I certainly hope so. I am confident it benefited our chamber in subtle ways, but it was also valuable for his professional development and career advancement. I have since employed that same strategy with two other rising chamber professionals – once to get our state chamber accredited and once to earn our re-accreditation.

Once accreditation is earned, it must be re-earned and the five-year sunset of a chamber's accredited status puts a certain burden on the organization to maintain that status. If it were to lapse and the forfeiture were noticed by the chamber's board of directors, it could be a blemish on the reputation of the chamber CEO – a blemish that perhaps would weigh heavier than the initial rewards of obtaining accreditation in the first place.

Considering the sum of the factors mentioned above, I am a fan of accreditation and, if I were to move to an unaccredited chamber, I would look for an early opportunity to pursue it. Moreover, in viewing accreditation from a 30,000-foot level, I'm very appreciative that the U.S. Chamber has a process in place to create a common understanding – in effect, an industry standard – of what the basic organizational expectations are for a professionally managed chamber of commerce.

> The U.S. Chamber has a process in place to create a common understanding – in effect, an industry standard – of what the basic organizational expectations are for a professionally managed chamber of commerce.

■ ■ ■

At the core of being an effective chamber executive is the willingness to consciously and efficiently manage the organization. Just as a chef pays close attention to the ingredients required for an appetizing dinner, a chamber exec must recognize and pay close attention to the details of governance that serve as the recipe for a successful chamber. Dismissing those issues as burdensome details that must be tolerated by a chamber CEO who believes he or she has more important things to do will lead to organizational dysfunction, diminished effectiveness and possible career jeopardy.

Excellent resources for effectively managing the governance requirements of a non-profit organization are available from Robert Harris, CAE, and his Nonprofit Center at www.nonprofitcenter.com. With publications on association management, seminars, consulting services and a wealth of online information, Bob was the first person I called when I arrived at the Kentucky Chamber and realized we needed a strategic plan. He has helped countless chamber CEOs and a wide variety of chambers to evaluate their missions and their operations.

CHAPTER 10
CHAMBERS INTERACTING WITH GOVERNMENT

Chambers exist outside government, firmly rooted in the private community with business leaders directing the organization and private enterprises providing the core funding. But chambers also have overlapping interests with government in promoting the public good. There are occasions when government decides that the business community can provide certain services more efficiently than government – services such as economic development, business recruitment, downtown development, marketing the community and workforce training. To that end, public-private partnerships are sometimes effective ways to administer specific services that promote the public good, and those partnerships can often involve public (taxpayer) money being appropriated for programs managed by chambers of commerce. While those partnerships can be mutually beneficial, there are also risks that are inherent in those relationships.

The Complications with Accepting Public Funding

Many local and some state chambers receive an element of public funding, either as membership fees, sponsorships, contracts for specific services or all of the above. It is not uncommon for chambers to play the primary marketing and new business attraction role for a city, county or region through public-private partnerships with local governments. In other cases, chambers have contracts to run Main Street programs, manage tourism bureaus or provide small business assistance. In many cases, these partnerships also involve one or more public officials having a seat at the table, either on the chamber's board or on the governing council of a particular program.

Many state chambers, on the other hand, consider their advocacy role central to their reason to exist and therefore avoid accepting public funds through grants or contracts. They want to avoid a conflict of interest and being compromised when speaking to government on contentious issues. Some state chambers even have formal prohibitions against accepting government funds written into their bylaws. In the case of our state chamber, we allowed local governments and school boards to join our chamber in order to receive discounts on some of our affinity programs, and we allowed government agencies to sponsor some of our events, such as the state employment office sponsoring our human resources conference. However, accepting public grant money through a contract with state government was a more complicated issue. When I took the issue to our executive committee as a part of a process of updating our bylaws, I was surprised that our board leaders – a relatively conservative group of free enterprise advocates – decided that while our chamber itself should not accept direct grants or contracts, our chamber's charitable foundation could enter into public-private partnerships and by doing so, accept public money. Therefore, we incorporated one of our most ambitious chamber programs – our Chamber Workforce Center – as a separate legal entity (technically an SMLLC, i.e. a single-member LLC) under our chamber foundation to allow it to enter into a two-year contract with our state education and workforce department for specific services.

There is no universal right or wrong answer to the question of whether to accept government money. However, one of the most delicate relationships for a chamber executive to manage is the day-to-day political relationship with the predominant government(s) in the chamber's service area. Those relationships can become much more complicated if the chamber accepts public money in the form of substantial membership dues, sponsorships or a contract for services. If a mayor or county executive wants a seat on the board of directors in return for the public funding, things become even more challenging. During my career, I found that chamber board members – even strong-willed, outspoken business leaders – were often overly deferential to elected officials and considerably less candid with their input when an elected official was in the room during the chamber's deliberations. It's often hard to openly disagree with a mayor, county council president or governor who is in the room when chamber decisions are being made. The danger is that the voice of the business community can be subdued when business leaders consciously or unconsciously defer to elected officials.

A chamber's delicate relationship with government can become much more complicated if the chamber accepts public money in the form of substantial membership dues, sponsorships or a contract for services.

Managing the expectations of local and state government officials can be difficult, sometimes nearly impossible. I've seen chamber CEOs and economic development executives raked over the coals in city council meetings because, according to a council member from an economically disadvantaged council district, the chamber hasn't recruited an industry or a Walmart or a movie theater to a neighborhood in that district. The chamber is cast as the bad guy and inaccurately portrayed as not caring about disadvantaged parts of town and only being interested in serving the interests of big companies.

Admittedly, our decision to keep our state chamber free of government money while allowing our foundation to accept public funds through public-private partnerships may eventually inhibit the chamber's advocacy efforts, but it seemed to be a rational, pragmatic solution for our chamber at the time and has worked well for several years – even with specific programs and the underlying management contracts surviving the transition of the governor's office from one political party to the other.

Maintaining a central chamber function as the voice of business can become very difficult if a mayor is angry with the chamber and the economic development contract, for example, is coming up for renewal. I observed one metro chamber that avoided taking a stand on several public policy issues that were clearly well-established in the business community because the chamber, as a practical and financial matter, needed a positive relationship with City Hall to maintain its economic development contract and its central role as the preeminent economic development agency for the region. After a new mayor unilaterally cancelled the chamber contract to manage economic development while publicly insulting the chamber as not being very effective at business attraction, the chamber quickly adjusted its mission, prioritized advocacy as a core function and began speaking out on issues that had previously been too hot to touch, including opposing tax increases proposed by the mayor. While chamber purists might applaud that chamber for emerging from the shadow of City Hall and finally taking on tough issues, the short-term damage to its brand as the region's economic development agency, the financial blow from the loss of public funds and private investments, and the subsequent layoffs of several veteran staff members defined a painful chapter that none of us would want to experience.

While it might be easy for some chambers – especially state chambers or the U.S. Chamber – to refuse direct public dollars and to proclaim ideological purity, there are many more chambers who must regularly navigate the nuances of public-private partnerships and associated political sensitivities. When considering the appropriate circumstances under which a chamber can accept public funding, I would consider this hypothetical question: Even if my chamber refuses direct government funding in the form of membership dues or service contracts, would it be equally hesitant to refuse a sponsorship from a public agency for a chamber-hosted conference or refuse a substantial membership investment by a government agency such as the local airport, transit authority, school system or public hospital? I suspect not. Those represent gray areas between the black-and-white options of eagerly accepting and categorically refusing public money. Having chamber board leaders consider the sensitivities associated with public funds and approve written policies for the practice will ultimately protect – or at least cushion – chambers from the tough situations that will surely arise.

The New Mayor Syndrome

Another issue related to a chamber's independence and a difficult minefield for chamber execs to navigate is what I call "the new mayor syndrome" – which by the way, has a closely associated affliction, "the new governor syndrome." Anyone who has been elected to the chief administrative office of a city, county or state has probably overcome significant personal and political challenges to do so. Very few citizens merely file for election and breeze into office. Successful candidates have usually sacrificed personal time, probably encountered scrutiny and criticism from the media, overcome negative opponents and finally attained a position they have coveted for a long time. However, even if an elected official wins with only a razor-thin margin, he/she considers the electoral success a strong mandate for his/her political agenda. That individual has emerged at the top of the heap and psychologically assumes that surely everyone knows that it's a new day. As a former political candidate and mayor, I admit that it's a pretty heady experience on election night and during the initial honeymoon period. And it's easy to assume that everyone is on board with you. The fever of now being in charge and assuming everyone is in lockstep behind you is one defining symptom of the new mayor syndrome.

So how does this affect a chamber CEO? A newly minted mayor cannot imagine that anyone on the city council, at the local newspaper or the chamber of commerce could disagree with his or her agenda. After all, the new mayor has just won a mandate from the public and truly wants what's best for the community, right? Why wouldn't everyone share his/her goals and get on board? The learning curve for a recently elected official can be painful as various interest groups, other elected officials, editorial page writers, bloggers and community gadflies take exception to specific aspects of the office holder's agenda and begin openly criticizing the new mayor. For a chamber to take exception to portions of the mayor's agenda is unthinkable to the new mayor. "Why wouldn't the chamber of commerce openly advocate what I (the victorious new mayor) think is best for the community?" That's when the fireworks usually take place.

Even if a chamber stakes out its independence from a newly elected official, the expectations of that official can continue to be unrealistic. A chamber exec can receive a call from the mayor who wants the business community to show overwhelming support at a council meeting for the mayor's latest priority – as though you'll rent buses to get your members to City Hall. It's difficult to temper those expectations while avoiding antagonizing the mayor. I once had a notoriously strong-willed mayor respond to my hesitance, "So you're telling me you can't get your members to support my proposal?!" Ugh.

If you can imagine a 1-to-10 scale that represents a spectrum of cooperation with government ranging from a 1, offering total cooperation to the point of relative obedience to governmental authority, to a 10, asserting total and vocal independence, it's important to try to find relatively peaceful ways in the mid-range – perhaps a 6, 7 or 8 – to resolve issues while keeping an arm's-length distance and maintaining healthy independence. Private conversations, perhaps first with aides to government officials or through well-placed business leaders who have personal or political standing with the mayor, can break the ice and offer the chamber's different perspective while affirming mutual long-term goals for the community. (It's worth checking publicly available records of political contributions from your board members and other friends of your chamber to the mayor's or governor's campaign as you think of building bridges to a new administration.)

Situations are always different, and I have observed well-run chambers that wore their confrontational style on their sleeves as a badge of courage. Maybe that works in certain situations when the political climate is conspicuously anti-business or anti-chamber and chamber board members are united behind the chamber exec in speaking out. However, in my experience of working with challenging political personalities and having served in elective office myself, it's my sense that private diplomacy and finesse usually serve a chamber far better than direct confrontation with the political powers-that-be. Chambers are often well advised to play the long game with steady resolve and great finesse while exercising their independence from government.

Private diplomacy and finesse usually serve a chamber far better than direct confrontation with the political powers-that-be.

Community Dysfunction and the Need for a Chamber

When I arrived at the Birmingham (Alabama) Chamber of Commerce in 1999, I made it a priority to methodically meet hundreds of business and civic leaders in the first few months. I received a warm welcome from my new southern neighbors and as I listened to their opinions about the community, a similar comment offered by several caught my attention; I was surprised by the number of times I was greeted with some version of, "We need you." They knew very little about me personally and had no reason to need me as the new chamber guy in town, but I soon learned they wanted (needed) a strong, effective chamber.

There was a perception that the multiple local governments in the metro region didn't cooperate, that the political leadership was dysfunctional and that the region was not growing nearly as well as other metro areas in the South. There was a racial overlay to most community issues that added a level of complexity and divisiveness to virtually every public issue. While they didn't know enough about me to need me personally, they were expressing a hopeful desire to have a chamber that could make sense out of what they perceived to be a fragmented and contentious political environment.

I also noticed for the first time a paradox that seemed initially counterintuitive but which I have now experienced in other chamber settings: the more dysfunctional a governmental and political environment is perceived to be, the greater the opportunity for a chamber to fill the void, offer a vision, build bridges and tactfully assert itself. In a sense, this simple equation of more-dysfunction-equals-more-opportunity is a logical extension of the opportunity chambers inherit from the political and social polarization described in Chapter 12. A chamber can emerge as the glue for a more cohesive civic culture and a higher functioning community.

The more dysfunctional a governmental and political environment is perceived to be, the greater the opportunity for a chamber to fill the void, offer a vision, build bridges and tactfully assert itself.

In some regions where there is a decentralized assortment of multiple cities and counties or there exists a conspicuous vacuum in political leadership, a chamber executive has an incredible opportunity to play a cohesive role as a convener and even as the spokesperson for the community. For example, I've observed that in Northern Kentucky – a multi-county collection of cities, counties and Cincinnati suburbs on the Kentucky side of the Ohio River – the chamber president's position practically offers him a de facto role as the mayor (with a small "m") of a region that has a population of a half million people. Of course, he has to be careful not to overstate or overplay his role with the local elected officials, but the opportunity to pull a sprawling, amorphous region together and to speak for that region is enormous.

In contrast, I've noticed a nearly opposite situation in some communities in which a charismatic and effective political leader – generally but not always the mayor – is perceived by the public as a progressive, business-friendly leader and as the go-to person for quarterbacking major projects. In those circumstances, a chamber exec can be relegated to playing a relatively lower-profile, supportive role – working to be at the table on major issues of the day but trying not to upstage a business-friendly and effective mayor who is a natural ally of the business community.

■ ■ ■

The relationship between a chamber and the governments having jurisdiction in the chamber's service area is one that is constantly evolving as issues, personalities and politics reshape the chamber's external environment. Being able to work effectively with governments while also maintaining a healthy independence from them requires a delicate balancing act that must be thoughtfully orchestrated so a chamber exec can achieve positive results for chamber members and for the broader community.

Being able to work effectively with governments while also maintaining a healthy independence from them requires a delicate balancing act that must be thoughtfully orchestrated.

PART III
IT'S ABOUT YOU AND YOUR COMMUNITY

Chambers can shape their communities in profound ways. By recognizing and skillfully navigating the ever-changing political and cultural forces that affect a community, a chamber can reach beyond its traditional functions of providing member services and help create a vision and action plan for its community. What are some of the forces shaping our communities and chambers? What are practical steps a chamber can take to navigate those currents? Can a chamber really shape a community or are we destined to play the role of community cheerleaders from the sidelines?

CHAPTER 11
HELPING OUR COMMUNITIES NAVIGATE CHANGE

Recognizing and understanding the trends that are shaping our communities and the external environment in which chambers must operate is the first step toward a chamber positioning itself to help its community navigate change.

Cultural Trends Shaping our Communities

While technological changes such as the advent of smartphones and the prospect of driverless vehicles often capture our imaginations, there are powerful cultural and economic changes disrupting our communities as well. Cultural institutions are evolving in profound ways. Traditional, once monolithic institutions such as political parties, labor unions, churches, governments and mainstream media organizations have lost much of their ability to command loyal followings as they once did.

The public – especially the younger public – is increasingly skeptical of these and other traditional institutions.

The ways we affiliate with these institutions have changed dramatically. Robert Putnam, in his book *Bowling Alone*, documented the decline of society's sense of civic obligation and personal inclination to join community organizations. Membership in Rotary Clubs, Kiwanis Clubs, Junior Leagues and other service organizations peaked in the late 1970s and has continued to fall, with many of those traditional service clubs now out of business. Veteran chamber execs will remember the Jaycees, an international organization with thousands of robust local chapters that helped millions of young men (and later women) develop leadership skills; Jaycees International – at least in the U.S. – is now merely a shadow of its former self. The days when more than one third of the private workforce belonged to a labor union have long since passed. And the regular church attendance that characterized the childhood of most Baby Boomers in the 1950s and '60s has experienced a steady decline in the decades since.

The disinclination of millennials to join traditional organizations and the myriad ways technology allows us to join with people of similar interests have changed the way we connect socially and how we belong. Through modern communications technology, we can connect with a network of our peers or with strangers who share a common interest anywhere in the world; we can have countless virtual meetings without attending a physical gathering.

Cultural attitudes have also changed in profound ways. The rapid shift of attitudes in support of diversity and inclusion, the changing dynamics between men and women in the workplace, the rapidly increasing acceptance of LGBTQ rights, the widening demands for racial justice, the angry resistance to these cultural trends and the fragmentation of our political culture all create a new environment for communities and chambers.

The number and variety of cause-based organizations have grown dramatically, creating competition for chambers in relevance and resources. At the local, state and national levels, the number of nonprofit organizations has grown far faster than the for-profit sector. One 2016 study documented that the number of nonprofit organizations had grown 20% in the previous decade while for-profit organizations had grown less than 3%. According to the Urban Institute, the nonprofit sector has the third-largest workforce, behind retail and manufacturing, and represents 10% of the total. Most nonprofits are dedicated to a cause: enhancing life for a segment of our society or a particular community. Within the growing constellation of causes and organizations, chambers have to continually demonstrate their relevance and compete for resources to survive.

The sheer number of government agencies, boards, commissions and regulatory bodies has grown at an astonishing rate, creating complexity that is increasingly challenging for citizens and businesses. Many chambers are now seeing that complexity as an opportunity to serve as navigators for their members and the broader public.

The number and variety of cause-based organizations have grown dramatically, creating competition for chambers in relevance and resources.

Occupational specialties have emerged within the space chambers have traditionally occupied. For example, the economic development profession as we know it is only a few decades old. Now almost any community of significant size that wants to compete for jobs and prosperity has economic development specialists working on its behalf – often under the umbrella of a chamber. Fundraising specialists, workforce development specialists, lobbyists, grant writers, and IT specialists that are common occupations in today's Chamber World were relatively rare just a few years ago. Who would have predicted ten years ago that some chambers would employ social media specialists as an integral part of their communications strategies? I certainly could not have predicted just a few years ago that our chamber would create a nine-member workforce staff or that our chamber would obtain a grant to hire two addiction specialists who would work exclusively to help employers deal with the impact of the opioid crisis on their workforces.

Add to the growing complexity of our world the dizzying rate of change taking place. As Thomas Friedman describes in his best-selling *Thank You For Being Late,* an exponential increase in computing power and the impact of globalization are out-pacing our societies' ability to absorb the changes and manage them. He concludes that nations and individuals (and, I presume, chambers) must learn to be fast (innovative and quick to adapt), fair (prepared to help the casualties of change) and slow (adept at shutting out the noise and accessing their deepest values). His observations provide an excellent description of the fast-moving world that chamber professionals are called upon to navigate.

By understanding major trends that are causing major cultural changes, the increasing complexity and the accelerating pace of change, chambers can increase their relevance to their members and their communities.

Change within the world of commerce is advancing at a rate that intimidates even the most flexible organizations. Many businesses now frame their long-range planning in two- and three- year segments instead of trying to imagine a decade or more into the future. A business that prospers today could find itself struggling to survive five years from now due to international competition, corporate buy-outs, advances in technology, online competition, workforce deficiencies or in many cases, all of the above.

As our communities are shaped by these and many other cultural shifts and technological innovations, the businesses in our communities must adapt to survive, and chambers will find it necessary to re-evaluate their missions and their basic value proposition for members. Chambers and chamber leaders will have to become more specialized and more sophisticated in how they serve their members and help their communities navigate the outside world.

■ ■ ■

Navigating the cultural currents and complexity of our world is increasingly challenging for citizens and businesses, but by understanding major trends that are causing these changes, the increasing complexity and the accelerating pace of change, chambers can increase their relevance to their members and their communities.

CHAPTER 12
ACCE'S "HORIZON INITIATIVE"

The Association of Chamber of Commerce Executives (ACCE) decided in 2014 to gaze into its crystal ball by creating the Horizon Initiative Task Force to try to predict what chamber life might look like in 2025. The publication they produced, in my opinion, is one of the most thoughtful and profound products ACCE has ever created for chamber professionals, and its value will last long past 2025.

After considerable brainstorming on the front end of their deliberation, the task force decided against the crystal ball approach of trying to predict what a chamber would look like in 2025. Chambers are too diverse to be easily confined to a cookie-cutter description today – to say nothing of an attempt to predict what they will be a decade from now. The task force instead focused on major trends affecting chambers and communities that are likely to influence chambers in the foreseeable future. ACCE said its long-term goal was "to help business-led, economic-civic entities of every size and type thrive in a world shaped by these oncoming pressures and opportunities."

The task force produced a ground-breaking report, "Horizon Initiative: Chambers 2025,"subtitled "Eight Influences Shaping the Next Decade for Chambers of Commerce." The task force invited feedback from chamber professionals across the country, and based on that feedback, subsequently added a ninth influence to its final report.

The ACCE task force decided against the crystal ball approach and instead focused on major trends affecting chambers and communities that are likely to influence chambers in the foreseeable future.

With great respect and appreciation to ACCE and the chamber professionals on the Horizon Task Force for their great work, I attempt to briefly summarize a few of their key observations while occasionally adding an illustration or observation of my own.

Nine Influences That Will Shape Chambers

1) The Nature of Belonging and Gathering

Business people who join chambers are doing so for different reasons than in the past. While a sense of civic obligation compelled our grandfathers to join chambers and Rotary Clubs, today members are looking for a cause they want to support or some direct benefit from belonging.

The declining loyalty to traditional institutions, the different approach younger adults take to belonging and gathering, the time pressures of business life, the urgency of communications in a digital world, the plethora of nonprofit groups competing for time and talent, and the competition for dollars from the budgets of businesses are all factors that put pressure on the traditional membership model of chambers of commerce. To succinctly summarize the problem these trends pose for the basic "join and get involved" membership model that chambers have traditionally offered, the Horizon report quotes membership guru Kyle Sexton from his book, *Remembership*. "Eighty percent of your members don't show up for anything, yet you still tout participation as the best way to get value from your membership." In other words, equating attendance with value or success as butts-in-seats is a less relevant indicator of viability and more likely a recipe for a steady decline in relevance.

Chambers will have to redefine the notion of membership and distinguish among the interests of their various constituencies. The Horizon report suggests that "the chamber of the future may not identify members the way most chambers do today. They will have customers, clients, investors, partners, some of which will be called 'member.'" Some of those members may actually pay dues. A chamber may have a member company – for example a CPA firm – that pays $500 in dues, spends $1,000 for a table at the annual dinner, pays $5,000 to be the presenting sponsor for a tax seminar and also donates $10,000 to the chamber's foundation for a program to assist tech entrepreneurs. In effect, the member is joining the organization, purchasing services, investing in its own marketing <u>and</u> donating to a cause - clearly expanding the traditional definition of "joining" a chamber.

> A CPA firm that pays $500 in dues, spends $1,000 for a table at the annual dinner, pays $5,000 to be the presenting sponsor for a tax seminar and also donates $10,000 to the chamber's foundation for a program to assist tech entrepreneurs, clearly expands the traditional definition of "joining" a chamber.

There are opportunities for chambers in this evolving environment. Chambers must evaluate the individual motivations of their members and provide specialized programming and networking options to meet those needs. While technology is changing the ways various chamber constituents belong to a chamber, the impersonal nature of certain technologies may also increase the desire for high-touch human connectivity that chambers have traditionally offered. Chambers that can find proper balance on the high-tech/high-touch continuum can occupy a valuable space within their business communities.

2) Communications and Technology

In the past, chambers have typically held a unique position in their communities as the only chamber in town and as the exclusive clearinghouse for certain basic information about the community. Many mid-size and larger chambers employed a research director to answer phone inquiries, to answer surveys from prospective new businesses and to monitor indicators of business activity in the community (housing starts, airport enplanements, bank deposits, etc.). Today, communication technologies make a wealth of community data much more available on a mobile device in seconds. Alexa and Siri know infinitely more facts about a community than the most capable research director. Where does this leave the chamber? How does a chamber add value for its members and other constituents by providing information?

The Horizon report answers with a quote from a McKinsey and Company report: "How well we use these new lines of communication and technology tools to capture information, seek input from others, utilize the collective response to frame decisions and then implement them to shape our economic future will determine our effectiveness in growing healthy, sustainable communities." With businesspeople bombarded by an endless flow of real-time information, a chamber can become a valuable resource if it can carve out space as a viable, trusted source of processed information. "To add value, the chamber must be a filter and an analyst to help determine the value of information," according to the Horizon report.

With businesspeople bombarded by an endless flow of real-time information, a chamber can become a valuable resource if it can carve out space as a viable, trusted source of processed information.

Following the Great Recession, as newspapers continued to downsize and lay off veteran reporters, our chamber concluded there were major issues not being covered by the traditional media. Exacerbating the dearth of coverage was the editorial slant of our daily newspapers – frequently antagonistic toward the business community. After seriously considering purchasing the state's leading business journal in order to have our own media outlet, we decided instead to become our own news source. We hired a talented political reporter to cover import- ant state issues, becoming the first state chamber to hire a journalist to report news for a business audience. Our news blog called "The Bottom Line" soon partnered with the statewide business journal and became the state capital bureau for that online publication and hardcopy magazine.

Communicating with a chamber's various constituencies must change. Broad, generic messaging sent out by news releases to vacant newsrooms and faceless audiences is no longer effective for chambers. Customizing messages to specific audiences is required, along with robust feedback loops that allow chamber audiences to communicate back to their chamber. The ability to frame a conversation, analyze the feedback and use it to create a shared vision for a community is the challenge and the opportunity for chambers. Doing it within increasingly tight timelines is required.

Several action steps were recommended by the Horizon Task Force. Because information dissemination is losing its value as web sources multiply, chambers must adopt an "analyze and filter" culture to deter- mine the value of information for their multiple constituencies instead of maintaining a "push information style." Resist the temptation to try to simply keep up with technology. Instead, use whatever tech tools you can afford to establish and maintain personal relationships and personalized services. Two-way communication – feedback loops – will be needed and expected in the future, even if they are maintained via a video phone on your wrist. The technology-communications challenge requires chamber staff members to spend as much time examining their communications model to keep it fresh as they spend meeting their monthly newsletter deadlines. Look to other chambers – especially those who have been recognized for pioneering new methods – as models.

3) Scarcity and Abundance

Events are moving at an increasing pace due to technology innovations, but the impact is far greater than just the speed of communications. Changing technology can spur abundance in natural resources and shape political movements. For example, consider the impact of fracking on the boom in natural gas supplies and lower energy prices while, conversely, that same technology caused a Depression-era impact on coal-producing regions in central Appalachia. In considering the impact on our communities, the Horizon report quotes Jim Clifton, author of *The Coming Jobs War*: "Some gotta win, some gotta lose."

But it's not just energy resources that will affect populations with abundance or scarcity; it's water, agricultural products, the availability of broadband, the occurrence of natural disasters and pandemics, the consolidation of businesses, the quantity and quality of the available workforce and other factors. For example, an announcement that one airline is merging with another and closing a major hub in your region can create economic hardship for laid off workers and area employers and affect the community's growth trajectory for decades. Because the world of commerce is moving faster and becoming more interdependent each year, these game-changing surges of abundance and scarcity will impact communities more frequently.

Not the least of concerns for most communities and chambers is the supply – or lack thereof – of human resources available for local employers. The current skills gap between available jobs and adequately trained job candidates became a critical issue for employers during the recovery from the Great Recession of 2007-2009, and that gap becomes more acute when the domestic economy improves, occupational categories evolve with new technologies and as a massive demographic wave of Baby Boomers continue to retire. A shortage of medical professionals or software developers or bachelor's degree holders or welders or farm workers or maintenance technicians can hamstring whole industry sectors that could otherwise expand and thrive in a community.

The Horizon report summarizes the impact on chambers: "A chamber that is absent from resource discussions, unaware of the issues, or resigned to letting government alone solve them, risks certain competition from organizations that choose to play in this arena." A helpful exercise for chambers is to engage a group of civic leaders in simply identifying areas in which the community is facing abundance and scarcity and evaluating how those factors might shape the community's prospects for growth.

> "A chamber that is absent from resource discussions, unaware of the issues, or resigned to letting government alone solve them, risks certain competition from organizations that choose to play in this arena."

4) Global Impacts

We are inextricably linked across the globe by commerce, geopolitics, terrorism, energy prices, food supply, disease and labor markets. Who would have guessed a few years ago that our 401K retirement accounts would be damaged by protests in Greece over public pensions? Or that a virus in China could cause massive unemployment in the U.S.? Or that the anger of young, unemployed, radical Islamists in the Middle East would force us to take off our shoes and carry our shampoo in small containers before boarding a flight from Des Moines to Chicago? Who would have guessed that my former chamber would sell hundreds of thousands of protective face masks to employers in response to the COVID-19 global pandemic?

Chambers have traditionally focused on trade as the primary reason to engage internationally. As Chris Mead points out in his book,

The Magicians of Main Street, increasing trade was a central motivating tenet of trade organizations centuries ago and, more recently,
of chambers of commerce. Today, with the vast majority of global
consumers living outside the U.S. and with globalization expanding
the middle classes and the purchasing power of hundreds of millions
in emerging economies, our communities will find that more and
more economic opportunities will
come through global engagement.
A community's or region's brand
will be increasingly important to
attracting international investment and commerce. Chambers
must be prepared to facilitate
their communities' strategies for
capitalizing on these trends.

Today, with the vast majority of global consumers living outside the U.S. and with globalization expanding, our communities will find that more and more economic opportunities will come through global engagement.

But it's more than international trade. Climate change and its impact
on agriculture, coastal communities, tourism, infrastructure, insurance
rates and energy demands will force chambers to respond to challenges never before envisioned. Population growth and its impact on
the environment will have profound implications for communities,
businesses and chambers.

While these impacts present new opportunities, there are also global
threats. The public library in my hometown was closed for more than
a week because its central computer that controls almost every function in the library was hacked from a foreign source that demanded
ransom in untraceable cryptocurrency to deactivate the ransomware
it had planted. A few years ago, IT specialists at the U.S. Chamber
noticed frequent hits on their computer network from Chinese servers,
not coincidentally as Chamber CEO Tom Donohue was preparing to
lead a trade delegation to that country. It's no wonder that increasingly
chambers are offering their members courses and services in cyberse-
curity in an effort to cope with new global threats.

As the Horizon report states, "The volatility of the global stage will increase over the next ten years. But the world is made up of regions, cities, communities, neighborhoods, each with a meaningful role to play on the international stage."

At the Kentucky Chamber we attempted to position ourselves for greater international engagement by forging a formal partnership with our statewide World Trade Center. We even hired former Kentucky Governor Martha Layne Collins as a consultant and as our "ambassador at-large for international trade" to promote exporting across the state. (Her legacy had been cemented by recruiting Toyota Motor Manufacturing to Kentucky and spurring more than 150 Japanese companies to subsequently establish operations in the state.) Her high-profile role served us well, and she was a compelling speaker for groups across the state. However, our partnership with the Trade Center organization wasn't structured solidly and we discontinued it after a couple of years. Nonetheless, the potential for chambers to engage in international affairs remains strong and deserves serious exploration.

The Horizon report points to four avenues for chambers to consider in developing international strategies: export support for local companies, proactive attraction of foreign direct investment, facilitation of international networks, and instruction/awareness about the global trends, dangers and opportunities likely to affect local companies. Chambers developing programs and products in these areas will make themselves more relevant for many of their members. Getting closer to the companies in your region that have overseas interests and connections will identify relationships that can be harnessed. Creating partnerships with port authorities, freight forwarders, government agencies, consultants and corporations with experience and expertise in international trade will help chambers chart their courses. And significantly for chambers wanting to monetize these strategies, treating international trade as a mission and purpose-driven undertaking will attract financial resources to that cause.

5) Population Shifts

Demographic change is shaping politics, markets, workforces, communities and neighborhoods. Recognizing the changing diversity of our communities and developing strategies for including non-traditional populations in our organizations are imperatives for chambers. Chambers ignoring these population shifts risk irrelevance with various segments of their members — many of whom are responding proactively to these new realities — and with the broader community.

Chambers ignoring these population shifts risk irrelevance with various segments of their members – many of whom are responding proactively to these new realities – and with the broader community.

No longer is diversity just the high-minded concern of large chambers in metropolitan areas. Chambers of all sizes should look at how their organizations are perceived by non-white populations, millennials, the economically disadvantaged and other non-traditional chamber constituencies.

"Every perennial chamber priority, from education to transportation, to business climate, to place-making is affected by demographic changes," according to the Horizon report. "Failure to recognize the continuing population changes will negatively affect membership, audience, clout and future funding streams."

Demographic diversity means more than considering racial inclusion; generational change is also having a profound effect on communities and workplaces and must be factored into the discussion of diversity. Chambers must consider how to include younger constituents in more than Business After Hours gatherings and young professional programs; we must learn how to engage them in decision-making. There are already 70 million millennials in the U.S. In just a few short years, they will be the majority in the workforce. The chamber from which

I recently retired provides a vivid illustration of this rapidly unfolding reality: millennials already comprise the largest age cohort within the 40-person staff, and one of those young professionals was selected as my replacement as CEO. Not insignificantly, she was chosen after a serious, eight-month search conducted by a committee of prominent, blue-chip CEOs – four males and four females – all Baby Boomers. A major generational transfer is taking place.

An additional diversity issue for chambers is the social-economic disparities that are growing in America. College-educated members of our society who have done relatively well navigating our information-based economy are increasingly segregated in social and political attitudes from those in the lesser-educated population who have been victims of technology and globalization and who are increasingly frustrated by income inequality and with our political and social institutions. Chambers – composed mostly of business leaders – are usually aligned with and perceived to be the domain of the "have's" rather than the "have-nots." Attempting to be effective in the broader community that encompasses both ends of that spectrum is an increasing challenge for chambers, especially as they try to effect change in the public policy arena.

If chambers are going to rise above a reputation for being old, white, male and elite, they must be strategic and intentional with strategies for inclusion of a broader range of community stakeholders. They can't build future-focused chambers without those strategies. I learned in my own hiring decisions that diversity doesn't just happen to a chamber; there has to be a precise decision – i.e. conscious, deliberate intentionality – to pursue and accomplish diversity. Chamber leaders must consider gender, age, race, culture, economic status and lifestyle and how we can model inclusiveness at the board level, with our staffs, within our mem-

> *Diversity doesn't just happen to a chamber; there has to be a precise decision – i.e. conscious, deliberate intentionality – to pursue and accomplish diversity.*

bership, in our programming and with our advocacy efforts in the broader community.

6) Political and Social Fragmentation

Political and social fragmentation has increased in our country in recent years and reflects more than partisan divisions and the racial and generational divisions discussed earlier. It's how we think, where we live, how we shop, who we associate with, how we get our news and how we see the world. It's more than cable news that divides us into political tribes, and it's more than the gerrymandering of political districts that polarizes our nation and our communities; it's also our self-segregation as we choose to live in neighborhoods with people who look and think like we do.

When our presidential campaigns are reduced to mind-numbing political attack ads and when city council meetings or zoning hearings become shouting matches between the perceived "haves" and "have-nots," how does a chamber position itself? As the Horizon report states, "....for two centuries, chambers' work has depended on bringing people together around common causes like growth, jobs, kids, advocacy, infrastructure, and celebration." In our current environment, we are forced to ask: Is that common ground all but impossible to achieve?

Actually, the fragmented political and social landscape that appears unlikely to dissipate in the foreseeable future simultaneously creates dysfunctionality and enormous potential for chambers of commerce to grow and provide leadership. Chambers have experience at consensus-building, maintain a position of trust in the community, have a positive brand and often function as conveners of stakeholders. Chambers represent businesspeople who, regardless of their political affiliation and social values, are generally results-oriented and pragmatic about getting those results. Chambers have the opportunity to serve as the voice of reason or as some call it, "the sane middle."

In an environment of controversy, a chamber can often be the only organization with the standing, a problem-solving inclination, a mission that supports economic progress and the resources to play a critical role between opposing sides. In an effort to plan the future and help a community process decisions, a chamber can play a central role among businesses, citizens and governments, facilitating and mediating a common vision that leads to a collaborative and positive future.

Political and social fragmentation has increased in our country in recent years. Chambers have the opportunity to serve as the voice of reason or as some call it, "the sane middle."

It's not that a chamber can dictate solutions and the world passively falls in line. Thankfully, gone are the days of a handful of older white men in a wood-paneled boardroom at the local bank dictating who will get elected and how the community will move forward. In today's more complex world, with complex problems demanding complex solutions, a chamber that is properly prepared, presents itself as an honest broker and is truly focused on pulling diverse stakeholders together to solve problems can be more relevant and valuable to its community than ever before.

7) Resource Alignment

To chamber executives, the term resources generally means membership sales and/or fundraising. The never-ending challenge to recruit new members and raise money to sustain and expand a chamber's programming is a reality faced by nearly every chamber in the country. To the Horizon Task Force, the expanded terminology of resource alignment offers a deeper meaning and suggests a much stronger connection between resources and the purposes for which a chamber seeks them. As the Horizon's report puts it, the notion describes a closer alignment in which the "what" (asking for money) and the "why" (for what purpose) are strategically coordinated.

As noted in Chapter 8, chambers will continue to offer fee-for-service transactions such as seminars, events, advertising, and publications, and access-pass investments such as tiered dues with graduated benefits in return for greater investments. As the Horizon report suggests, "Transaction-driven revenue will always be part of chamber revenue. Companies will pay for services and network access provided by a trusted source. Alignment of resources, however, revolves around finding ways to secure more funding targeted to support the stated mission and vision of the chamber." Increasingly, chambers are being drawn to cause-based fundraising where substantial dollars are committed to specific community-building purposes such as economic development and education.

Increasingly, chambers are being drawn to cause-based fundraising where substantial dollars are committed to specific community-building purposes such as economic development and education.

Some chambers have seen a dramatic increase in the activity of their 501-c-3 charitable foundations. Whereas chamber foundations were once passive vehicles for accepting charitable contributions from occasional donors, they are now being utilized to actively align chamber goals with external, philanthropic resources. Those resources are not exclusively available from member companies; quite often they come from foundations affiliated with chamber member companies (the JP Morgan Chase Foundation), from national foundations with specific philanthropic goals (the Ford Foundation) or from wealthy individuals – often local individuals who support the particular causes a chamber is championing (e.g. the Jane and John Smith Education Fund).

Chambers will have tough resource alignment decisions to make in the future: How much casework – the care and feeding of individual member requests -- can a chamber offer if it can't generate revenue to support those services? How much time do you dedicate to member services vs. trying to advance your community? Does a traditional membership sales staff have the right skills and the time necessary to raise substantial dollars from chamber members for a particular cause? Does anyone on the chamber staff have the experience to write a time-consuming application for a national foundation grant? If you do pursue substantial dollars from private foundations, how do you resist the temptation to adopt the priorities of those funding sources, inadvertently causing mission creep that can distort your chamber's priorities, its brand and even its mission?

Given the kinds of resource opportunities created by the accumulation of private wealth in our country, chambers that are in constant need of funds to support their programs must develop the skills and devote the time to strategically match causes with available sources of funding.

8) Catalytic Leadership

The eighth influence gets to the heart of the special role chamber leaders play and is especially relevant for those who have dedicated all or a substantial part of their careers to chamber work. Leadership makes the critical difference in the success of companies, churches, armies and families. Hundreds of self-help books offer their angles on this simple truth: For positive results in any social group, capable leaders must emerge.

"This is not a theoretical consideration for chambers and communities. Leadership, both by volunteers and paid executives, is arguably the biggest factor in determining the future of chambers and, by extension, the success of communities." The Horizon report articulates why the notion of catalytic leadership takes on powerful meaning within a chamber of commerce context: For a chamber to provide its community catalytic leadership, "it will need to focus on what it wants to be in the community more than on what it will do."

If the chamber sees itself as a change agent for the community, there will be an increasing demand on the professional chamber executive to provide catalytic leadership and to recruit capable volunteers who want to see progress. "Civic entrepreneurs ten years from now will crave results because they are comfortable with change and uncomfortable with the status quo." A catalytic chamber will see itself as an instigator of change, rather than merely a resource to help people cope with change. Instead of saying "Well, we've got a new mayor; let's go meet with her and see what she's planning," the chamber should be proactively saying, "Hey, Helen Johnson is planning to run for mayor; let's go meet with her and lay out what we think needs to be accomplished in this city." In other words, a leader can observe the change at City Hall and organize a meeting with the new mayor; a catalytic leader is proactive and wants to engage with a prospective mayor on how she frames the opportunities ahead and her agenda to tackle those opportunities.

> *A catalytic chamber will see itself as an instigator of change, rather than merely a resource to help people cope with change. Professional leadership – the executives hired by chamber boards – will become increasingly important for the success of chambers.*

Chambers are controlled by volunteer leaders who are taking time away from their places of business to serve in a civic role. There are varying opinions about whether the quantity and quality of volunteer leaders from the business community is decreasing. I have no reason to believe leadership talent within the business community itself is in short supply, but I am convinced the availability of capable business leaders for engagement in chamber programs and causes is increasingly scarce. Finding capable volunteer leaders who have the time, professional flexibility and appetite for tackling seemingly intractable community problems like poverty, low educational attainment, poor health and racial tension has become more difficult. This will make professional leadership – the executives hired by chamber boards – increasingly important for the success of chambers. Staff-level leadership that rises to the level of catalytic leadership provides greater value to the broader community.

The Horizon report calls for us to move beyond the admirable notion of servant leader. While the description of a leading servant captures a large part of the disposition, the mission and the management style of many successful chamber leaders, the more ambitious notion of catalytic leader is even more compelling, especially when aligned with the higher expectations of a modern chamber – a catalytic chamber – that seeks to create change. The discreet notions of servant leader and catalytic leader need not be mutually exclusive.

The concept of catalytic leadership, as ambitious as it is and as aggressive as it may sound, should not be misconstrued as fostering a solo act by a dynamic, charismatic chamber executive. It connotes the ability to pull people together through communication, collaboration, negotiation, and humility. Ted Abernathy, an economist, futurist and consultant to multiple chambers including mine, calls this kind of leadership "networked leadership" and maintains that it will transcend traditional hierarchies and pinnacles of authority. A chamber executive's ability to align influential stakeholders with a specific challenge at hand – the matchmaking function of chamber leadership – is essential to tackling major challenges and seizing major opportunities for our communities.

Catalytic leadership calls for chamber professionals to advance beyond simply managing a successful chamber (more members, more income, more ad hoc projects and greater profile) to seeing oneself as an activist team builder to accomplish community goals. The Horizon report predicts that by 2025, "only people who were hired for, or learn to take responsibility for catalytic, prosperity-focused change are likely to occupy CEO positions in large and mid-sized chambers." And in spite of all the competition that will exist to provide traditional chamber-like services to businesses (networking, advocacy, etc.), a chamber can rise above that traditional role and provide catalytic leadership in the community. A chamber of commerce is probably in a better position than any other community organization to recruit talented leaders from the business community and match them with the community's most compelling causes. A chamber with mission-driven volunteers and a highly motivated professional staff will be well-positioned to provide that kind of catalytic leadership.

9) The Limitations of Government

A ninth influence was added two years after the original publication of the Horizon report in direct response to feedback from chamber professionals across the country. In a variety of ways, chamber professionals noted that government inadequacy was often a factor affecting their chambers. They described a reality that extends well beyond the partisanship and polarization described earlier as the 6th influence. Interactions with school boards, zoning commissions, historic districts, downtown development authorities, city councils, state regulatory boards, the legislature, federal agencies and Congress create an environment in which a chamber exists and through which it attempts to create change. To be effective for its members and for the community, a chamber must skillfully navigate the ever-widening constellation of agencies and entities in the public sector.

To be effective for its members and for the community, a chamber must skillfully navigate the ever-widening constellation of agencies and entities in the public sector.

Apparently there was some concern expressed within ACCE about the original title of a ninth influence that centered on the term inadequacy – perhaps because it sounded overly negative or appeared to be an indictment of all elements of government and all policymakers. The ninth influence was subsequently revised with the publication of a helpful ACCE how-to guide for working with the public sector called, "Engaging the Public Sector." I've noticed various online references to the ninth influence under the original "Limitations" title and others with the "Engaging" title. Frankly, I identify more with the original version. After spending more than three decades in Chamber World and more than one decade in government at the local and federal levels, I don't consider an observation about the limitations of government to be in and of itself pejorative – any more than an objective discussion of the limitations or inadequacy of chambers of commerce is necessarily an indictment. Whatever title we use to describe the limitations of government, it represents a reality that plays a major role in defining the individual political environments of every chamber and every chamber executive in the country.

As a former elected official, I have a deep appreciation for the role of government and the fact that the private and public sectors necessarily operate by different rules. A business operates with its own money and in most cases, I – as a customer – can choose whether to interact with that business. Government however, operates with my money and I don't have much choice about whether to interact with it. Therefore, I want a different set of rules for a monopolistic government and a different level of transparency for how it conducts its affairs. That expectation, shared by most citizens, necessitates public decision-making processes and some level of bureaucracy that are inherently more deliberative and often more cumbersome than private sector decision-making.

The Horizon's report suggests four roles for chambers to consider in the face of the reality of public sector limitations: 1) Fixer. A chamber can use its many connections and deep understanding of local policy to help its members and community navigate the public sector. 2) Windows of Opportunity. Chambers can seize the moment when solutions emerge from public-private dilemmas and use those solutions to broaden the benefit for a larger segment of the business community. 3) Persistence. A chamber that stays focused on the end goal and that keeps on keeping on can outlast political intransigence and countless barriers that stymie progress. 4) Instructor. Using chamber networks that encourage the sharing of information and best practices, a chamber can bring ideas, lessons and solutions to its own community. I would suggest another role: 5) Translator. Chambers can help translate the political, policy and bureaucratic language coming from government into Main Street language for their business audiences which are often too busy to absorb all of the nuance, complexity, red tape and jargon emanating from the public sector.

Political Polarization and the Opportunity for Chambers

To expand on the notion of political and social fragmentation described earlier, I offer the following reprint of a column I submitted as my chairman's column to ACCE's "Chamber Executive" magazine in 2010. In it, I suggested that chambers have a profound opportunity to fill the vacuum caused by increasing polarization, and I was delighted to see the notion incorporated by the Horizon Task Force in its 2015 report.

The polarization phenomenon has only grown more pronounced in the years since I wrote the column. According to the Pew Research Center, "Republicans and Democrats are more divided along ideological lines – and partisan acrimony is deeper and more extensive – than at any point in recent history. And these trends manifest themselves in myriad ways, both in politics and in everyday life." That analysis by Pew conducted in 2014 – the same year the Horizon task force was deliberating and two years before the bitter 2016 Trump vs. Clinton presidential election and five years before the Trump impeachment drama exposed an even deeper divide in our country.

Political Polarization: A Great Opportunity for Chambers

Everybody is sick of the partisan polarization in Washington and to varying degrees, in statehouses and city halls across the country.

Even those of us who believe divided legislatures are part of the brilliant national experiment we call democracy, the gamesmanship displayed in Congress and the partisan wrangling over serious issues of global consequence are insulting. If you add to the mix the talking heads on dozens of cable channels, the mind-numbing blather on talk radio and the ideological smack-down available in cyberspace, we wonder if our "experiment in democracy" - a phrase used by Thomas Jefferson - will ultimately succeed.

But amidst all the political sound and fury, there is a tremendous opportunity for our chambers of commerce. Consider the following:

- **Chambers want results.** *Our members – business owners and managers – are generally pragmatic and, at the end of the day, are primarily interested in results. While they hold strong philosophical beliefs and political attitudes that are typically right of center, they are less ideological and certainly less partisan than the two main political parties. On social issues – the ones that the political parties enjoy using as weapons against each other – the business community is more often than not agnostic and/or silent.*

- **Chambers can be "the voice of reason".** *An effective chamber that has a solid government relations function, an appropriate committee structure, guiding principles and policies and a member contact program in place, can position itself as "the voice of reason" on many policy issues facing local communities and states. A chamber that does its research, deliberates seriously on community issues and points out the economic consequences of various policy alternatives can not only be at the table, it can provide expertise and valuable insight from a business perspective to policy-makers.*

- **Chambers represent a positive brand.** *The chamber brand is stronger than the reputation of the Democrat and Republican parties. Both parties are perceived very negatively by the public in national surveys. The public doesn't trust them to solve our problems. On the other hand, countless surveys demonstrate empirically that the name "chamber of commerce" carries substantial positive*

> A chamber of commerce has an unprecedented opportunity in today's balkanized political climate to walk through the middle of that battlefield and play a unique leadership role in shaping its community.

weight. Candidates, companies, communities and bars of soap all sell better if they are associated with the chamber of commerce.

A chamber of commerce that wants to truly provide leadership in its sphere of influence has an unprecedented opportunity in today's balkanized political climate to walk through the middle of that battlefield and play a unique leadership role in shaping its community.

■ ■ ■

The full ACCE Horizon report, available at www.acce.org, provides far more insights into the nine influences. It also offers action steps in each of the nine areas and suggests ways that engagement with specific ACCE divisions can help chamber leaders stay attuned to trends and sharpen their skills in each of the areas.

CHAPTER 13
COLLECTING IDEAS AND CAPTURING A VISION

When questioned during a presidential debate about his vision for the country, former President George H.W. Bush dismissively referred to "the vision thing," unintentionally revealing an absent-minded disregard for the value of articulating a vision for the country. Political opponents and late-night television comedians ridiculed the remark, characterizing Bush as an intellectual lightweight who couldn't see a bigger picture and grasp a broader vision for the nation. In contrast, Ronald Reagan defined his optimistic vision for the county as "the shining city upon a hill" and much of his political messaging and his administration's policies tied back to that vision.

Just as a country needs a vision that captures its aspirations and sets its priorities, communities need a coherent vision for where they are headed. Chambers are uniquely suited to help craft such a vision.

The range of options for developing a community vision is very broad – from sponsoring a town hall conversation facilitated by a local volunteer to employing specialized consultants to conduct formal studies. What role should a chamber play in such a visioning process – and by extension – what role should the chamber executive play?

Just as a country needs a vision that captures its aspirations and sets its priorities, communities need a coherent vision for where they are headed. Chambers are uniquely suited to help craft such a vision.

How to be Smarter Than You Are

It's easy in the daily crush of organizational demands that weigh on a chamber executive to fail to notice the need for an external vision for the community or if recognizing the need, to feel overwhelmed by the idea of pursuing a visioning project. The notion can seem hopelessly vague and the burden of managing such a project horribly time-intensive. Meanwhile, the chamber exec is pressured to balance the chamber's budget, raise money, schedule countless meetings, plan events – all required to keep the doors open.

A chamber executive who makes the conscious decision to pursue a visioning project doesn't have to feel personally responsible for identifying and articulating that vision. Initiating a chamber-led process that facilitates the development of a vision and creates an idea-friendly culture within the chamber can form the foundation on which the community itself develops its particular vision for the future. The chamber can serve as the forum for ideas and be the honest broker – the relatively neutral party that cares about the community and invites citizens to be involved in shaping its own future.

When considering a visioning process, one of the best skills a chamber executive can bring to his/her organization is the ability to "be smarter than you are". That notion involves consciously leveraging outside resources for your chamber and community from beyond your own expertise. None of us is clairvoyant or has a crystal ball for reading the future, but we can use practical methods to reach beyond our own knowledge base and our own limited ability to visualize the future. By doing so, we can be smarter than we are.

After I spent nearly eight years as mayor of my hometown, the newspaper editorialized about my tenure at City Hall and used the term visionary to describe my administration. I was flattered by the comment but felt somewhat uncomfortable. I didn't feel I had been visionary enough. Although we had clearly pushed the envelope of the civic culture in progressive ways and had several high-profile successes to show for it, I had a nagging regret that I hadn't articulated a more precise vision for my community, like Reagan's succinct vision with a capital "V". I felt I should have concentrated harder, been more insightful, done a better job of predicting and somehow painted a clearer picture for my community. Perhaps I should have identified a more concise, unifying dream of my community becoming the "_____ Capital of America". What I failed to realize was that by reaching outside our community for ideas and inspiration and constantly pursuing progress on multiple fronts (like strategically advancing the pieces on a chessboard) we were leaning into the future and in effect, creating a vision for our community. We just didn't capture our aspirations in a single tagline.

As Peter Drucker said, "The best way to predict the future is to create it." And the best way to create it is to constantly observe what other communities are doing and what other ideas are circulating. Seeing an outdoor sports complex or a business incubator in a nearby community, or a major streetscape project in a downtown you visited while on vacation, can provide clues for opportunities for your own community's development. While I was in college, I toured a performing arts auditorium in Danville, Kentucky, on the campus of Centre College. A few years later, while attending a symphony concert in a high school auditorium back in my hometown, with its rows of folding wooden seats and acoustically challenged concrete block walls, I decided our community needed a performing arts center if we were going to expand our arts programs and be competitive for the professionals we needed to recruit and retain.

We didn't just snap our fingers and create a major new complex. Even after we created a chamber work group to explore the possibility of a new arts center, various setbacks and delays consumed time, and it was nearly a decade before we celebrated opening night of the RiverPark (performing arts) Center. It had been a full two decades after originally touring the college arts center where the seed of an idea was planted. It took time – two decades – before we were able, in effect, to move that particular piece on our community's chessboard. Having a dream – a vision – for such a facility was obviously critical, but having the desire to see our community advance and the determination – the grit – to stay with the idea in spite of significant discouragement, was more important to its realization.

A chamber colleague of mine once suggested that chambers have the opportunity – and even the obligation – to own the vision for their community. In other words, because chambers usually provide the central forum for businesses and serve as the primary advocate for economic growth in their respective communities, they have the opportunity and even an obligation to create a process by which a community vision is developed. One could argue that a chamber is often in the <u>best</u> position to artic-ulate and pursue that vision, better than a mayor who might not be in office past the next election or might not have the personal ability or forward-leaning inclination to lead the community toward the future.

Chambers have the opportunity – and even the obligation – to own the vision for their community. A chamber is often in the best position to articulate and pursue that vision.

In 2017, I surveyed all 46 state chambers for a presentation about visioning that I was preparing for the Council of State Chambers and asked about visioning projects they had conducted in their states. Thirteen responded that they has published a vision for their states and most had packaged their strategies with titles such as "The Four Pillars of Prosperity," the "Five Cornerstones of Progress," the "Six Bold Steps Toward 2025" or as the recommendations of a blue-ribbon task force such as "The Commonwealth Commission." The most common themes and accompanying strategies cited by the chamber executives were education and workforce (virtually all had addressed this issue), competitive business climate, infrastructure, innovation and entrepreneurism, economic development and jobs, government effectiveness, and quality of life. Most of the studies focused on four or five of these broad priorities.

While chambers can be influential in shaping a vision, they are not in a position to impose their vision on a state or a community. For one thing, there will always be important and powerful players in the community with ideas of their own. A wealthy entrepreneur who wants to recruit a sports team, the editor of the paper who persistently champions government reform and the recently elected mayor with a reform agenda will always have the ability to capture the attention of the community and shape its aspirations, as they should. But the chamber can serve as a respected forum for those ideas and a vehicle for pursuing certain initiatives, adding important support for sound ideas and asking constructive questions when rough ideas need polishing. Helping shape those ideas and developing practical strategies for the best timing of key initiatives (deciding which chess pieces to move in what sequence) can be critical to the pace of progress in a community. By constantly surveying the chessboard and the position of the key pieces, one can begin to visualize how the game of creating progress can be won.

There are multiple tools available to chamber executives who want to begin a visioning process – practical ways in which you as the chamber exec can become smarter than you are and provide a powerful service for your chamber and community.

Board Retreats

One of the most valuable ways to gather new ideas and insights is by using the talent of your board of directors and engaging them in a conscious visioning exercise – perhaps in an isolated retreat setting – to produce valuable ideas for your chamber and the community. At my hometown chamber, an annual board retreat became a much-anticipated highlight of the organization's calendar. Every January after the rush of the holidays, our board members and their spouses went to a resort two hours away and spent the weekend. It was an enjoyable get-away for socializing and having a more thoughtful dialogue about our chamber and our community.

One of the most valuable ways to gather new ideas and insights is by using the talent of your board of directors and engaging them in a conscious visioning exercise.

The board members and I spent most of a Saturday in a planning session. We reviewed the progress of our chamber during the previous year, engaged in a structured SWOT analysis of the community as described in a section below and suggested goals. We prioritized those goals by board members voting their preferences. We reminded ourselves that we had to be willing to eliminate some of our old programs if we were going to add goals to our agenda. We discussed our chamber's operations and what our chamber could do to advance the goals we set for the community. Following the board retreat, I summarized the notes and drafted a detailed business plan for consideration at the next board meeting.

We had excellent participation in those board retreats and a high level of buy-in by the board for our plan of action. Moreover, the retreat was fun, and it served as our single greatest tool for creating camaraderie among board members. Because of that team culture, I don't recall a single split vote or contentious decision at the board level during my tenure as their chamber exec.

When I was invited to lead the significantly larger Birmingham Regional Chamber, I learned that my key leaders – most of whom were high-level corporate executives with many demands on their schedules – didn't have the appetite for a board retreat, and the key officers seemed willing to place a huge amount of the strategic planning function on my shoulders. When one of my board chairs said, "That's why we hired you," I felt responsible for developing a plan, but I also worried about getting buy-in for our goals from individual board members and key community influencers. My senior staff and I went through a strategic planning process, the product of which was readily adopted by the board. However, I never thought the plan carried the weight or the profound potential of a board-developed plan.

As with the state chamber I later served, we only had quarterly board meetings, and they were relatively formal affairs with routine chamber business handled by key officers and formal presentations by guest speakers. Asking for a weekend of planning was impractical, given the professional responsibilities and the travel obligations associated with the board members' corporate roles, but we were able to occasionally convene a half-day planning session that was piggybacked onto our quarterly board meeting, or we dedicated the lion's share of a board meeting to a planning exercise. Meanwhile, our 15-member executive committee was willing to spend more time engaged in a focused dialogue about the direction of our community and the chamber, and that smaller group became a critical working group for our planning process. In addition, I worked to find other ways to engage individual board members in the process, often visiting them, listening to their concerns and factoring their thoughts into the process.

Engaging Staff

If more responsibility is placed on the staff for planning the future of the chamber and addressing the critical issues of the community or region, engaging a small group of senior staff members, key officers of the chamber and/or trusted advisors in the process is critical. At my larger chambers, I included our senior staff in regular planning meetings and occasional staff retreats in isolated settings. The retreats were loosely structured around our business plan or more formally structured around a SWOT analysis. We discussed opportunities and challenges we saw in the immediate future, those starting to emerge on the more distant horizon and even some so-called BHAGs (Big, Hairy, Audacious Goals). It doesn't take a trained facilitator or paid consultant to structure a discussion that will help a group focus on practical goals and gain consensus around charting a direction. I occasionally led planning sessions to engage our full staff in a discussion of where we stood and where we needed to go. In those sessions, I attempted to play a facilitator role more than a participant role so I didn't inhibit engagement and discourage fresh ideas from our staff.

One such session, which I described in Chapter 4, focused on simply making a list on a marker board of the functions for which our chamber was recognized or for which our chamber was the exclusive provider. We listed about three dozen items during our exercise. As you might expect, not everyone on the staff was as comfortable brainstorming as others. But we got surprising input from a broad group of participants, and even those who held back from offering suggestions observed the discussion first-hand and were reminded of the distinct role our chamber plays in the life of our state. Moreover, much of the mystery and perceptions of top-down decision making by the bosses (senior staff who were routinely planning and making decisions within the organization) were taken out of the planning process – or at least minimized.

Our annual, confidential workplace survey of our staff, conducted through an independent third party, indicated a strong sense that staff members agreed with the statements that they "have a sense of how decisions are made in the organization" and "the organization keeps me informed of things that will affect my job." Our occasional full-staff planning sessions created a participatory platform for gathering solid input and maintaining staff cohesion. In addition, the senior members of the staff got to hear valuable insights from other staff members who didn't normally participate in planning sessions, including the person who greeted our walk-in visitors, the membership sales person who received unfiltered feedback about our organization from members and prospective members, the staff member who worked on membership renewals and the young communications manager who monitored the metrics of who was watching, interacting with and sometimes trolling our chamber on social media platforms.

Our occasional full-staff planning sessions created a participatory platform for gathering solid input and maintaining staff cohesion.

Town Hall Visioning Sessions

Offering a public forum can be a valuable way to engage everyday citizens in creating a vision. Citizens generally want to be heard but not everyone is comfortable thinking abstractly about the future. I learned a valuable lesson early in my career about the challenges of engaging average citizens in discussions of the future.

I ran for mayor of my hometown because I was dissatisfied with the slow pace of change in our community, and I wanted to help the community recover from a severe recession in which unemployment reached a Depression-level 14.3%. When my main opponent – the incumbent mayor – dropped out of the race one day before the filing deadline, he left me a conspicuously open path to winning the fall election. However, two underfunded opponents were encouraged by their buddies to jump into the race just hours before the filing deadline. They both revealed to the local newspaper that they didn't have any particular ideas or a campaign platform on which to actively campaign. They just thought it would be interesting to run for mayor. Wow! That vacuum of campaign substance created an awkward campaign environment.

I didn't want to appear that I was taking the election for granted or was too confident or arrogant to actively campaign for the office so I decided to pivot with my strategy. Instead of mounting a traditional campaign about my qualifications for office and the planks of my campaign platform, I literally went door-to-door, handing people a campaign brochure that included a return card asking for their ideas about the future of our community. I genuinely wanted average citizens to give their best ideas about where our community could be in five or ten years. I collected the names of several hundred people who volunteered ideas so I could later consider appointing them to local boards, commissions and ad hoc task forces, and I appointed many of them to various volunteer positions during my first term in office. Meanwhile, I collected hundreds of ideas ranging from minor complaints (the pothole at the corner of Main and Orchard Streets) to the grandiose (we should build an international airport with direct flights to Paris).

After my election, I continued the ideas-for-the-future theme by sponsoring several listening sessions that were hosted in private homes by volunteers who had worked in my campaign. The newspaper and television stations were very interested in this non-traditional approach to governing and covered several of the sessions, giving our campaign and my first weeks in office an unusually high profile in the tri-state television market.

A campaign volunteer arranged for one of those sessions to be hosted by a woman who lived in a large public housing project. She invited a dozen or more people into her living room, and I opened the session by asking everyone to make suggestions about where the community could be in five or ten years. I was young, enthusiastic and – as the session would reveal – a bit naive about gathering futuristic input.

The first woman to speak said she lived nearby and that her next door neighbor had more than a dozen cats. The cats posed a nuisance and created a horrible odor during the summer that permeated the woman's open screens. She pointedly asked me what I was going to do about it. I stammered and stuttered about our department of building code enforcement and how I would have someone come and inspect the problem. But the lesson for me was more profound: Many people don't have the luxury of daydreaming about the future of their communities; they live their lives trying to manage everyday concerns. Even on our chamber boards, which are populated with civic-minded business people, you have members who are very comfortable attempting to peer into the future and others who are uncomfortable with abstract, theoretical talk. The latter type of board member would rather get down to business and, for example, hear which businesses had dropped their memberships during the previous month, who our annual dinner speaker would be, and whether we were staying on budget for the year.

I had the pleasure of sponsoring a variety of town hall meetings to gain feedback from our community and our chamber – some with paid consultants as facilitators, some with volunteer leaders. I was always amazed at the variety of ideas that came forward. Early in my first term at City Hall, I put together a six-hour community brainstorming session called "100 Ideas for the Future of Owensboro." It was a low-budget session with box lunches for the first 100 participants who registered. It got a tremendous amount of publicity and conveyed the message to the broader community that we were looking to the future, and that we were reaching out to citizens for ideas. It was an interesting and productive exercise.

I invited a friend of mine, the charismatic mayor of Louisville, to give the opening address and to get people thinking about how a community can make progress. After the high-energy opening session, we asked participants to choose among ten breakout groups stationed around the room – groups focused on tourism, transportation, the arts, education, health care, sports and recreation, downtown development, youth activities, economic development and community appearance. Everyone chose a break-out group with a facilitator who led a rapid-fire exercise to capture ideas. When time was up, the group went through a voting exercise to select their top ideas. After a quick break, everyone moved to a second group and repeated the process. The responses from the two sessions were merged, ballots were prepared during lunch with the most popular ideas from all the groups, everyone voted for their favorites and the results were reported back to the entire group of participants. Some ideas were practical and easily achievable. Others were more grandiose and would take decades – if ever – to implement.

The event was highlighted in the newspaper the following day with a major layout of the 100 ideas along with an editorial that complimented the community's engagement. A year later, the newspaper followed up with a major Sunday feature about areas where progress had been made and other areas where results were not yet visible. The community brainstorming exercise reinforced the future-oriented culture we were working to create, gave the general public an inside view of the planning process, provided the community with 100 specific ideas as food for thought and, more important, helped shape the public dialogue about specific challenges and opportunities facing our community.

The community brainstorming exercise reinforced the future-oriented culture we were working to create and helped shape the public dialogue about specific challenges and opportunities facing our community.

While I sponsored the event as a newly elected mayor, a chamber can host a similar town hall forum as a general idea-gathering exercise or to focus on a specific issue facing the community. There are individuals who are trained to facilitate community forums, and there are national organizations such as AmericaSpeaks that encourage civic dialogue and offer resources that can be identified through an online search.

Listening to Members and Opinion Leaders

Another valuable way to be smarter than you are is to seek out and listen to smart people around you. While that might appear obvious, it's sometimes difficult to actually take the time to process what we see and hear. The following story illustrates the challenge of hearing an idea, processing it and figuring out a way to implement it.

The publisher of my hometown paper was a brilliant lawyer and an astute observer of our community. He had noticed that while we had three solid school systems in our community and two independent colleges, the on-to-college rate among our high school graduates was only 43%, ranking us substantially below the state and national averages. He concluded that a major contributing factor was the lack of a state-supported university or a community college that could offer our region (including the state's third-largest city) affordable access to higher education.

He approached our chamber and expressed his concern about the economic prospects of our community and the dismal career prospects of high school graduates who didn't have sufficient access to higher education. While I was easily convinced of his assessment, I admit I didn't immediately see a way to address the problem. My initial reaction: The state's not going to create another regional university or community college; we already have too many and the legislature doesn't have enough tax dollars for the existing institutions. Moreover, we have two small colleges in our community with loyal alumni/ae, a substantial amount of political standing in the community and day-to-day financial challenges to keep their doors open. They would probably oppose, openly or surreptitiously, any attempt to disrupt the local market for high school graduates by creating taxpayer-subsidized competition. In other words, the reality of our local situation restricted my vision – it was the only reality I knew – and I couldn't see the forest for the trees.

The newspaper publisher suggested the chamber create a higher education committee to address the issue, and I immediately recommended it to our board. Not only did I agree with the problem he had diagnosed but, after all, he was the highly influential publisher of the local paper to whom a chamber exec would naturally pay considerable deference. I staffed the committee which met countless times. We brought in state officials and higher education consultants (paid for by the publisher) and worked diligently without a particular solution in mind. The chamber committee eventually morphed into a freestanding nonprofit called The Citizens Committee on Higher Education. I continued to staff the effort which at times felt tedious and exhausting.

But as the Citizens Committee continued its research and advocacy, various political stars lined up with a new governor, a local legislator elected speaker of the house and a prominent local lawyer becoming chair of the state's higher education authority. Fast forward thirty years. Today the freestanding community and technical college that emerged from those efforts enrolls more than 4,000 students and has produced thousands of trained graduates who have been crucial for the region's workforce. Moreover, the state university an hour away subsequently developed its own extension campus across the road from the community college, offering a "2+2" option for two-year associate degree graduates to continue their education toward a four-year bachelor's degree.

The community's on-to-college rate increased from 43% of local graduates to nearly 70%, and the two local independent colleges continued to successfully fulfill their missions and even expand their campus facilities. During the ensuing decades, the higher on-to-college rate represented more than an interesting statistic; it represented a transformational change for the community, greatly enhancing its future economic prospects and, more important, enriching the lives of thousands of its citizens – many of whom would have never attended college otherwise or stayed in their home community.

The vision for this game-changing institution was not the vision of the chamber exec, the chamber itself or even the publisher who provided the initial spark. It was the outcome of a committed community leader identifying a problem, tirelessly focusing on the details of the problem, utilizing the chamber as the initial vehicle for developing a vision, persisting in advancing the issue and eventually finding a solution. Through that process, the chamber profoundly shaped the future of its community as a catalytic agent of change – not because it performed a solo act but because it was the best vehicle for analyzing a problem, creating a compelling vision, incubating a powerful solution and developing consensus and political support.

What's the lesson for chamber execs? Simply, chamber execs don't have to have all the answers or all the ideas. We don't have to have a crystal clear vision of a precise outcome. Regardless of how much experience we have or how many ideas we personally bring to the community table, there are more and often better ideas swirling around us. By listening to smart and committed community citizens – even to people we might be tempted to dismiss as unrealistic, naïve or overly obsessed with a pet project – we can capture the best ideas available and help actualize the highest potential of our communities. Our personal experience, our circle of informal confidants and the collective wisdom of our boards of directors will help us filter the ideas and know when and how to push specific ideas forward. In other words, they will help us determine when we can make another strategic move on the chessboard.

Chamber execs don't have to have all the answers or all the ideas. We don't have to have a crystal clear vision of a precise outcome.

Intercity Leadership Visits

Many local chambers sponsor annual intercity leadership visits to gain ideas and inspiration from other cities. Typically the visiting chamber chooses a community that has excelled in a particular way – developing arts programs, pursuing historic preservation, nurturing entrepreneurism, implementing government reforms, promoting town-gown relations with their universities or producing other notable accomplishments. Typically, a two- or three-day program is carefully planned around unique assets and accomplishments of the host community, and the agenda features speakers from the ranks of local elected officials, journalists, community activists and historians.

The ideas flowing from such sessions are priceless, and the camaraderie produced by community leaders spending quality time together "on the road" is incalculable. Either from a sense of creative inspiration or good old-fashioned jealousy of the host city, the ideas gleaned by the delegation can take root back home in countless ways through individual and collective action. I've seen major community innovations sparked by such visitations. In my view, these leadership visits are excellent ways to help shape a community vision, and sponsoring them lies directly within the wheelhouse of an effective chamber.

Leadership visits are excellent ways to help shape a community vision, and sponsoring them lies directly within the wheelhouse of an effective chamber.

Commerce Lexington, the local chamber in Lexington, Kentucky, boasts perhaps the nation's longest record of consecutive annual leadership visits, having sponsored them for more than 80 years. They routinely take an impressive delegation of more than 200, including a significant portion of the city council and a group of up-and-coming civic leaders who have earned scholarships from local businesses to participate. The chamber proudly lists the communities they have visited over the years along with specific local accomplishments such as the merger in the 1970s of Lexington's city-county government that were either inspired or accelerated by an intercity leadership visit.

After sponsoring similar trips on an ad hoc basis in my hometown, I worked to replicate the practice at my new chamber in Birmingham, Alabama. One of my board chairs was especially enthusiastic about the idea and committed to seeing the chamber sponsor such trips. We traveled to Charlotte, St. Louis, Baltimore and other metro areas. While each city had incredibly valuable lessons for Birmingham, the more immediate value of the visits emerged from the camaraderie among the participants. In a metro area with a large African-American urban core, a predominantly white ring of suburbs and a largely white cadre of corporate leaders, the trips created a civic bridge between the minority-dominated political powers of Birmingham's City Hall and the predominantly white corporate leaders. They provided an enjoyable social setting for developing much-needed professional relationships and creating friendships.

There are countless ways to gather new ideas and inspiration. The list of ideas that were planted in my chambers and my communities from success stories we observed and imported from other communities is lengthy. In Chamber World, plagiarism is a good thing. Copying the best practices you can find in other communities is a solid way to be smarter than you are and to serve as a source of creativity for your community.

State Associations of Chamber Executives

One of the most cost-effective and accessible ways to get ideas for your community and especially for your chamber is to lean on colleagues in your region or state. Most states have an association of local chamber executives – sometimes affiliated closely with the state chamber, sometimes independent. Some have a staff person; others are run by volunteers. With periodic meetings to exchange best practices and new ideas, a chamber executive can come back full of practical ideas for seizing opportunities and solving problems – to say nothing of gaining moral support from peers who are experiencing many of the same challenges and job pressures in their own communities.

With periodic meetings with chamber colleagues to exchange best practices and new ideas, a chamber executive can come back full of practical ideas for seizing opportunities and solving problems.

When I was with the Birmingham Chamber, I observed a great approach by the state chamber to strengthen the peer network among local chambers. The Business Council of Alabama (Alabama's state chamber) had a senior staff person whose full-time job was to serve as the executive director of the local chamber association (CCAA) and as a liaison between the local chambers and the state chamber. I copied that model when I returned to my home state as president of the Kentucky Chamber.

I offered a proposal to our Kentucky Chamber of Commerce Executives association (KCCE), that they split the costs with us of a full-time executive director who would function in roughly a 50/50 capacity as the association's executive director and as our state chamber's liaison to local chambers. The executive director would focus on professional development for the association while simultaneously making our state chamber policy materials available to local chambers, thus extending the reach of our state chamber's advocacy network. We determined that collectively, there were more than ten times as many members of local chambers across the state – at least 25,000 – as there were dues-paying members of our state chamber, and reaching that larger footprint of members was incredibly important for our state chamber in terms of our effectiveness at the state capital.

That organizational structure produced tremendous benefits to both organizations over the years. One manifestation of the strong culture of professionalism among our local chambers was their active participation in professional development programs offered by the national association of chambers, ACCE. For example, Kentucky routinely produces one of the largest state delegations at ACCE's annual convention and by 2019, more local chambers in Kentucky had competed for the title of Chamber of the Year, more had been named as a finalist in their category of similar-size chambers and more had won the title than in any other state – a tribute to our strong peer network of chambers leaning on, learning from and encouraging each other.

Meanwhile, our state chamber benefited tremendously by engaging more local chambers and their members in our government affairs efforts. For example in 2013, more than 30 local chambers joined a coalition of some 50 employer groups convened by our state chamber, demanding reforms of the state pension systems. Pension reform is a complex, relatively abstract issue for any state and not one that most local chambers would normally address. In spite of that, our coalition came together almost overnight. Years of trust-building and open communication created an environment in which a sizable chorus of local chambers voluntarily joined our coalition around a cause that was critical for our state but was politically sensitive for many local chambers and their boards of directors.

Because local chambers are autonomous and independent, our state chamber was in no position to tell them what they should think about an issue or whether they should get involved. We had to make information available to them that would build their brand and their relevance to their members, even if short term it was at our expense. As I told local chamber execs, issues as nebulous and unexciting as workers' comp reform or environmental regulations might seem esoteric and boring, but one of those specific issues might be the pressing issue for a few of their local businesses. If the state chamber can deliver valuable information to those companies through the local chamber, the local chamber might earn the loyalty of those dues-paying members for years to come.

We experimented with a variety of methods to financially coordinate our efforts with local chambers, to combine our memberships through a dues-sharing formula or to provide free e-memberships for members of local chambers. We settled on an associate member category for our state chamber, offering a free membership to any small business that had fewer than ten employees and was a member of its local chamber. While we didn't find a dues-sharing proposition that we could offer jointly, we succeeded in developing a strong working partnership that yielded meaningful benefits for the state chamber, great peer-to-peer exchanges among local chambers and substantial value to the members of each.

Other Peer Networks

Professional chamber associations like ACCE and the Council of State Chambers (COSC), if properly utilized, are terrific sources of inspiration, ideas and support, and the specialized conferences they offer can help you be "smarter than you are." The U.S. Chamber also pulls together groups of chambers around specific policy issues through its chamber federation network, its U.S. Chamber Foundation's outreach efforts and its Committee of 100 (for larger, advocacy-oriented chambers).

In my Birmingham and state chamber experiences, I also participated in or observed informal peer networks that provided great support for their members. When I first moved to a metro chamber in Birmingham, I found myself in a bigger league and had to adapt quickly. Expectations were higher, and I needed to step up. I found two extremely valuable networks: an informal group of the four metro chamber execs (the CEOs in Mobile, Huntsville, Montgomery and Birmingham) who met informally a couple of times a year and an ACCE-sponsored network of about a dozen metro chamber executives in the Southeast – from Orlando to Louisville and from Memphis to Raleigh. Our twice-a-year meetings were a tremendous source of ideas and inspiration and provided an extra set of shoulders for me to lean on when dealing with the political realities of my own chamber position. I always came home with a legal pad full of ideas that I wanted to pursue and the encouragement to plow ahead. In addition, our informal meetings created the collegial relationships that allowed us to be only a phone call away when controversies or sensitive issues arose.

In a similar way, I observed a group of female chamber execs from mid-sized communities in western Kentucky who met periodically and leaned on each other for professional and personal support. Such informal associations can serve as critically important peer networks for professionals striving to improve themselves, their chambers and their communities.

ACCE and COSC have both created specialized peer networks for CEOs, governmental affairs professionals, finance and administrative officers, education and workforce specialists, membership development executives and other subsets of chamber professionals.

> *Such informal associations can serve as critically important peer networks for professionals striving to improve themselves, their chambers and their communities.*

They provide excellent forums for chamber professionals who speak a common language to share best practices and encourage each other.

Professional Conferences

I am an enthusiastic advocate of attending professional conferences to collect new ideas; I almost always came away with valuable ideas that I was glad I had heard. Several years ago, I attended a Council of State Chambers (COSC) meeting where we shared our "Best and Worst Ideas of the Year" – a roundtable exercise that was a perennial highlight of COSC meetings. My counterpart from the Oklahoma Chamber mentioned that he had challenged the IRS over unrelated business income (UBIT) taxes paid on the royalties the chamber had earned from its health insurance program. His chamber claimed that the revenue wasn't unrelated business income that was derived from competing with private businesses in the marketplace; it was "related" income that was a perfectly germane member benefit they offered their chamber members. He won the appeal, got back a few hundred thousand dollars and offered to connect us with the lawyers who handled his appeal. I returned home to my chamber, decided we had similar legal standing to contest several years of our UBIT taxes and finally, after two years of a hurry-up-and-wait appeal process, we received a refund of more than $45,000 from the IRS. My chamber would not have gotten that check if I had not been in the room when that specific discussion took place and the seed of a valuable idea was planted.

My chamber would not have gotten that $45,000 check if I had not been in the room when that specific discussion took place and the seed of a valuable idea was planted.

An experience I had with the U. S. Chamber Foundation is another example of being in a professional situation where ideas are flowing and being able to tap unexpected opportunities. I volunteered to serve on the U.S. Chamber's Education, Employment and Training Council, primarily to keep up with issues relating to education and workforce, priorities of my state chamber. During those meetings, I heard about a new concept of talent pipeline management (TPM) and a national implementation program the Foundation would be rolling out in selected areas across the country. After a few conversations with the staff and consultants, I volunteered my chamber to serve as a guinea pig for the program, rolling it out on a state level. Two years later, with a startup grant of $200,000 (not from the U.S. Chamber but from a partner foundation interested in TPM), and subsequent contracts with our state government of more than $2 million, the Kentucky Chamber Workforce Center quickly grew to a full-time staff of nine people and has since implemented TPM across our state. That would have not happened without my being in the room where the discussion was taking place, trying to discover ways for my chamber to address a priority need of our state.

While those specific examples might not apply to many chambers, the moral of the story applies to all chambers: Valuable ideas come from conversations with professionals in similar circumstances as your own. I can recall example after example of conferences I attended in which valuable ideas were born – ideas that in many cases carried a more substantial monetary benefit for my chamber than the cost of travel and the time away from my chamber.

A SWOT Analysis

Conducting a SWOT analysis – a very simple method for looking at the future of your chamber or community by identifying its Strengths, Weaknesses, Opportunities and Threats – can seem daunting, but we often do something very similar in our everyday lives. Consider the analogy of buying an older home and trying to create a comprehensive list of tasks needed to modernize it. You first identify the immediate needs of the home (fix the leak in the roof), then make your wish list of items which might not be as urgent but which you would like to consider as you can afford them (a new countertop in the kitchen). After making the raw list of needs and wishes, you start to focus on the costs and relative urgency of each improvement and develop a practical sequence for pursuing the items – like moving the pieces on your chessboard.

A SWOT analysis takes you through a similar process. All it takes is a capable facilitator who is willing to listen and honor the variety of ideas produced by a group of participants and capture those ideas on a marker board for all to see. Usually after a freewheeling, rapid-fire session to generate as many suggestions as possible within each of the four categories, the leader follows with a balloting process by which members of the group prioritize the most compelling and practical ideas.

The process can be very revealing by bringing into focus key elements of the community's self-image, its challenges and its aspirations. It produces a list of ideas that is more comprehensive than any one individual could produce alone. And it doesn't take a team of futurists to conduct it; it's available to chambers of any size that are willing to lean into the future and think about ambitious goals.

A SWOT analysis offers a very simple method for looking at the future of your community by identifying its Strengths, Weaknesses, Opportunities and Threats.

Professional Consultants

A chamber colleague and good friend of mine wanted to apply for an open chamber CEO position. He felt he had the requisite experience in the community, a successful professional background outside the chamber, the essential management skills, an understanding of the chamber culture and a people-oriented personality. I agreed; I thought he checked all of the boxes for being an excellent chamber CEO. However, when seeking my advice, he said he lacked what he called "the vision thing."

My quick, off-hand response was, "Don't worry. You can buy the vision thing." I was not being facetious; I genuinely felt he had the requisite skills to be a very successful chamber president and that he didn't need to feel personally responsible for offering a comprehensive vision for the chamber or for the community. Rather, if he had a basic appreciation of the role a chamber can play in articulating a vision for itself and its community (which he did), he could reach out to others who could facilitate the development of that vision and engage them to manage that process. He could use one or more of the methods mentioned above, and/or he could use outside experts as consultants for the chamber.

As noted earlier, I sometimes used outside consultants who brought a variety of special skills and expertise to the table. An experienced planning facilitator can probably be arranged through a local community college or member company. If the community needs a more in-depth economic development strategy, a master plan for the historic downtown area, a marketing plan for increasing the tourism in the region, a strategy for recruiting a major sports team or a plan to mitigate the damage of a major industry or a military base closing, experts with specific technical skills may be necessary. People who have a different experience base and fresh perspective can bring added expertise to a community's challenges and opportunities. They can play a catalytic role in developing and helping implement strategies for the progress you hope to create.

While it's easy to dismiss the idea of hiring expensive consultants and paying for a study that might gather dust, engaging qualified consultants can bring brainpower to your chamber that you could never afford to hire in staff positions. Someone with expertise in a particular area can introduce a new perspective from similar work in other communities or provide a priceless idea that otherwise would have never occurred to you or your locally focused volunteers. I saw consultants earn their entire fee in a single meeting by helping a group of people see a challenge from a completely new angle. My chambers benefited greatly from consultants with expertise in fundraising, downtown design, public policy, state budgets, economic analysis, market analysis, workforce analysis and other specialties at various times.

With the world around us and within our chambers becoming increasingly fast-paced and complex, the specialties available through consultants are a critical element of achieving success. There is a growing trend toward engaging specialists on a temporary basis, so-called "ten-99s" whose earnings are reported on the IRS 1099 form instead of the W-2 form that traditional employees receive. Sometimes referred to collectively as the gigasphere (workers who go from one temporary gig or project to another), the opportunities for renting such talent vs. owning (employing) such talent are an increasingly valuable source for expanding a chamber's talent pool.

With the world around us and within our chambers becoming increasingly fast-paced and complex, the specialties available through consultants are a critical element of achieving success.

The traditional stereotype of consultants is "a man with a briefcase from at least fifty miles away." However, increasingly, talented individuals of all ages are offering their specialized skills as contract employees. Whether it's redesigning a website, leading a small business seminar, developing a technology masterplan for your community or lobbying for a particular bill at the state legislature, contracted talent can play a meaningful – and affordable – role. Sometimes, one-time consulting projects can be funded by a sponsorship from an interested chamber member firm or with a grant from a charitable foundation or government agency that supports such projects. And it's helpful to engage a few of your volunteer leaders in the selection so you have multiple perspectives at the table, your volunteer leaders have buy-in, and you have cover in case things don't go well with a particular project.

Chamber execs with limited resources must be able to sift through the various promoters and focus on precisely what product – what deliverables – they expect from a consultant. It is critical to review their individual methodologies, their references, their credentials and samples of work they have done for other clients. Imagine that you received a similar report at the end of your project. Would you be satisfied with those types of data, those sorts of recommendations? Would the recommendations be actionable or simply restating the obvious and offering vague platitudes? Does the previous work of the consultant seem to be boilerplate jargon, using a particular formula so that all of his/her reports basically recommend the same thing and only the name of your community is substituted for a previous community? (I once saw a consultant's report that failed to change the name of the previous community in the text. Oops!) Would the consultant simply put a pretty cover on what you already know? You want a product that truly recognizes the particular nuances of your community and its current challenges.

When my chamber was pursuing a more precise vision for tourism development in our region, I contacted a few firms with expertise in the hospitality industry. One, an international firm that regularly provided economic advisory services for corporate clients and for our state economic development department, submitted an impressive proposal that along with an accompanying masterplan, would cost more than $250,000. Because of the price, I decided not to recommend it to my leadership at that early stage in our project, but I briefed them on it and said, "If we were the Walt Disney Corporation looking to develop a new theme park, I'd hire these folks." But we didn't have that kind of money. Instead, I found an experienced developer of tourism destinations through an industry association and offered to pay his daily rate for a two-day visit and a follow-up memo advising us on how we should proceed. Total cost: about $4,000. That memo gave us a more focused vision that was exactly what we needed at that point in our project.

Groups like ACCE and the American Society of Association Executives (ASAE) can provide information on consultants who can help chambers in a wide variety of ways. Also, the faculty of the U.S. Chamber's Institute for Organization Management (IOM) includes a wealth of experts who regularly consult with chambers.

Engaging the most talent and intelligence possible – either by *renting* or *owning* the talent – is essential for a chamber to be relevant, to articulate a vision for its community and to help its members navigate the complexity of issues, government agencies and other competing interest groups that shape the external environment in which chambers operate.

■ ■ ■

There are myriad ways for a chamber to gather and process ideas for its community. A chamber executive only has to reach beyond him/herself to be smarter and to serve as a critical pipeline for valuable ideas to flow through the chamber, into the community.

CHAPTER 14
DEVELOPING A STRATEGIC PLAN

When developing a vision, a critical next step is to shape it into a strategic plan. It's one thing to make a list of needed home improvements; it's another thing to prioritize those tasks, to weigh the dollars and time required for each individual project, and to decide the sequence for executing those tasks. How does one go about developing a practical implementation plan for pursuing a compelling vision for a chamber and/or its community?

Internal vs. External Plans

When a chamber decides to actively pursue a strategic plan, an important early decision is whether to focus on an internal plan for the chamber itself, an external plan for the broader community, or a combination of the two. When I first arrived at the Kentucky Chamber, the organization had been through a difficult ordeal and so the strategic plan our board developed in my first few months was almost exclusively about rebuilding the reputation and standing of our state chamber – in other words, an internally focused plan. Several years later with the chamber on sound footing and feeling more ambitious, a special chamber task force laid out a vision for the Commonwealth of Kentucky called "The New Agenda for Kentucky" and immediately followed it with a separate three-year strategic plan for our chamber. Our internal chamber plan attempted to answer two questions: 1) What can the chamber do in the next three years to fulfill portions of the "New Agenda" (external) plan? 2) What should we do internally to strengthen the chamber as an organization? That three-year strategic plan was then supplemented each year with one-year business plans, the documents that focused on the practical, operational requirements for advancing the chamber's strategic plan in one-year segments and which built in an accountability component by encouraging regular reporting.

When considering a strategic plan, an important early decision is whether to focus on an internal plan for the chamber itself, an external plan for the community or a combination of the two.

Another important decision is about setting the time frame. Strategic plans are generally meant to address broad aspirations and, therefore, usually span a multi-year time frame. I've heard technology company executives say that three years is much too long and that technology moves too quickly to create a formal plan for three years out. One could argue that the conditions in your community move equally fast and three-year futures are too hard to predict. But remember: strategic planning is not an exercise in predicting a precise future; it's an exercise in trying to combine your aspirations for your community with a practical overlay of what is reasonable to accomplish in the next few years.

A well-designed plan is the best means of determining focus and priorities, including what the chamber should stop doing. To the extent possible, any chamber project, program or service should satisfy three elements: 1) Is a proposed project, program or issue a priority that is truly consistent with your chamber's mission? 2) Is the chamber the best/only agent to address a genuine need? 3) Is there some kind of financial motivation for the endeavor that adds to or detracts from its relevance to the chamber?

When I reviewed our previous strategic plans after their three-year time frames, I was usually struck by how outdated some aspects seemed to be. Conditions had changed so drastically in some areas that parts of the original plans seemed hopelessly off the mark. However, I was generally pleased that by staying focused for three years on what we said we hoped to accomplish, we achieved remarkable and sometimes unexpected results for our chamber and our community.

I also noticed that when I reported annually on the progress of our chamber relative to our strategic plan, many of our accomplishments were due to our chamber being nimble and opportunistic, taking advantage of unforeseen situations that arose and opportunities we couldn't have predicted. For example, during one planning period our chamber received hundreds of thousands of dollars in grants and contributions, primarily for our educational programs. I could not have anticipated that level of support three years earlier. Because of some of our ambitious programs which were outlined – at least in general terms – in our strategic plans and the relationships one of our policy consultants had developed, we caught the attention of external funders who came to us with support we had not anticipated. On another occasion, one of our staff members was in the right meeting on a particular topic at the right time, was alert and savvy enough to connect a few dots of the conversation with our chamber's policy goals and concluded we should apply for a grant. A single serendipitous moment laid the groundwork for a grant of several hundred thousand dollars. Our strategic plan had outlined our desire to address an important issue but had not anticipated a precise approach or the resources that might become available.

Both the scope of the planning process (internal vs. external vs. both) and the timeframe for the plan can be decided based on some very practical considerations about what your chamber leaders want to accomplish over a particular period of time. You might consider what key events could affect your planning process. Political circumstances might be one such factor. Our chamber admittedly fast-tracked one of our strategic plans for our state because our primary goal was to affect the political dialogue of the upcoming governor's race, putting a spotlight on issues we considered critical to the future of the state.

An anticipated change in your next mayor's election might affect whether you want your plan to span three years or five years. Perhaps the anticipated opening of a major new company or the downsizing by a major employer might be a dominant issue that will affect the timeframe you choose. If you are preparing an internal strategic plan for your chamber, an anticipated retirement of the chamber CEO might trigger a planning process that is designed to address that transition during a period of some uncertainty. A few months prior to my retirement, our chamber decided to go forward – rather than wait for the new CEO – by creating a new three-year strategic plan because continuity and continued momentum for our chamber were stated priorities of our top chamber officers.

Visioning and creating a formal plan can shape an organization and a community in powerful ways. Conversely, a chamber that expends an inordinate amount of its energy on budgets, bylaws and the minutiae of keeping the doors open has robbed itself of the valuable opportunity to strategically shape itself and the broader community – the opportunity to think bigger and have a greater impact. The hours of the day and days of the year present a zero-sum reality; spending time in one area inherently takes time from another, potentially more valuable area. Carving out time to plan strategically is a key ingredient to building a high-performing chamber.

Reporting on Progress

As important as putting a plan on paper is the follow up, specifically the reporting that keeps the plan fresh and helps your leaders and staff remain focused on the plan. Because my board only met four times a year, I included a written update of our annual business plan in the directors' board materials at each meeting. Prepared by our four senior vice presidents who oversaw our four operating divisions, the reports contained brief, candid updates under each stated goal and objective. Concise statements such as "Done," "50% Complete," "Delayed due to maternity leave of project manager" or "Executive Committee decided to postpone kick-off until next fall" were included under each item. I encouraged the vice presidents to avoid candy-coating the progress. Admitting a delay or even a failure gained credibility with our board members who wanted to know the document was not just the staff patting itself on the back.

The quarterly updates of our one-year business plan, in an outline format, were usually ten to fifteen pages long. At the board meetings, we didn't dwell on the document but simply announced that it was available for board members to peruse as they wished. In some cases, I verbally highlighted a few items to give the board a general overview of the year's progress – or lack thereof – and how it tied back to our strategic plan. Because we had four vice chairs on our board who were connected by a dotted line on the organizational chart to our four operating divisions and the four vice presidents who managed those divisions, the volunteer vice chairs had a regular written update they could rely on to monitor the progress of their respective divisions. I realized it was unlikely that more than a handful of other board members with an above-average appetite for engagement actually read the quarterly updates, but I was more interested in the entire board knowing our

As important as putting a plan on paper is the follow up, specifically the reporting that keeps the plan fresh and helps your leaders and staff remain focused on the plan.

organization held itself accountable and our volunteer leaders were not left to wonder what happened on a particular project, program or priority. In addition, the updates served as an internal tool for our staff as they paced their progress toward fulfilling their objectives throughout the year.

■ ■ ■

Developing clearly stated strategic plans for your chamber and your community is THE essential building block for a chamber to play a leadership role in its community, and regular reporting of the progress instills accountability and builds credibility with the chamber board and other key stakeholders. Objectively communicating the progress at regular intervals also sustains the focus and pace a chamber needs to stay on course and achieve maximum effectiveness.

CHAPTER 15
THE HISTORICAL IMPACT OF CHAMBERS

Chambers tend to think in one-year segments with their budgets, the turnover of their officers and board members, their annual meetings and so forth. It's certainly important for a chamber's effectiveness to track its progress on the short-term – from board meeting to board meeting and from annual report to annual report. However, it's even more revealing to consider a chamber's progress and its impact on its community in a historical context – a context spanning multiple years and even decades. That's a tall order. Chamber executives have huge short-term demands and often feel like Sisyphus, the character of Greek mythology who was cursed by the gods to roll an immense boulder up a hill again and again, only to have it tumble

It's even more revealing to consider a chamber's progress and its impact on its community in a historical context – a context spanning multiple years and even decades.

back down each time. That overwhelming sense of a constant grind – running on a treadmill that has no off button – makes it very difficult to stand back from the day-to-day frenzy to gain a deeper perspective of a chamber's impact. How does a chamber executive ascertain a chamber's legacy and place in history? Here I offer three examples of ways to think about the longer-term impact of chambers: a chamber in a small city, a chamber in a metro area and the collective impact of chambers on a nation.

A Chamber Shapes a Small City

To illustrate how chambers can have such a profound impact, I contributed the following column (slightly updated here) about my hometown chamber to ACCE's "Chamber Executive" magazine more than a decade after I left that chamber and had ample time to reflect on its historic role in the community. Some of its most noteworthy accomplishments occurred long before my arrival at that chamber, some during my tenure and others after my departure.

Judge a Chamber by Decades, Not Years

Leading a chamber is like spinning plates. On any given day, the whirling political environment and managerial responsibilities can be all-consuming: prepare an agenda for next week's board meeting, call two membership prospects, return calls to a reporter and a board member, solicit a chairman for the membership drive, book a speaker for the fast-approaching annual meeting, order new chairs for the board room. The tasks may change depending on chamber size, but the rigor required to juggle the important, the urgent, and the unimportant-but-necessary tasks is essentially the same.

Chamber execs must master the art of time management because all these tasks and many more are required to keep the doors open. On a good day, you get scores of tasks completed and go home with a sense of accomplishment.

On a bad day (or in the middle of the night), each task seems like one more layer on a suffocating pile of duties and deadlines.

It's important to reflect on achievements and savor successes, but we should occasionally take an even longer view of our work. I learned to appreciate this when I headed the chamber in Owensboro, Ky. We were developing a newspaper insert to celebrate our new building, and I decided to chronicle the institutions that had been created from within the chamber and that had helped shape the community over a period of decades. I was surprised to discover a long list of established organizations, each with its own history of community impact, which had grown from seeds sown by our chamber.

- *The local industrial foundation was created in the early 1960s to purchase, hold and develop land for new industries and to develop industrial parks that would be shovel-ready. During the ensuing years, dozens of companies were attracted and created thousands of jobs. The spin-off in indirect employment has been even greater.*

- *The convention and visitors bureau was created when the chamber championed the enactment of a bed tax to promote tourism in the 1970s.*

- *The RiverPark Center, a two-theatre performing arts center over-looking the beautiful Ohio River, hosts more than 250 events per year. It's the home venue of the Owensboro Symphony Orchestra and several other arts organizations. The complex began as the chamber's Civic Center Committee in the early 1980s.*

- *The International Bar-B-Q Festival was created by the chamber more than 40 years ago after an annual hydroplane race festival closed. The Bar-B-Q Festival annually attracts tens of thousands of people for a cooking competition on the riverfront. It's the signature event defining the culture of the community, and it celebrates the unique culinary heritage of its people.*

- *A new four-lane bridge across the Ohio River between Kentucky and Indiana and its associated highway connections were ideas* incubated when an Indiana businessman was invited to make his pitch at our monthly chamber breakfast in the late 1970s. The chamber picked up the torch on the Kentucky side of the river, and after 25 years of planning, promoting and lobbying the state and Congress, the massive $300 million bridge was constructed, forever altering the transportation network and the prospects for commerce within the two-state region.

- The chamber's Citizens Committee on Education was formed in the mid-1980s when the local newspaper publisher expressed concern that the college readiness of our high school graduates trailed state and national averages. Numerous studies, consultants and lobbying trips later, the state legislature authorized the development of a community college that now enrolls more than 4,000 students.

- Our downtown development organization, Downtown Owensboro, Inc., was created by the chamber and a former board chairman in the late 1970s, following a mass exodus of downtown merchants to a new suburban mall. While the organization morphed into several different forms during the ensuing years, it has had a profound impact on revitalizing the urban core.

- Leadership Owensboro is a 35-year-old idea that was inspired by the leadership program in nearby Evansville, Indiana, after a local college professor and civic activist advocated that our chamber establish a local version.

- The monthly chamber breakfast (with the curious but memorable name, "Rooster Booster Breakfast") was copied directly from the "Rooster Breakfast" of a local chamber in Alabama in the 1960s. It has provided a platform for guest speakers, project announcements, political speeches, policy debates and civic boosterism for more than 50 years. It routinely draws 300 attendees and is broadcast live on a local radio station.

- "The Bluegrass Music Capital of the World" grew from a conversation with a local judge who said that Owensboro had a stronger *claim to bluegrass music than some of the festivals he observed on TV. After all, Bill Monroe, considered the father of bluegrass music, was born and raised in adjoining Ohio County. Those conversations at the chamber led to a master plan for bluegrass, an eventual Hall of Fame awards show, the recruitment of the International Bluegrass Music Association (which eventually outgrew Owensboro's hotel capacity and was lured to Nashville), the vision for a $15 million Bluegrass Music Hall of Fame and Museum and an annual bluegrass music festival that showcases leading performers.*

- *The Greater Owensboro Economic Development agency was created by business leaders in the early 1980s to accelerate the recruitment of new businesses. First incubated within the chamber, an autonomous economic development corporation was later created and has been the constant marketing arm for the business community, the city, the county and the region.*

- *The local community foundation was created independently, but was quickly embraced by the chamber and given staff support and office space. After more than a decade of partnership, it routinely makes grants for educational and community improvement projects from an endowment that has grown to millions of dollars.*

These examples from one small city in Kentucky demonstrate the power of a chamber's influence and its dramatic impact over a period of decades. These are community institutions incubated within the chamber, not merely ideas that the chamber passively endorsed. Each is an accomplishment for which the chamber was a catalyst or the primary vehicle for implementation.

Would they have happened without a chamber? Maybe. But these accomplishments came about because the chamber was doing its job, looking for ways to boost civic and economic success and providing an institutional mechanism to convert the community's best motives and altruistic energies into realities.

A chamber, like any human enterprise, will invariably have its ups and downs as leadership, talent, resources and opportunities ebb and flow. But when viewed over decades, the work of a well-oiled chamber can be critical in shaping its community in profound ways.

Major community institutions were incubated within the chamber, not merely ideas that the chamber passively endorsed.

A Chamber Works to Shape a Metropolitan Area

Another example – this case study from a metropolitan area – describes how the Birmingham, AL, Chamber worked to help its community manage a time of social crisis. The story provides a glimpse of a local chamber's behind-the-scenes efforts during the 1960's Civil Rights movement, a culturally and racially pivotal chapter for that community and our nation.

When I arrived as the new CEO of the Birmingham Chamber in 1999, the chamber owned and occupied a handsome 1920's-era, 14-story, landmark building which had been donated to the chamber by the Protective Life Insurance Company. On the top floor, just outside my office, was a large wall safe which once held valuable documents of the insurance company.

I was given the combination to the safe and told that it contained boxes of records from the Civil Rights era and the proceedings of the chamber's Senior Citizens Committee, a secret chamber committee formed in the 1960s to privately communicate with Dr. Martin Luther King, Jr. and local leaders of the protest movement. (The term senior citizens in the 1960s referred to the social status of the participants as the senior leaders of the business community, not to the age of the participants.)

The racial situation in Alabama in the 60s, specifically in Birmingham, was combustible and highly controversial within the business community. Likewise, it was controversial within the Birmingham Chamber, as local industrialists generally favored the status quo and its dependable supply of low-skilled, low-wage Black workers while the retail community was more progressive and open to adapting to the changing times. Downtown department store owners wanted to sell Easter dresses to all customers regardless of race and had a more pragmatic outlook toward integration. While working to navigate that divide within the business community, chamber leaders were also concerned about the negative influence of Bull Connor, a powerful police commissioner and racist demagogue who was politically more influential than the sitting mayor and who regularly played to the lowest common denominator of racial prejudices. Community leaders and especially the chamber were increasingly concerned with the bad publicity about Birmingham that was broadcast coast-to-coast each evening on the national TV networks.

The Chamber's Senior Citizens Committee was quietly appointed to try to resolve the growing tensions, and its meetings were to be kept confidential. At a time when racist thugs were bombing the homes of civil rights leaders, there was a palpable fear of what could happen to any whites who were seen collaborating with the so-called outside agitators like Dr. King and local firebrands like Rev. Shuttlesworth. Outspoken advocates and progressive business leaders were afraid for their families and their property and were probably nervous about alienating a portion of the white clientele of their businesses. According to my predecessor, who held the chamber CEO position for more than twenty years, the minutes of the Senior Citizens Committee meetings were to be kept secret according to an original agreement when the Committee was formed and safely stored under lock and key until all members of the committee were deceased. I had never thought of chamber minutes – certainly not committee minutes – having such significance and mystery surrounding them.

I took on my new job with a vengeance. Even with the mystique of secret papers in a wall safe outside my office and my fascination with reading several books on the history of Birmingham, I was operating in a whirlwind of day-to-day demands and didn't take time to open the safe until months after I arrived. Once I did, I found committee minutes and at least a partial list of committee members, but I was somewhat underwhelmed by the contents; I wondered if the records had already been culled by someone interested in minimizing any lingering controversy. Most of the material was information I had already read. I straightened the papers, closed the boxes and resealed them in the safe.

I didn't give the papers much more thought until a few years later when we decided to sell our building and relocate the chamber to a modern office tower in the heart of downtown. We found a buyer and started planning a major clean-out of our building and its massive basement. With my interest in history, we tried to responsibly separate the material worth archiving from the surplus materials that we felt were best suited for the dumpster.

My responsibility for stewardship of the secret papers started to weigh on me. I decided to engage the chief archivist from the Birmingham Public Library to review the papers, to evaluate their historical significance and to prepare a written appraisal that I could take to my executive committee for possible action. We arranged a visit to my office where I asked him to sign a confidentiality agreement and where he could spread out the papers on a large conference table.

After a few sessions in my office, he reached a similar conclusion to mine – that most of the information in the secret files was already available in the public domain. He suspected – as I did – that the files had been purged during the 30-plus years since they were first secured. Based on his assessment and with the concurrence of my volunteer leaders, we transferred ownership of the papers to the Birmingham Public Library for permanent cataloging and preservation.

The documents didn't contain the documentation of the committee's actions I had hoped to find, but their existence helped illuminate a pivotal period of history in which the business leaders of Birmingham attempted to create a dialogue with the African-American community – albeit in secrecy – and address highly sensitive desegregation issues faced by the community. The secret documents also illustrated for me an important lesson about chambers of commerce. When a community is in dire straits and its political institutions have failed it (which occurs from time to time in virtually every community), having solid civic institutions like a respected chamber that can work to resolve conflicts is fundamental to the orderly growth and development of those communities.

> When a community's political institutions have failed it (which occurs from time to time in virtually every community), having solid civic institutions like a respected chamber that can work to resolve conflicts is fundamental to the orderly development of those communities.

Chambers Shape a Nation

Not only can chambers play a profound role in shaping the history of their respective communities, some have also profoundly shaped our country. ACCE's former senior vice president Chris Mead spent years researching notable contributions by chambers to major achievements that shaped our country. The product of his research, published in 2014 as *The Magicians of Main Street: America and its Chambers of Commerce, 1768-1945*, represents a significant milestone in documenting the collective history of the chamber of commerce movement in the United States and should be on the reference shelf of every chamber executive in the country.

> Chris Mead's book, The Magicians of Main Street documents the collective history of the chamber of commerce movement in the United States.

I was honored when Chris asked me to review and comment on his manuscript prior to its publication. I offered the following:

> *"An amazing body of work, Chris Mead's* Magicians of Main Street *offers – for the first time – a compendium of the pivotal roles chambers have played in building American communities and, thereby, the nation itself. For those of us who are chamber of commerce practitioners, this exhaustively researched book serves as a cornerstone in the foundation on which we have built our professional lives and provides a valuable lens through which we can view the history and development of our communities."*

Mead chronicles notable chamber accomplishments ranging from Washington's Cherry Blossom Festival to New York City's subway system to Chicago's Board of Trade to the gaming industry in Las Vegas and the stars on the Hollywood Walk of Fame. He tells the stories of business people combining their efforts through associations – usually chambers of commerce or chamber-like organizations operating under similar names – to take collective action and to actualize their shared aspirations.

Although *Magicians* primarily spans the early years of our nation from the colonial period to World War II, Chris is planning a second volume that will explore common, post-war chamber initiatives in areas such as transportation, community image and promotion, downtown development, civil rights, economic development, education improvement, government reform, international trade and e-commerce.

■ ■ ■

Former Memphis Chamber CEO Marc Jordan is credited with saying, "Chambers do the things in town that everybody thinks just happen." Former ACCE president Mick Fleming added to Jordan's observation by saying, "Chambers do the things that could not have been done any other way." As Frenchman Alexis de Tocqueville documented in 1835 with the publication of his *Democracy in America* after touring the young country, Americans possess a unique inclination to form associations for collective action. Citizens form associations around a multitude of causes and, likewise, business people organize themselves – frequently as chambers of commerce – for collective public engagement. This tendency has manifested itself across countless communities and across centuries, thereby creating profound chapters of those communities' progress and a prominent place in America's history.

PART IV
IT'S ABOUT YOU AND YOUR CAREER

A career in chamber management has sometimes been characterized as an accidental career because so few of its practitioners entered the field with a premeditated plan to someday manage a chamber of commerce. More typically, chamber executives arrive in their positions through a circuitous path of education and career discovery in which the opportunity to lead a chamber is the result of gaining experience in nonprofit management, politics or some other related field. Regardless, there are many chamber executives who – once exposed to the variety and fulfillment of working for a chamber of commerce – begin thinking of their chamber occupation as a longer-term career opportunity and a role from which they can derive great meaning and personal satisfaction. To some it becomes so interconnected with the person's identity and sense of purpose, it takes on the profound significance of a calling.

CHAPTER 16
THINKING ABOUT CHAMBER MANAGEMENT AS A CAREER

There are chamber executives who serve their hometowns, sometimes for decades, and have no desire to relocate to another chamber. They have deep personal ties to their communities and are essentially place bound, by professional choice or family necessity. They grow in their positions, make meaningful contributions over the years to their communities and create a legacy of civic achievement.

There are chamber execs who don't see themselves staying in the chamber business long term but because a job opportunity at a chamber opened up for them, they view it as a promising, relatively high-profile stepping stone toward other possibilities. Perhaps they anticipate spending a few years at the chamber before going back into banking or public affairs or real estate with a broader understanding of the community, more experience managing an organization, a higher profile in the community and a host of connections from which to leverage their careers.

There are others who, having been bitten by the bug of life in Chamber World, can't imagine doing anything more fulfilling, and they gradually become interested in professional advancement as other chamber doors open. They become transient chamber professionals, willing to look at new chambers that offer increasing responsibility, higher compensation and the opportunity to play in a bigger arena.

An Accidental Start

After college, I returned to my hometown with a vague aspiration of getting involved in the community and perhaps in politics. I had enjoyed studying political science in college and grad school but I had enjoyed working in student government even more. Returning to Kentucky and looking to get my feet on the ground, I found an entry-level job selling men's clothing at minimum wage in the downtown department store and joined the Jaycees, a service club for men under 40. Within weeks, I had a chance encounter with the head of the local chamber who, after hearing of my interest in the community, offered to meet with me about his soon-to-be-vacant No. 2 position, that of project manager. Of course, I had heard of chambers of commerce, but I knew almost nothing about them. After he described some of the chamber's activities and the assistance he needed, I responded enthusiastically, "Oh good, it sounds like student government!" During a second meeting, he asked how much I would need to make. I told him I was getting married in a few months and that I

A career in chamber management has sometimes been characterized as an accidental career because so few of its practitioners entered the field with a premeditated plan to someday manage a chamber of commerce.

needed to buy some business clothes to work at a chamber of commerce, so "I think I'll need $7,500". He quickly responded, "Make it $8,500 and we've got a deal!" With that bit of tough negotiation and the first pay raise of my career behind me, he hired me into Chamber World. Within a few short weeks, I was absolutely enthralled with the work and immersed myself in my job and my community – still not imagining it as a career but frankly as a stepping stone toward something else.

I became extremely passionate about my hometown and worked to advance it through my role at the chamber. I had countless ideas and unlimited youthful enthusiasm. I really enjoyed the volunteers and staff and still think of many of them as my closest friends decades later. I couldn't imagine developing a comparable loyalty or the same level of enthusiasm in another community. I had no desire to move and when other chambers occasionally called, I declined and recommended other emerging chamber professionals who I felt might be a good match and possibly available.

I worked as project manager for four years before my boss left for another chamber. Within weeks, the board of directors decided to take a chance on me – a 25-year-old eager beaver – and put me in charge. I spent the next three years as executive vice president (the terminology commonly used in those days for many chamber CEOs). I enjoyed it tremendously, and we made some notable progress. But when the senior U.S. Senator from Kentucky called and invited me to join his staff as his in-state assistant, I decided to try my hand in the political realm. I traveled the state for him for about four years, meeting his political contacts in all 120 counties and learning from a master politician how retail politics was practiced.

During that time I missed the chamber and its hands-on, project-oriented work in the community. An opportunity opened up for me to run for mayor, and that successful campaign led to eight very positive years (two terms) in office. While at City Hall, I had many contacts with the chamber I had previously led. Chamber leaders were great partners for the economic agenda I put forward and for eight years, I delivered my annual "State of the City" address to several hundred chamber members at the monthly membership breakfast.

One thing about the chamber I noticed during my time as mayor was that it was just one of many voices that I heard on civic issues; there were environmental activists, women's rights advocates, union leaders, African-American pastors, senior citizens and countless others. While I came to the office with a chamber-centric view of the world, I had to learn to listen to all voices and balance the interests of those voices to be responsible to my community. I had a very positive relationship with the chamber overall, but there were a few situations when chamber leaders assumed, for example, that I would fill out the planning and zoning commission by appointing developers and homebuilders the chamber had recommended. When I opted instead for a balanced set of voices on that important board and appointed a well-known environmental activist, I temporarily stood at odds with some key chamber leaders who, I felt, had a rather myopic view of the chamber's role and influence in the community. I believe those experiences helped me later in my chamber career by instilling in me a bone-deep appreciation for elected officials and the realization that when I was lobbying a mayor or a legislator or a governor on behalf of my chamber, I was just one of the many legitimate voices he was hearing. I had to make a compelling case for our chamber's agenda, knowing there were other stakeholders in the wings (some with much closer personal ties to that official), waiting for their chance to sway the policymaker in a different direction.

As I neared the end of my second term at City Hall, chamber leaders approached me and asked me to come back to the chamber because they were combining it with the economic development corporation under one president and CEO. They wanted me to run the combined organization. At first reluctant – "been there, done that" – I decided that I really wanted my kids to finish high school in that community and after all, I knew I would love the work. That certainly turned out to be the case; I loved being back at the chamber.

After four more years during my second stint at the hometown chamber, a search firm approached me unexpectedly about the Birmingham

Chamber. I said, "No thanks, but if I hear of someone, I'll let you know." I had visited my brother and his family in Birmingham several times and admired the city during those visits. However, I couldn't imagine pulling up stakes in my hometown after more than ten years of chamber work and two terms as mayor. Not only were our family friends and my chamber friends our closest friends, our kids had grown up from the cradle through high school in that community. It took my wife asking, "Why wouldn't you talk to Birmingham?" for a light bulb to go off in my head with the realization that perhaps I should consider a new opportunity. Within a few days, I called the headhunter back and told him I would be willing to have a conversation about the chamber and possibly visit the community, but it had to be strictly confidential. I didn't want to start rumors in my home community or burn any bridges with my chamber leaders who had been very good to me. After a few conversations with the search firm, I agreed to go for an interview and within a few weeks, I was selected to head the Birmingham Chamber.

I was now moving to a brand new chamber position in a metro area 10 times as large, with a staff four times larger than my hometown chamber and with a budget to match. Their board meetings were completely different – much more formal and businesslike. I soon realized I had to dress differently and started investing in nicer suits for downtown meetings in a distinctly southern city. No more blue blazers and khaki slacks during the work day. My symbolic role in the community as the CEO of the metro chamber was different from my down-home political and professional profile as "Chamber Dave" in my hometown. I hit the ground running, drinking from the proverbial fire hose and soaking up the warm hospitality of a gracious southern city. What I learned in the first six months was, of course, infinitely greater than what I had absorbed after two friendly interviews, a couple of meals with chamber board members and a tour of the city. There were organizational challenges – primarily a few sensitive personnel issues to resolve – and there were political realities and cultural differences in the community that I had no idea I would face. As with any new CEO coming from outside, I was very green.

Look Before You Leap

Looking back on the experience of entering a new chamber as president, there were a few things I should have considered more seriously before I accepted the position. I should have done more due diligence before risking my career on a huge set of unknowns. Fortunately for me, things worked out well. I was energized by the new environment and the hundreds of welcoming people I met in the first several weeks. The chamber's finances were solid, and a few difficult situations during the early months turned out to be brush fires that were quietly extinguished without major controversy.

Not all transitions go so well. I have seen newly appointed chamber executives land in organizational quagmires that apparently no one warned them about or which were glossed over during a short-term, relatively superficial search process. At both of the chambers I entered from outside the community, I inherited very challenging political environments and relatively delicate personnel issues, but nothing compared to what I had seen other newly chosen chamber execs face. Some had inherited surprising internal situations such as the chamber's depleted finances that were somehow overlooked during the search process, while other colleagues were forced to navigate difficult external situations such as long-standing animosity at City Hall.

I have seen newly appointed chamber executives land in organizational quagmires that apparently no one warned them about or which were glossed over during a short-term, relatively superficial search process.

It's encouraging to have a prospective chamber interested in you and your abilities. It's flattering when they pitch you on relocating to their community. But it's important to look before you leap – to dispassion-ately assess the personal and professional risks involved with taking a leadership role at a new, unfamiliar chamber and to force yourself to make an objective list of pluses and minuses.

One critical body of information I should have requested was the financial and organizational metrics mentioned in Chapter 9. A simple request via the search committee chair to the chamber's finance director, probably during the late stages of negotiation between being named a finalist and eventually agreeing to take the offered position, would not have been considered intrusive or burdensome. On the contrary, it might have impressed the search committee with my diligence and my keen interest in the finances. A capable finance director would have been able to produce key bits of data and construct important trend lines from the past several audits in a matter of a few hours. Learning that the chamber had recently been dipping into its reserves to make payroll, for example, would have been a troubling sign worthy of further investigation. Hearing how board members talked about those trends would have given me a quick idea about whether I was being asked to build a chamber or rescue a chamber. Fortunately for me, I didn't inherit that particular problem with the finances.

There are countless factors to consider: the finances, any legal issues hanging over the chamber, organizational stability, the culture at the staff level, board support, the relative unity of the board's top officers, any in-house candidates for the job who were passed over, the cost of living and cost of relocating, opportunities for your spouse, your longer term goals, the political environment in the community, your commute, your children's schools, the distance from your extended family and, not least, the compensation package.

Probably the biggest negative is the inherent risk of walking into the unknown. You might detect some troubling issues, but regardless of your due diligence, there are many unknowns in a new environment. You simply don't know what you don't know, and you can't see around every corner. Is there a pending lawsuit from a disgruntled former employee? Is the chamber's board divided over your selection as CEO? Is the mayor carrying a grudge because the chamber opposed his proposed tax increase? Did the wife of one of your key officers or a long-time employee of the chamber not make the final cut of applicants for your new job? Any of these would be a red flag, alerting you to a potential brushfire that could spread out of control. Being able to navigate unknowns as they present themselves is critical to success in a new setting and the support of your top officers – knowing they've got your back – will be critical to your ability to navigate those situations.

Hitting the Ground Running as a New CEO: The First 100 Days

In two of my three chamber positions, I was invited to a new community and a completely new cultural and political environment where I was an unknown. In the Birmingham case, I was approached by a search consultant who specialized in chamber and economic development placements. He offered to come to my community and based on a one-on-one interview and a few backdoor references he had checked, he subsequently asked me to be one of the five finalists that he would present to the search committee. As I prepared for my interview with the committee, he suggested I present them a to-do list for my first 100 days in order to demonstrate that, even though I was an outsider (there were numerous local candidates seeking the job), I would hit the ground running, and my learning curve would not prevent me from being effective from the start.

It turned out to be a very valuable exercise for me personally, and I was later told that it contributed to my being selected. I highly recommend the practice to any prospective CEO preparing for an interview. Among the items on my list were the following:

1. Have one-on-one meetings with every board member (in this case, approximately 60) at his/her respective place of business.

2. Have one-on-one meetings with at least 140 other community leaders to gather their opinions about the chamber and the community, for a total of at least 200 leaders within the first 100 days – an average of two a day.

3. Have a one-on-one meeting with every staff person (approximately 40 at the time).

4. Read at least three histories of the community (one per month).

5. Ask the CFO to produce a spreadsheet charting at least 30 organizational metrics I needed to see, such as membership revenue, personnel expenses and staff turnover, for at least the previous five years. (This is the list which – looking back – I should have requested before agreeing to take the position.)

6. Review the chamber's previous strategic plans, annual business plans and/or annual reports to determine what the organization aspired to do and what it had accomplished. Learn how the chamber has talked about its role and its successes.

7. Attend at least one major community event per week.

8. Determine the status of job descriptions and/or position profiles of all staff and report to the board about the staffing structure, compensation issues, and related matters.

9. Determine the condition of internal financial controls and personnel policies and make recommendations to the board about any needed improvements.

10. At the end of the first 100 days, prepare a preliminary report to the board about the organization's current structure along with the feedback I was getting from the community and make detailed recommendations about how to establish the strategic direction going forward.

I extended my first 100-day listening tour throughout most of my first year. Meeting political leaders, key investors, ministers and rabbis, the media and many other community leaders allowed me to take the pulse of the community and begin to understand how the chamber could provide leadership for the next big challenges. By taking immediate steps, and hitting the ground running, a chamber exec who begins his/her tenure in listening mode can build goodwill with the chamber's leaders who are getting their first impressions and with a broad range of constituencies in the community that will be critical for the chamber's effectiveness in the years ahead.

A chamber exec who begins his/her tenure in listening mode can build goodwill with the chamber's leaders who are getting their first impressions and with a broad range of constituencies in the community.

■ ■ ■

For those who decide to pursue a longer-term career in the chamber of commerce field and seek upward mobility, relocations are often involved. Getting started at a new chamber is just that, but actively listening and absorbing as much as possible about the new environment in the early weeks is important for building goodwill and establishing a base of relationships that will strengthen the chamber executive in his/her new position and benefit the chamber in the years ahead. Community leaders are generally flattered to be approached and eager to share their opinions with the new chamber executive. The knowledge accumulated during those conversations will prove invaluable. Building on those relationships will help inoculate the chamber exec for any personality conflicts and political skirmishes that subsequently occur.

CHAPTER 17
GROWING AS A CHAMBER PROFESSIONAL

Much of the professional growth of a chamber executive comes from day-to-day, shoulder-to-the-wheel hard work and making countless decisions required to keep the doors open and the organization humming. Every day is an education as you navigate the tasks, deadlines and personalities. However, allowing yourself to be swallowed by your daily responsibilities without budgeting dedicated time for personal growth and professional development inhibits your growth as a human being and reduces your career potential. Below I recommend some of the opportunities my chambers provided me during my career to grow and advance professionally.

Step One: "Know Thyself!"

"Know thyself!" was the Greek motto inscribed at the entry to the Temple of Apollo at Delphi, and it was the sage advice Socrates gave his students. It comes to mind as I reflect on the various forms of professional development that can benefit a chamber professional. As stated in Chapter 2, "The Personality of a Chamber Leader," self-awareness is such a critical component for a chamber executive because the position requires constant interaction with a wide variety of people. Someone whose co-workers, board members or other constituents think "doesn't get it" in social and professional settings is probably not going to do well in a chamber leadership role. My first and most basic suggestion for professional development is to take specific steps to gain personal awareness.

Self-awareness is such a critical component for a chamber executive because the position requires constant interaction with a wide variety of people.

Personality profiles such as the Myers-Briggs Type Indicator, the Enneagram of Personality and the Predictive Index are three examples of well-established social science that can be very helpful tools to understand yourself, what makes you tick and, perhaps more important, what characteristics of your personality might become career obstacles. I was fortunate at mid-career that my chamber and ACCE made a week-long leadership program available to me at the Center for Creative Leadership in Greensboro, North Carolina. (CCL has sister campuses in Colorado, California and at least nine foreign countries.) It was a profoundly valuable experience because it required me to recognize my particular personality traits – good and bad – and how they might shape my effectiveness and my career. The week-long program involved several assessments of my personality and leadership style along with class exercises and one-on-one coaching. (The program made such a positive impression on me that many years later at the Kentucky Chamber, we created the Leadership Institute for School Principals and invested more than $3 million over nine years, offering the same professional experience to more than 400 education leaders.)

Employers and their human resource professionals are increasingly using various personality and psychological profiles to better understand what motivates a person and specifically what makes a job candidate tick. Is the candidate an extrovert or introvert? A visionary or more detailed oriented? Comfortable with or bored by having to manage repetitive tasks? Many sophisticated organizations will no longer hire or promote individuals without having such a profile created for each of their leading candidates. Some national search firms have in-house psychologists who routinely conduct such profiles on select candidates before their consultants will recommend those candidates to their clients.

I've become a staunch advocate for using such profiles. They probe the distinguishing motivations and behaviors that are hard-wired in our DNA, are shaped by our life experiences and profoundly affect how we view our work, our coworkers, our board members and others. Those differences shape others' perceptions of us, our individual work ethic and our ability to successfully interact.

After I had been invited to interview with the Kentucky Chamber and I had accepted the invitation, the search committee chair asked me to participate in a ten minute online exercise to determine my Predictive Index (PI) profile. I first had to select characteristics I attributed to myself from a list of a few dozen, choosing from pairs of words and phrases such as cautious vs. risk-taking and opinion-ated vs. open-minded. The second half of my exercise was to choose attributes from a similar list of binary options, but this time I was to select words that I thought others would use to describe me. That was it. No psychiatrist. No couch. No inkblots, truth serums or electrodes connected to my scalp.

I was unaware at the time that the committee had already completed the other half of the exercise where the employer (or in this case, the search committee) chose from a list of words that defined what skills, behaviors and attributes they considered critical for success in the position they were filling. The social science behind such tools allows the employer (or more accurately, the employer's computers) to determine how good a match the candidate will be with the expectations of the employer. The computers compared my responses to the committee's preferred traits and determined that I would be a fit for the chamber position. I was later told that less than a handful of applicants were considered a fit for this particular position.

The subsequent written report provided to me was extremely instructive, albeit a little eerie in terms of how they got inside my head and analyzed my motivations. It described what energized me for certain tasks, what I considered boring and many other characteristics. It indicated my relative level of need for encouragement and public recognition, my relative appetite for change, my tolerance for detail and so forth. And it was basically dead on. The employer receives a slightly more candid and in-depth profile and an outline of management strategies for the employer to use to make a particular candidate successful in the new job.

While such tools should never be the sole litmus test for a hiring decision, I found them to be very helpful in my hiring decisions, and I learned the hard way not to ignore their findings. I once narrowed a lengthy search down to two finalists for my chamber, only to have the personality profiler (who admittedly, I should have consulted earlier) tell me that neither of the candidates had the energy level needed to excel in the position I was filling. That's not what I wanted to hear.

I found such profiles extremely valuable in the "know thyself" department. An objective analysis of a person's unique strengths and weaknesses can provide a leader with a clearer sense of him/herself and how he/she might be perceived by people with a different personality profile.

There are other tools for gaining greater self-awareness and various 360-degree instruments that provide feedback about how those in your work environment – bosses, peers and direct reports – perceive your strengths and weaknesses. These types of tools are widely available, often through human resource executives and consultants, local community colleges, universities, hiring agencies and online.

Formal Education Options

While attaining an associate or bachelor's degree, getting a masters or completing a certification program in a specialized area is almost too obvious a professional development step to mention here, I include it because of what I consider its relative value – its currency – in Chamber World.

Does formal education matter? Generally, yes, for its inherent value in broadening one's perspective and ability to make decisions. But it also matters in a more pragmatic sense because it provides a chamber selection committee some level of insight into your motivation, your career path and your commitment, and it might provide one more data point that distinguishes you from other applicants. For example, a chamber search committee might eliminate any applicant lacking a four-year degree to pare 50 resumes down to 25. Unfortunately, a talented, possibly late-blooming go-getter who happens to lack a degree gets cut from the stack of applicants before having an opportunity to interview or even shake hands. Meanwhile, the guy with a master's degree in 18th century French literature who has been driving a taxi for the past two years just made it to the next stage of consideration. Unfair? Of course. But the hiring process is one of elimination, and the screens used by an employer to cut a stack of resumes from 50 to 25 aren't always fair. Just expedient. And having a degree or

Formal education also matters in a more pragmatic sense because it provides a chamber selection committee some level of insight into your motivation, your career path and your commitment, and it might provide one more data point that distinguishes you from other applicants.

degrees is still a common screen by which employers narrow the field of candidates.

Going back to school is, I believe, inherently valuable for personal development and professional mobility. My chamber paid for up to three courses a year for any staff member enrolled in a two-year or four-year degree program – whether directly job-related or not – or taking individual courses that were deemed job-related. Does a specific degree, for example an MBA, give a critical advantage to a candidate? Not necessarily, but it does provide one more distinguishing feature to a candidate's overall record and some assurance that the candidate has been exposed to basic managerial principles.

My master's degree is from a high-profile university, the reputation of which I believe has been a net positive in my career, but my degrees are in philosophy and ethics – disciplines not exactly required by chamber search committees. As my father, an electrical engineer, once asked only half-jokingly, "Is anyone hiring philosophers these days?" In spite of that "encouragement", I suggest that attaining additional formal education – especially in one's early and mid-career phases – is a solid personal and professional advancement tool.

There are literally dozens of conscious and unconscious factors, such as body language, appropriate dress, eye contact, punctuality and social graces that go into a hiring decision. Formal education might represent only one of these, but it is frequently a factor in the elimination process for hiring managers and executives. The lack of such credentials could consciously or unconsciously raise red flags in the minds of the hiring committee members about a candidate's lack of career direction, personal investment in career preparation, discipline and/or general preparedness to interact comfortably with business professionals and navigate a complex world.

How to Keep Growing: Continuing Education for Chamber Professionals

There are countless opportunities for professional education for chamber professionals. Among the most popular and relevant to chamber of commerce careers are:

> **The Institute for Organization Management (IOM).** The U.S. Chamber offers a four-year program that typically involves one week of on-site instruction per year, offered at several universities across the country. The curriculum is based on the knowledge requirements for the Certified Association Executive (CAE) and the Certified Chamber Executive (CCE) industry certifications. Each year attendees take six core courses and select three elective courses that allow participants to focus on particular areas of interest. Upon graduation, a student will have earned a total of 96 credit hours.
>
> The professional designation of IOM is often listed behind the names of chamber professionals who have earned the Institute designation and, I believe, denotes a person committed to self-improvement and to his/her profession as a chamber or association professional. The Institute program typically features courses in finance, law, marketing, budgeting, communications and other areas. My personal experience at the Institute and the consensus I hear from other participants are universally positive. My first boss sent a co-worker and me to the Institute within the first few weeks of my joining his staff as his project manager, and I completely bought in. I can't imagine a better introduction to chamber management than the one I received there. At the time, I had no interest in obtaining the IOM or CCE credential (primarily because I didn't yet see myself as a chamber careerist), but the intensive

I can't imagine a better introduction to chamber management than the one I received at the Institute for Organization Management.

exposure to the basic concepts of chamber management was an exhilarating, fun and eye-opening experience.

Certified Chamber Executive (CCE). This professional certification program is owned and administered by our primary professional association, ACCE, and serves as a designation for chamber professionals (not just CEOs) who have qualified through a multiphase process. There is a user-friendly, online application that allows you to privately score yourself and determine if you are prepared to proceed through the program. You get points for each year you've been in the chamber business, for your years enrolled in the Institute, for serving as a volunteer on a nonprofit board outside the chamber, for chairing a nonprofit board, for publishing professional articles, for participating in ACCE conventions and other related accomplishments. If you score enough points, you can proceed through the other phases. Various reading materials are prescribed, and you eventually take a four-hour exam on specific areas of chamber administration such as finance, governance and human resources. You take the test under the monitoring of a proctor who is a chamber executive, who has earned his/her CCE and who is usually chosen based on geographic proximity to you. Eventually you are interviewed about your career and your professional knowledge by a panel of your peers.

State-Specific Recognitions. There are a few state associations of local chambers that offer designations for chamber executives who perhaps cannot afford the Institute or cannot pursue the CCE certification. Contacting your state chamber can quickly determine if your state or a nearby state or regional association offers such a program. For example, the Western Association of Chamber Executives, which is managed by the California Chamber for multiple western states, offers an Accredited Chamber Executive program.

Other Chamber-Related Certifications. Economic development professionals often enroll in the Economic Development Institute

(EDI) at the University of Oklahoma. For professionals more interested in association management, the Certified Association Executive (CAE) certification earned through the American Society of Association Executives (ASAE) can provide a valuable professional development experience and a certification that carries positive weight, especially with trade associations and larger chambers.

Mentors

I admit that I sometimes feel slighted when I hear my colleagues talk about their mentors. To my knowledge, I did not have a particular teacher during my career who made it a conscious goal to help chart a career path for me. Have I learned a tremendous amount about leadership from some of my former bosses? Absolutely. Have I on occasion discussed career opportunities and job offers with my bosses or seasoned professionals in our field? Certainly. Have there been people who, in retrospect, have been incredibly generous with their time, compassion and counsel? Yes. I consider several of them major role models for myself. I've had great teachers who either by instruction, advice or as role models have taught me valuable lessons about navigating tough situations, dealing with troublesome volunteers and managing countless other aspects of developing skills conducive to success in a chamber career.

Perhaps my concept of a mentor – someone standing beside me, consciously choreographing my career moves, opening doors, making valuable introductions, coaching me over an extended period of time – is too narrow. Perhaps it's more accurate and useful to think in terms of key influencers who shaped my career

Perhaps my concept of a mentor – someone standing beside me, consciously choreographing my career moves, opening doors, making valuable introductions, coaching me over an extended period of time – is too narrow.

over an extended period. Most of my experiences with those more senior influencers were positive and friendly encounters; a few were less comfortable but nonetheless provided incredibly valuable lessons.

When I reflect on my career, I remember specific conversations – where I was sitting 45 years ago, who else was in the room and what was said – that proved pivotal in my education, development and career path. An interesting and valuable exercise is to "map yourself backward." Think retrospectively about your career. What was the main influence on which college or university you chose? What door opened and who opened it for your first job interview? Was there a painful disappointment that proved pivotal in your career choices? Was there a particular point or a specific conversation when you decided, for example, to major in political science instead of accounting? Was there a summer job that affected your interests and your subsequent choices? It's interesting and enlightening to reflect and attempt to connect the dots backward. There are probably specific life events and key people who influenced you and who, in retrospect, played the role – if not carried the title – of mentor.

For those who are still shaping your careers, don't hesitate to approach a more senior professional you admire and ask if he/she would be willing to serve as a mentor to help you advance your career goals. Who isn't flattered by being asked for advice? Such a suggestion will probably be welcomed by the prospective mentor and could lead to a more intentional approach and richer relationship built on that person's career advice.

Coaches

For me, the term coaching connotes something different from mentoring. When I think of coaches, I think of specialists who help in a specific way based on their particular expertise and usually for a shorter period of time.

There is tremendous personal and professional value of engaging writing coaches, speech coaches, media coaches and other professionals to polish your abilities. For example, even though I had been speaking publicly for more than 30 years and felt quite comfortable in front of a small civic club or even a large audience, I once engaged a speaking coach to offer her critique and suggestions. She attended several of my presentations and offered a set of recommendations, none of which suddenly made me a dynamic professional speaker but several of which helped me improve my effectiveness. For example, she suggested that if I used a PowerPoint on a screen in the front corner of the room, I shouldn't stand at a podium in the other front corner of the room. The audience would suffer whiplash glancing back and forth between the screen and me standing at the podium. Her simple suggestion: go over and stand beside the screen – or better yet, ask your host to set up the podium by the screen or give you a lavaliere mike so you can move around. Other suggestions: Try to convert policy messages into stories and use statistics only to the extent that they illustrate the points you're making with the stories. Common sense stuff, but I needed someone other than myself and someone more knowledgeable of these basic methods to help me improve.

When I think of coaches, I think of specialists who help in a specific way based on their particular expertise and usually for a shorter period of time.

With the writing project that led to this book, I engaged a writing coach to give me pointers via a few webinars and, more important, to crack the whip and build some discipline into my scattered attempts to set aside time to actually write. Later in the process, finding the right editor – a former journalist and communications consultant who would push back on some of my assertions and illustrations – was also critical.

I've benefited from media coaches who advised me how to look into a television camera with an open face instead of grimacing and looking like I'm defending myself against a criminal indictment. I've never engaged a life coach, but I have known people who have benefited greatly. I participated in an intensive leadership training program that concluded with a one-on-one coaching session and very candid, practical advice about work-life balance, about possibly inflicting burn-out on my coworkers and about possibly taking up meditation. I needed that kind of input from an objective third party.

Recently, our chamber engaged an executive coach to present a two-hour training session for our entire staff on executive presence – from appropriate dress for specific occasions to body language, from making eye contact during conversations to cell phone etiquette and pointers about how to approach and engage people. Even if I picked up only one new tool from such an exercise, it is well worth my time and money to use experienced coaches for specific areas of improvement.

Recently I have seen two chambers make an executive coach available to their newly selected CEOs as part of their compensation packages – not in an effort to address perceived weaknesses but to give the new CEOs another tool for reflection, self-evaluation, achieving work-life balance in high pressure positions and for overall professional development.

Peer Networks for Professional Support

ACCE reports that the decentralization of the traditional news media and today's widespread mistrust of institutions have caused more and more chamber professionals to look for peer-to-peer networks that offer a reliable source of information in an environment of mutual trust. Of course, ACCE offers chamber professionals opportunities to network on a national level through meetings, conferences, peer groups, online discussions and other forums. Many states have an association of local chambers that can be extremely valuable for professional support and development.

An innovative vice president who worked with me at the Kentucky Chamber and handled our events, publications and seminars (and produced more than half our chamber's revenue) met once a year in an informal retreat setting with his counterparts from two other, roughly comparable state chambers. They had become close friends, shared with each other the

> More and more chamber professionals look for peer-to-peer networks that offer a reliable source of information in an environment of mutual trust.

programs they were initiating and managing, and enjoyed friendly competition with each other over the results they were producing. I jokingly accused my co-worker of disguising his annual junkets with his friends to a high-end resort as a bogus excuse for an outing but in truth, I appreciated and encouraged him and others on our team to seek out such peer-to-peer growth opportunities.

There are many peer-to-peer networks that exist outside the chamber profession but which offer value to a chamber professional. It can be an economic development group or a group of nonprofit execs in your region. Maybe it's a monthly breakfast with a small group of leaders in your community that allows you to lean on other professionals and learn from their successes, frustrations and disappointments.

Chamber-to-Chamber Exchanges

A low-cost but effective way for gaining a deeper understanding of your chamber is to look in a mirror and study what you see. That "mirror" can be a similar chamber that resembles yours – in size, scope, service area, staff and/or budget.

While serving at a state chamber, our best comparisons were with similar state chambers. Having been an admirer of my counterpart at the Georgia Chamber, I asked him if I could bring my senior team to spend a day with our counterparts at his chamber. He quickly agreed, and six of us from Kentucky made the trip to Atlanta. The dozen of us spent the entire day in his conference room, trading ideas and posing questions to each other. We talked about everything from workplace policies to staff structure, from policy issues to board meeting dynamics.

A low-cost but effective way for gaining a deeper understanding of your chamber is to look at a similar chamber that resembles yours – in size, scope, service area, staff and/or budget.

On the way home, four of us who were riding together decided to compile a list of all of the specific differences we had noticed about how our chamber operated vis-a-vis what we heard in Georgia. We agreed not to pass judgment on whether their approach was better, worse or just different; we wanted to simply capture the distinguishing characteristics of their chamber. The way the Georgia Chamber divided its operational divisions, the fact that they had elevated their chief communications officer to a vice president level, the fact that their board of directors of several hundred members was primarily an honorary board rather than a governing board – were all characteristics we found instructive by comparison.

After our return, I compiled notes from our list of differences and presented a summary at our next all-staff meeting – our once-a-month casual lunch where we discussed what was going on in our organization. I also gave an abbreviated version of that summary to our board of directors at its next meeting. After all, most of our board members had never been exposed to another state chamber and had no points for comparison.

We made some operational adjustments after our visit to Georgia. The visit affirmed some of the ways we were doing things and made us question others. With some of the differences, I concluded that if we were forming our chamber from scratch, we would do it the way Georgia was doing it, but because of the particular talent we had on our staff and the history of some of our programs, we needed to continue with our current approach.

The whole exercise served to let us look in a mirror – to look beyond our immediate surroundings and take note of what was on the horizon. It provided us a better sense of our direction and gave us an extremely valuable exercise of introspection about how we could do things better.

Useful Publications

ACCE offers an online library of useful materials for professional development, a help desk for specific inquiries and the ACCE "Chamber Executive" magazine, a wealth of timely reporting on best practices, issues facing chambers, ideas for professional development and much more.

In addition, chamber execs can access local resources and determine which might constitute a must read. Perhaps it's a regional business journal or a community magazine. Knowing the issues, the developments and the people who are making news can be critical to a chamber executive. Just as keeping up with your area's favorite sports teams helps you quickly establish common ground with strangers at a cocktail reception, staying abreast of the headlines in business and politics can build bridges to many of your key constituents – and helps you avoid landmines when navigating the politics of your community.

I also suggest selecting one or two magazines that offer a broader context, perhaps in political affairs or world events. You don't have to be versed in the intricacies of Middle Eastern politics to do your job as a chamber leader, but staying abreast of national and international events – at least at the level of being conversant – deepens your own understanding, helps you make more solid decisions and positions you better with important leaders in your community who stay abreast of such matters. Being able to engage in higher level conversations regarding politics, literature, business and travel allows a chamber exec to develop greater standing and rapport with the top echelon of the business community.

Print publications are no longer the media of choice for many chamber professionals. The young public affairs staffers at my chamber were far more attuned to their Twitter feeds than to hardcopy publications, and they monitored their social media apps for the latest happenings in our state capital as they unfolded in real time. We are all moving in that direction, and our appetite for real-time information – filtered by our own tastes and interests – continues to grow. Regardless of one's preferred method for staying up to date, it is important to look for solid reporting from reputable sources and to constantly strive to attain deeper understanding of events as they unfold.

A chamber colleague of mine recently asked, "Given the state of today's polarized media, how do you know who to trust?" For me, I attempt to discern the truth by putting an emphasis on finding balance – a balance of media sources. For example, I watched the 2020 Republican National Convention on the left-leaning MSNBC and the Democratic National Convention on right-leaning Fox News. I wanted to hear the counterpoints to the self-serving rhetoric being spun by the political parties. Of my two favorite magazines, one is generally center-right and the other, center-left. My choice of online newspaper subscriptions are spread across the spectrum, from right to left and from national to community news. Being able to calibrate our personal opinions on various subjects in relation to the partisan extremes that divide our country allows us to establish our own equilibrium – to maintain our balance, regardless of where we personally stand on the political and social spectrum.

Being able to calibrate our personal opinions on various subjects in relation to the partisan extremes that divide our country allows us to establish our own equilibrium.

■ ■ ■

There are countless resources available for a chamber executive to grow as a professional and to become a more effective leader. Chambers of commerce and their communities will benefit when their chamber leaders make a commitment to invest in their own professional development. Because life in Chamber World is hectic and can be consuming, it takes personal discipline and determination for a chamber leader to consciously carve out time and to identify specific opportunities to grow as a human being and as an effective leader.

CHAPTER 18
PERFORMANCE REVIEW AND COMPENSATION

One of the most delicate areas of managing a chamber and managing one's career centers on issues of compensation: how to administer compensation for your staff and how to ask for additional compensation for yourself. How do you determine what is fair to pay your employees, and how do you position yourself for appropriate salary increases?

Performance Reviews

Evaluating the performance of individual staff members is essential for establishing a merit-based and fair system of compensation. Formal performance reviews seem to fall in and out of favor with management experts, but I found an annual review of each employee's performance extremely helpful for creating a feedback loop among our supervisors and the staff members who directly reported to them. There is a tendency for performance reviews to become a redundant, tedious ritual but when administered thoughtfully, they force a conversation between the employee and the supervisor that needs to occur periodically to maintain a healthy work environment. They encourage the exchange of ideas for improvement, and they create an opportunity from a management standpoint for developing a growth plan for each employee, a critically important paper trail for handling future promotions and the documentation an employer needs when considering a termination or planning an exit strategy for an employee.

There is a tendency for performance reviews to become a redundant, tedious ritual but when administered thoughtfully, they force a conversation between the employee and the supervisor that needs to occur.

A written performance review was required at our chamber for all employees, including me. The process typically began two to three months before the end of our fiscal year, with each of us conducting a required self-assessment of our performance during the previous year. We answered written questions in about a dozen categories of performance (responsiveness, job knowledge, communication, overall productivity and others). In addition to assessing our own performance, we were expected to offer our suggestions for how we could improve during the coming year. After staff members submitted their self-assessment to their supervisors, the supervisor responded in writing and offered additional suggestions for the coming year. The supervisor and the employee then had a conversation about the evaluation, and both were expected to sign the document acknowledging completion of the process, regardless of whether they agreed with each other on every point of the evaluation.

Occasionally in sensitive situations, I asked to see the two-way assessment before the supervisor returned it to the employee. After all, the supervisor's comments provided a formal written opinion rendered on behalf of the chamber and would thereby take on additional significance in the highly unlikely event of a future legal action involving the employee. I sometimes pushed the supervisor to be more objective

– perhaps less glowing – with the assessment because a) the employee deserved to know the objective truth about any concerns the chamber had and b) the paper trail left by the performance review could come back to haunt the chamber if a possible termination eventually became necessary and contentious.

In preparation for my own review each year, I reminded my immediate past board chair who had chaired my performance review committee a year earlier to deliver a confidential traveling notebook (essentially my personnel file) to my current chair for his/her review. It contained my original one-year contract, my compensation history and all my previous evaluations. The notebook provided a comprehensive summary of my tenure and provided context by which the current chair and the other two members of my performance review committee could evaluate my year's performance, decide any appropriate bonus and set my compensation for the coming year.

Meanwhile, using the same form that we used for all employees, I completed a written self-evaluation of my performance for the year and forwarded it to the three-member review committee (my board chair, my immediate past chair and my incoming chair). I encouraged the three of them to have a private conversation about my performance so the current chair could summarize the findings of the committee in a written evaluation. Naturally, the board chair was free to survey the executive committee, some or all board members, and even outside stakeholders to gather input. To my knowledge, however, I rarely had a board chair go the extra step of formally gathering input from outside the three-person committee. After they provided me their written evaluation, I sat down with the committee, and they presented their assessment and any suggestions for improvement. In some cases, they suggested specific goals for the coming year but more often, they relied on me to set goals for myself.

Sometime during that process I offered my board chair the most recent annual survey of compensation of state chamber executives (CEOs and about five other senior staff positions) conducted for the Council of State Chambers (COSC) by a professional compensation consultant. It was an extremely valuable tool by which my performance committee could calibrate appropriate salary levels for our chamber. ACCE also offers a wealth of salary data for local chambers.

Several years ago at my last chamber, we discontinued using numerical scores (scoring different parts of the evaluation on a 1-to-5 scale) as part of the evaluation process because we didn't tie compensation directly to the evaluations, and we didn't want to create an expectation that, for example, a 4.5 out of 5.0 on the evaluation necessarily triggered a certain salary increase. We did, however, attempt to complete the written evaluations prior to making our budget and compensation decisions each year. The evaluations could identify areas for needed improvement, and the employee-supervisor conversations required by the process could reveal concerns such as areas of employee dissatisfaction, an employee being impatient for a promotion, the possibility that an employee might be looking at other job opportunities or other human resource issues that could affect compensation decisions.

With the evaluations in hand each year, I worked with my senior team to determine who in their departments needed special consideration for salary increases – for example, who we were vulnerable to losing, who had excelled in their positions and who had perhaps topped out in terms of appropriate salary ranges for their particular functions. Making comparisons across the organization, attempting to be fair to all members of the chamber team and staying within our personnel budget allowed us to make salary decisions that promoted a healthy, highly effective and constantly improving workforce. I usually found myself giving extra consideration for increases to preserve our senior team and to reward high-performing team members. While there were inevitable issues of fairness weighing on my decisions, and I always tried to provide at least cost-of-living increases to virtually all staff members, the reality of the marketplace dictated certain advantages for our top performers and our senior staff members who enjoyed greater mobility in the job market. In that sense, I found our chamber to be a microcosm of the pay and equity tensions in society writ large; the folks at the top are inevitably better positioned to navigate the talent marketplace and benefit more in a knowledge-based economy.

CEO Compensation: Why Pay More?

Compensation – especially your compensation – is an awkward topic. It's generally off limits to discuss with peers, awkward to discuss with your board, awkward to advocate. Perhaps that's why in only four cases in my 45-year career did I request a specific salary level for myself – the three times I agreed to take on a new chamber and the one time when my board chair asked me, "What would it take to keep you until your retirement?"

Because a chamber is viewed, correctly, by the business leaders who decide our compensation as a nonprofit organization, I believe the compensation of chamber CEOs is often subconsciously grouped by those business people with that of other charitable organization executives such as the United Way director or the Red Cross director. While the compensation of executives of nonprofit organizations is readily available online at www.guidestar.org, chamber board members who haven't previously served on a compensation committee or executive committee – especially for mid-sized and larger chambers – are sometimes surprised when they discover what constitutes a competitive, market-based salary for a chamber executive. Businesspeople who routinely make compensation decisions for executive talent within their own companies based on a perceived market value for each position, apparently can view the chamber as a charitable service organization in the nonprofit sector and in that context hold preconceived notions about paying less-than-private-sector compensation.

Another factor that I believe negatively affects chamber salaries is the reality that chambers often choose a president from within the community, someone who has deep roots and strong relationships in that home community. While that can be commendable, it also creates an impression that the chamber exec is not going anywhere, is unlikely to pull up roots and go to another chamber. (I suspect but can't prove that this perception of relative immobility is an even greater factor for female chamber execs, especially ones who are married for example to a local professional who is unlikely to relocate his legal or medical practice or some other business to another community. If I'm correct and this phenomenon more commonly affects females in chamber roles than males, it represents a form of institutional sexism that many chamber boards composed predominantly of males might not ever notice or attempt to address by paying a competitive salary in that market.)

In cases of perceived or actual immobility, the risk of a chamber losing its exec is probably not from another chamber but from across the street at a bank that needs a new well-connected market president and approaches the chamber exec about making a lucrative career move. A chamber that doesn't pay an appropriate professional salary for the level of managerial skill and leadership talent its community deserves can find itself becoming a revolving door – a training ground for upwardly mobile young professionals. I observed one small chamber that had three capable CEOs in a five-year period, with each one going on to greener pastures within that same community.

A chamber that doesn't pay an appropriate professional salary can find itself becoming a revolving door – a training ground for upwardly mobile young professionals.

The best way for a chamber exec to counter preconceived notions about chamber compensation is not with personal appeals about how much money he/she wants or deserves; it's with data. ACCE has a very sophisticated salary comparison tool on its website for comparing a chamber executive's salary to comparable chambers across the country. You can compare salaries based on the size of the budget, the size of the staff and the population of the community. The annual ACCE Benchmarking Survey and subsequent reports provide a great way to see what the market is paying for chambers in comparable circumstances. There can be pretty wide variance, even among comparable communities, because of the relative tenure of the chamber executive and the perceived standing of the chamber in a particular community or region. If the chamber has enjoyed a long-standing reputation in the community as the go-to organization for getting things done, chamber leaders are probably willing to invest more in the president and senior staff leaders. If, on the other hand, the chamber is viewed somewhat dismissively as a feel-good civic organization that brags about the community and hands out awards, chamber leaders are probably only willing to pay for a friendly placeholder who can keep the doors open, keep the finances in order and represent them reasonably well.

State associations of chambers can also be good sources of benchmarked salary data for smaller chambers. The value of participating in salary studies, aside from the obvious benefit of providing insight for individual executives, search committees and volunteer leaders is the sharing of information about salary ranges. The more chamber volunteer leaders are inclined to meet or exceed the market levels for chambers their size and the more chamber leaders value the role of their chambers, the faster the average compensation rises for chamber professionals in general.

Why would one chamber pay more for its executive than another chamber of similar size or pay significantly more than it has in the past? Here are a couple of hypothetical ways of looking at chamber executive compensation.

First, imagine a hypothetical chamber in which the volunteer leaders decide to recruit a new exec and, for whatever reason, they end up paying double the salary the previous exec was paid. Why would they do that? Assuming it doesn't involve a dramatic restructuring of the chamber (merging with the economic development agency or the tourism bureau, for example) and the search committee didn't conspire to hire someone's out-of-work brother-in-law or political pal, what could possibly be the motive?

For the sake of discussion, let's assume the higher salary came from a good-faith, arms-length decision to pay substantially more. We could conclude that the leaders must have determined they wanted a higher level of executive leadership or more experience or both. In other words, they wanted more horsepower. They must have decided to *invest* in their CEO rather than to simply *spend* money to fill the position. Perhaps the community is in a recession with high unemployment and a nearby community that is viewed as a competitor seems to be growing more successfully. Perhaps business leaders have decided they need to kick-start their local efforts and they have agreed to invest more in order to attract a particularly aggressive individual with a track record of success.

Unlike a bank CEO who makes decisions that will directly affect the bank's individual shareholders who have substantial investments riding on the bank's performance or a hospital CEO who regularly makes strategic decisions that cost millions of dollars and/or save lives, chamber execs typically don't carry those types of big-dollar decisions directly on their shoulders. The bank board and the hospital board are willing to pay relatively high salaries in the talent marketplace to recruit experienced executives who have a track record of sound judgment and profitability when making financially consequential decisions.

So, in the case of our hypothetical chamber that is willing to pay significantly more, if it's not about million dollar decisions, what would make a chamber exec more or less valuable? Most likely, it's the perceived need within the community for a greater skill set – perhaps specialized skills – along with a solid track record of executive leadership and solid success.

I've seen communities in the South and Midwest pay economic developers substantially more than chamber execs in the same communities.

Why? Because the desire to create new jobs is often seen as more urgent and critical to local business leaders, whereas the chamber's role, absent the business recruitment function, is perhaps perceived as a community booster organization focused on retail promotions, networking events, awards banquets, slick community brochures and feel-good activities. It's all good work which chamber members say they value, but those functions and the associated reputation for providing those services are not perceived to directly affect the local economy in terms of greater bank deposits, new housing starts and more utility hook-ups.

In a second hypothetical scenario, imagine a community where a nearby military base with several thousand jobs is the primary economic engine for the region but is threatened with a BRAC (Base Realignment and Closure Commission) decision. Thousands of direct military jobs and indirect civilian jobs are at risk. A well-known and locally respected general is taking retirement in his late 50s but wants to stay in the area for family reasons. The chamber has a shot at hiring him, but it will require a compensation package that is much greater than the chamber is accustomed to providing. The sense of urgency and the availability of a uniquely qualified person to coordinate the community's response comes together, a couple of bankers decide to double their dues for the next five years, and suddenly the chamber is viewing its role, its importance and its resources in a completely new light. And it's willing to pay accordingly for the right person to fill a specific need.

Chamber execs and chamber volunteer leaders should view themselves as constantly building the value proposition of their chambers, making their organizations more relevant and indispensable in terms of achieving the aspirations of their communities. A chamber exec who is viewed as uniquely qualified to lead the community toward its highly focused vision is always going to command more within the marketplace. Also, a chamber exec who gets courted by another community and handles the situation professionally, can cause his/her volunteer leaders to suddenly take a fresh look at their own chamber, their compensation levels and their willingness to compete for talent. Ideally, the chamber exec finds him/herself in a discussion of "What will it take to keep you?" That's certainly a great place to be.

Hopefully, chamber board leaders are asking, "What kind of chamber leader does our community deserve?" rather than, "How much are we going to have to pay?"

The point of these two hypotheticals is that the perceived value of the chamber and of the chamber executive, which are often closely linked, creates the backdrop against which compensation decisions are made. Of course the size of the budget and the perceived mobility of the exec are relevant factors, but over time chamber volunteer leaders are collectively making conscious and unconscious decisions about how much the organization is worth to their community and their individual businesses. Hopefully, they are asking, "What kind of chamber leader does our community deserve?" rather than, "How much are we going to have to pay?"

When I was at a smaller chamber, the executive committee discussed my performance each year in a closed session and decided whether I would get a year-end bonus and/or an increase for the coming year. That process usually involved the full executive committee inviting me back into the room, and those conversations were generally very positive. As I moved to larger chambers, I found the compensation process more streamlined – much to my liking and in keeping with the volunteer leaders' time constraints. During my last twenty years at two chambers, I was accustomed to my annual performance review and compensation matters involving only the three most senior board officers mentioned earlier. After their evaluation, the chair of the committee communicated whatever bonus they had approved for the current year and any change in compensation for the coming year directly to our staff finance director who, in turn, built that salary into the coming year's personnel budget along with the other staff increases I had authorized. My compensation was not reported to the executive committee or the board nor did it require approval at those levels. Of course, my compensation along with that of our top staff members was later disclosed on the annual IRS 990 forms which were subsequently distributed to and approved by our board and eventually made public on the Internet.

Occasionally, and usually only if requested, I reported the salary levels of our senior staff members to my performance review committee and entertained their comments. If asked, I explained those compensation levels, my perceptions of market demand for those senior positions, and what comparative data and rationale I used to establish those salaries. I routinely attempted to survey other chambers and human resource materials to determine what constituted competitive salaries for our various positions. I did not volunteer salary or performance information for the remainder of our staff to my review committee, but our CFO showed a list of all salaries to our board treasurer once a year. I didn't want to burden the committee with that level of detail and frankly, I didn't want to invite them to delve into staff personalities, the minutia of compensation comparisons or a level of micromanagement that tends to be unhealthy for a professional organization.

It was my experience that having only a small group of top officers involved in compensation decisions was the healthiest approach. The top officers usually have the most direct interaction with the chamber exec and have usually worked with each other enough to have a comfortable rapport; confining the decisions to a small group limits the sensitive personnel discussion and the temptation to stir a wider rumor mill. Having the full executive committee or in some cases, the full board involved in compensation matters often leads to unhealthy interference and can lead to conflicts among the chamber's volunteer leaders.

Generally throughout my career, I had the good fortune to work with board chairs who were successful leaders of the business community and who, I assume, were making more – or many times more – than my position paid. I considered that a good thing. Assuming the chamber's budget was in relatively healthy shape, and the chamber was experiencing growth in its income, a board chair at higher compensation levels was probably not going to expend a lot of energy quibbling over the chamber exec receiving a year-end bonus or a salary increase for the coming year.

Employment Contracts

Many executive search consultants, compensation consultants and veteran chamber colleagues suggest that a chamber executive have an employment contract. I agree. However, I didn't take that advice and only had two, one-year contracts during my thirty-plus years as a chamber employee. When I twice made professional moves from one chamber to another, I was offered a first-year contract at each new chamber. In both cases I wanted a guarantee of the first year's compensation package to justify making the move and taking on the risk to my family and me that the new position might not work out. In hindsight, I neglected during the early period of our courtship to politely request an automatically renewable, evergreen contract that would give me at least one-year's guaranteed compensation in case things didn't work out or if I were terminated without cause – a specific infraction of chamber policy, professional standards or the law. Many contracts are for multiple years and define the conditions under which the CEO can be terminated.

During subsequent years as my annual evaluations were conducted and things were going well, I felt confident and secure in my position and frankly, I was timid about asking for a contract. Fortunately, things worked out well, but considering the precarious political situations in which chamber execs can find themselves, I feel in retrospect that I was performing on a tightrope without a net. It wasn't the smartest way to manage my career and protect my family.

The optimal time to request a contract is when you are in the process of accepting a new position and compensation is on the table; when you are still in a honeymoon period; at the time of your performance reviews – assuming they are positive; when you have a supportive board chair who has expressed interest in keeping you in your position; after receiving a bona fide offer from another employer and your current chamber leaders have

Considering the precarious political situations in which chamber execs can find themselves, working without an employment contract is like performing on a tightrope without a net.

expressed an interest in keeping you; or when changing political circumstances look precarious, such as when a new mayor who is antagonistic toward the chamber gets elected and your leadership shares your anxiety about the new political environment. If the committee that evaluates your performance is positive and encouraging, you may have the flexibility to position yourself to obtain the protection of a contract with a guarantee of severance pay if you were terminated in the future. That kind of conversation, however, should probably follow a heart-to-heart conversation with your board chair, assuming he/she is supportive and willing to endorse and personally carry the idea of an increase to your compensation committee or executive committee. It would be imprudent to bring up the topic cold in a group setting and invite an impromptu conversation about your performance.

To be sure, there is substantial risk of overplaying one's hand if the opinions of board leaders haven't been accurately assessed. A chamber exec might learn the hard way that the officers are not sufficiently convinced of his/her value to the organization, and the request for a contract, contract extension or salary increase is considered presumptuous and triggers an uncomfortable conversation about board members' previously unspoken performance concerns.

It's almost impossible to plan ahead for situations of termination. When you take a new position at a chamber, the last thing you're thinking about is termination. It's new, it's exciting, your picture is in the paper, board members who selected you are bragging on you, and there is usually a honeymoon period. It can be a heady experience. But it's best to use that period of optimism – both your optimism and the chamber volunteer leaders' optimism – to plan for a worst-case scenario.

Requesting an employment agreement that addresses such possibilities as termination and severance pay is the wise course to take. Neither of my two one-year contracts addressed causes for termination, but each guaranteed a payout of my first year if I were terminated. Fortunately many chamber executives are more far-sighted than I and arrange a longer-term cushion. A 2016 compensation survey of state chamber CEOs by a Minneapolis consulting firm showed 58% of those chamber execs were covered by employment agreements. I assume most of those agreements addressed termination, with or without cause, and severance pay.

I had the good fortune to work with consistently supportive boards and board chairs, so I never felt, except in the two cases noted above, the need to ask for a contract. I always felt confident enough that, even with a politically volatile turn of events, my board would either back me or at least give me a soft landing with severance pay, positive references and sufficient time to make a move of my choice. That was probably naïve on my part and, now that I am retired, I realize a negative turn of events could have been more threatening to my career than I imagined, especially as I moved through my late 50s and early 60s, and my marketability for making a comfortable move to another chamber naturally diminished.

Golden Handcuff Agreements

Golden handcuffs or stay bonuses are deferred compensation incentives that can be used effectively by chambers to encourage a chamber exec or staff member to stay with the chamber for an extended period of time.

They are relatively common in other fields, such as for high-profile athletic coaching jobs, providing incentives for performance and monetary encouragement to keep building a successful program.

Chambers that decide they are at risk of losing their CEO can offer such incentives to make it more appealing for the exec to stay put. If the board leaders say, "We know other organizations are looking at you," and "What would it take to keep you here?" the timing is probably right to plant the seed for a golden handcuff agreement. Chamber CEOs, likewise, can offer such incentives to key employees who might be tempted to jump ship.

Technically – at least in the way I used them – they are not agreements; they are unilateral promises made by a chamber to an employee. In the simplest terms, they are written, legally binding

If the board leaders say, "What would it take to keep you here?" the timing is probably right to plant the seed for a golden handcuff agreement.

offers by the organization to put aside a certain dollar amount or a percentage of the executive's annual compensation each year and protect it in escrow so, if the executive stays a certain number of additional years, he/she gets the defined bonus. If the exec leaves before the term of the agreement, the bonus is forfeited and the chamber keeps the money that has accrued in the escrow account. I don't believe a golden handcuff agreement typically carries the legal weight of an employment contract (except to the extent that it explicitly conveys the desire of the chamber for the exec to stay), and it usually doesn't require the employee to stay for the agreed-upon term. It simply offers an added incentive to stay for a certain number of extra years. I used these agreements in a rare number of cases in which I thought the chamber was particularly vulnerable to losing a valuable employee – someone who perhaps had a high profile outside the chamber and was being recruited by another employer.

When I offered such handcuffs on behalf of our chamber, I wrote a simple memo to the employee with a copy to the employee's personnel file, outlining the chamber's offer. For each agreement, our finance director deferred a proportionate amount during each pay period and the increasing total, with interest tied to federal treasury bills, was carried on our chamber's balance sheet as a deferred compensation liability – a debt our chamber owed certain employees.

Because as CEO I was authorized to set staff salaries, I typically did not ask the board or executive committee to approve such agreements. Admittedly, I probably should have run it by my board chair before making such an offer because the golden handcuff was a legally binding, multi-year, one-way pledge from the chamber to the employee, and I was incurring a liability for the chamber that would extend to the next CEO if I were to leave. However, I did report the agreements to my incoming board chair each year as part of an overall disclosure of our chamber's legal and financial obligations.

I occasionally used golden handcuff agreements to retain young talent on our staff. I always felt that recruiting young, talented people was relatively easy because they viewed the chamber as an interesting place to work, and many young candidates felt it would look good on their resumes. However, I found it a major challenge to retain those same individuals after two or three years. By then, our board members had noticed them, the community had noticed them and other chambers had perhaps noticed them. Therefore I sometimes – sparingly – used golden handcuff agreements after a person's first year of service. If our organization believed the staffer was someone with a bright future at our chamber, who had been approached with other opportunities and who we should try to keep as long as possible, we offered him/her a confidential handcuff agreement that added, for example, 10% per year or a flat dollar amount for staying three or four more years.

On the short term, young staffers probably didn't truly value the future monetary benefit of the deferred compensation and were probably more focused on their most recent pay stub, but the offer from the boss of a deferred bonus was a significant affirmation after a year of great work. The offer made them feel valued, more secure and more optimistic about the future. As time went on and the employee gained more tenure, the possibility of earning a bonus that would pay for a new car, pay down a student loan or help make a down payment on a house became much more inviting, and it encouraged them to stay. The bonuses I offered also assured them, in writing, that the agreement did not negate their opportunities for annual increases and/or promotions if proper conditions unfolded.

What if the staff member left right after our chamber had paid out a nice stay bonus? That situation didn't really concern me – other than the obvious loss of a talented colleague on our staff – because I knew I couldn't always compete for someone's entire career, and I might have lost that person sooner if I hadn't offered the incentive to stay. It was worth the extra cost for the chamber to retain that person's increasing capacity to contribute to our chamber rather than to have the alternative – an earlier departure, a loss for the chamber of talent and experience, and the negative effect on the organization of higher staff turnover.

Confidentiality is important in offering such packages because morale in the office can suffer if other staffers suspect preferential treatment of a co-worker. I didn't apologize for offering market-based compensation agreements to retain any of our key talent, but I wrote into the handcuff agreement a confidentiality clause, saying the bonus offer could be withdrawn if confidentiality were breached.

In my experience, approximately half of the selected staff members stayed for the entire term of their agreements and therefore, only half the bonuses were actually paid. In terms of cost to the chamber, that meant the bonuses eventually only cost about 50 cents for each dollar offered and carried on the chamber's balance sheet. When you hire sharp young people, opportunities are going to come their way, and some of those greener pastures can't be refused. In cases when I lost staffers who were covered by such agreements, I wished them well in their new positions and gave them a proper send-off. Meanwhile, the chamber had a minor windfall for the current year's balance sheet because the compensation we had deferred for that employee's golden-handcuff wasn't paid and no longer needed to be carried as a liability on the chamber's books.

Near-Death (Career) Experiences

Near-death career experiences or those unexpected, career-threatening turns of events when you see your career flash before your eyes, can happen to the best of chamber professionals. They can be triggered by a partner of the chamber going bankrupt and leaving the chamber holding the bag, by a scandal involving an unscrupulous chamber employee, by a chamber being on the wrong side of an election, by a major company pulling its membership over a petty slight or by a perceived downturn in the local economy. I remember distinctly where I was sitting when one of those moments happened to me nearly forty years ago.

I was the young CEO of my hometown chamber and things were going well. At least I thought so. Although the country was in a deep recession and my community was feeling it acutely, I had a very supportive board, an enthusiastic chair I considered a friend, and our chamber was setting records for growth and programming. We had created a community leadership program, we were working to create a community college, we had created a popular annual food festival, we were working to develop a performing arts center, and we were striving aggressively to revitalize our downtown. We operated from a multi-year strategic plan created by the board and one-year business plans created with significant board involvement. Our chamber earned accreditation for the first time from the U.S. Chamber, and we had emerged successfully from a financially difficult situation. Pretty solid record, right?

One day I received a call from a prominent businessman who wanted to know if I was in my office and whether he could drop by. He soon arrived and – surprising to me – he was accompanied by a very prominent local developer. Apparently they had talked to each other about the dire economic situation and how our community had failed to recruit any substantial industries in several years while a nearby community seemed to be announcing a new employer on a regular basis. That sister community, Bowling Green, Kentucky, had an impressive history of growth over several decades – growth fueled in large part by its enviable location on an interstate highway, its growing state university and its close proximity to the Nashville, Tennessee, International Airport. Our community, Owensboro, offered an outstanding quality of life and an idyllic location on a bluff with a panoramic view of the Ohio River but had none of those three strategic economic development advantages.

The unscheduled visit that morning by two of our most powerful community leaders (neither of whom happened to be on our chamber board at the time) was polite but direct. I concluded that they were privately wondering what the hell our chamber was doing. They were seemingly unaware of our chamber's most recent achievements and, when told, seemed unimpressed with the community development initiatives mentioned above. I suspect – although I don't know – that they considered such initiatives to be fluff. They were more interested in the community attracting jobs and wanted to know why the chamber wasn't chalking up economic development achievements with more announcements of new jobs.

Fortunately for me, I had been working behind the scenes with my board leaders' blessing to scrape together sufficient funds from the chamber, the local industrial foundation (a passive land-banking organization) and the local riverport authority to begin a partnership and commit the necessary funding so the chamber could hire the community's first full-time economic development director. Just a couple of weeks prior to the visit of these two business leaders, I had placed a want ad for our newly-created job opening in a national economic development newsletter, and I had a fresh copy on my desk. I was able to redirect the conversation by agreeing that we had to do more to recruit jobs and by showing them, in print, evidence that we were preparing as a chamber and as a community to shift gears and be more aggressive.

They left, apparently satisfied or at least appeased, but for the next few hours I could think of nothing else and I paced the floor. Needless to say, I felt I had dodged a bullet. I was in my late 20s and to have two, extremely influential leaders who were my father's age deliver a two-on-one, up-close-and-personal indictment of our chamber and its feel-good successes was a gut-punch that nearly floored me. While the episode sounds relatively benign – even comical – in retrospect, it was intense at the time as I momentarily saw my chamber career in profound jeopardy. What had felt like a very positive period of conspicuous successes and vocal support from my board was suddenly dismissed by two pillars of the community with a single phone call that led to an abrupt meeting and a strictly-business conversation.

During the subsequent years of my chamber career, I knew at least a half-dozen chamber executives who lost their jobs or were pressured out when a few community and/or political leaders – not necessarily chamber board members – concluded that the chamber wasn't getting the job done and had somehow lost its way. I saw some fall victim to the creation of a rival group of civic leaders – perhaps a Business Roundtable of CEOs in a metro area or on a statewide level – when the perception of the chamber took a negative turn. And I saw chamber careers derailed by a new mayor or – in the case of a state chamber, a new governor – who had it out for the chamber exec or in some way communicated to the chamber's leadership that he or she couldn't work with the sitting chamber exec.

I had good friends accept new chamber positions in good faith and with the apparent embrace of the local business community only to find themselves fall victim to politically turbulent winds that even the most skilled executive would have difficulty anticipating or navigating. Sure, you could say they should have seen this or known that, or reacted to things differently. But entering a new community only to find long-simmering political factions erupting through no neglect on your part can be disconcerting to say the least — and often career-threatening. Some have compared the precariousness of being a chamber CEO to the fragile tenure of a city manager — both are professional managers serving in politically volatile environments, juggling a host of personalities from a relatively high-profile but structurally subservient role and, as a result, having relatively limited life expectancies in their positions.

I knew at least a half-dozen chamber executives who lost their jobs when a few community and/or political leaders – not necessarily chamber board members – concluded that the chamber wasn't getting the job done and had somehow lost its way.

Unlike local elected officials who can fall back on their electoral mandate when they get into political skirmishes — at least until the next election – a chamber CEO serves at the pleasure of a volunteer board. While on a given day that relationship can feel relatively stable and secure, one shouldn't underestimate the fluid nature of local politics, especially when strong community leaders decide to publicly attack a chamber executive or put pressure on the chamber's volunteer leaders to make changes. It's not uncommon for your board leaders' own jobs and economic livelihoods – even if not directly dependent on other, more powerful community leaders – to be influenced by pressures from the local powers that be. A board chair who is a local developer and needs a favorable zoning decision from City Hall or a business person who needs a line of credit extended at the local bank can be unduly influenced by local power brokers and make things difficult for a chamber executive who has somehow gotten crossways with those powerbrokers. Having chamber board members who are strong and independent enough to withstand that kind of heat are essential when the local political currents become turbulent. In those circumstances, we all hope for board leaders — especially board chairs — who aren't easily pressured.

Termination

I had the good fortune to never face the harsh circumstance of being terminated, but I know that the political crosswinds of a community and a chamber board can shift abruptly and a chamber exec's career immediately suffers. I witnessed very capable and talented chamber colleagues fall victim to that occupational hazard. Not only does a termination cause at least a temporary if not permanent professional setback, it can be a traumatic personal experience that affects one's psyche and one's family for years. I knew friends who experienced the equivalent of post-traumatic stress disorder (PTSD) and one who, quite tragically, took his life after a forced separation from his position. Few of us can experience such an intense professional crisis and immediately and cheerfully pivot toward a new chapter in our careers.

Of course, no two termination situations are the same. If the dismissal is prompted by scandal or questionable behavior or, in contrast, it involves philosophical differences and a chamber board chair saying euphemistically, "We've decided to go in a different direction," a chamber exec going through a forced or mutual termination needs to keep an eye on the future and what options he or she might pursue. If and when termination appears inevitable, it's wise to try — to the extent possible — to orchestrate your own departure. While it may be difficult or impossible to negotiate your dismissal, you should request the opportunity to offer your resignation, even if it must be immediate. You'll be better positioned for the interviews for your next position, whether it's in the chamber arena or something outside the field.

Your public statements and private conversations as you exit are critical. This is the time to use lessons from crisis communications experts.

While it is very tempting to spit on the floor or throw a verbal hand grenade over your shoulder as you leave the chamber, taking the high road will serve your interests better. The temptation to tell them off, to save face, to fire off some expletives or simply to get even needs to take a back seat to the professional and practical advantages of taking the high road. Taking shots at the local chamber on the front page of the newspaper after a forced resignation or sending an overly defensive email to the full board might let you get something off your chest, but it will almost surely cause a self-inflicted wound and probably eliminate many of your best options for landing on your feet in another chamber or association.

In traumatic situations, it is tough to be magnanimous, but assuming there hasn't been a high-profile disagreement between you and your board leadership leading up to the termination, I suggest a public statement something like, "I've had the wonderful opportunity to work with some of the region's most talented business leaders, and

Taking shots at the local chamber on the front page of the newspaper after a forced resignation or sending an overly defensive email to the full board might let you get something off your chest, but it will almost surely cause a self-inflicted wound.

I thank them for that. There comes a time for new professional challenges, and my family and I look forward to those. I wish my friends and colleagues at the chamber continued success." That high-road approach will position a chamber exec much better for the next professional position, and it will certainly sound better to your remaining supporters, friends, and colleagues than a bitter, spiteful statement. It's far more advantageous to concentrate on your next position than to settle scores in an unfortunate situation that will soon be history.

In my nearly thirty years in Chamber World, I only terminated two or three employees by concluding that, "It's over; we've tried to make it work; this is your last day." And even in those cases, the termination followed a period in which I provided the employee a written improvement plan by which he/she could attempt to grow into a position and meet expectations. In a few other cases, I found it necessary to eliminate certain staff positions because the chamber had grown in ways that no longer matched certain employees' skills. In those cases where the employee's performance had been satisfactory or better, I offered a severance package using a formula I learned years ago from BellSouth: offering to pay 5% of salary for each year of service, up to 10 years – in other words, up to one half year's salary based on tenure. I felt that anyone who invested part of their career with our chamber and performed satisfactorily deserved a soft landing and the opportunity for a financially manageable transition. In those instances involving severance pay, I asked the employee to sign a separation agreement promising that neither party would speak ill of the other, that the amount of severance would be confidential, that the work they produced for the chamber was considered the intellectual property of the chamber and that they would not pursue any action or grievance against the chamber – all in return for the severance payment, favorable references and any other consideration we built in.

In other cases, for example in membership sales, staff members who burned out, lost interest, didn't make their sales goals or otherwise underperformed during a defined grace period, in effect, terminated themselves. Those situations were somewhat easier to manage because the performance goals were explicit up front, were easily quantifiable and were not so dependent on the manager's or the employee's subjective opinion.

Facing termination or terminating an employee is rarely easy – especially if you as CEO have been successful in developing a healthy, enjoyable workplace culture where co-workers are friends or at least genuinely respect each other. I lost more nights' sleep during my career over difficult personnel issues than I did fretting over relationships with board members, navigating City Hall politics, worrying about the success of particular chamber initiatives, being anxious about public speaking or dealing with hostile reporters. Other chamber execs may compartmentalize those difficult HR situations better than I could.

Succession, Retirement and Transition

Every management expert I know recommends succession planning for an orderly transition from one CEO to the next and from each staff person to the next. On a few occasions at my chambers, we interviewed each employee about his/her job satisfaction and career aspirations so we could put on paper a succession plan for every position in the organization. With some positions, an obvious successor was already on our staff while vacancies in other positions would necessitate recruiting from outside for a specific skill set or professional credential.

I didn't develop a formal succession plan for my position, but each year as my new board chair was taking office, I gave that person a detailed, confidential memo with suggestions about what he/she could do if something happened to me. It gave my candid assessment of the interpersonal dynamics within our staff, who internally might aspire to take my place, what the fallout would be among other staff members (especially within our senior team) if an internal candidate were promoted to my position, who outside the organization might be available for the position, who might be appropriate as an interim executive while a search process took place and so forth. I recommended resources for determining appropriate compensation levels, executive search firms that specialized in chamber executives and people in the industry, such as the presidents of ACCE and the Council of State Chambers, who could provide advice and resources. My memo also provided suggestions on how the board could maintain positive

Each year as my new board chair was taking office, I gave that person a detailed, confidential memo with suggestions about what he/she could do if something happened to me.

morale among the existing staff members during a search process involving uncertainty and heightened anxiety.

As part of my annual performance reviews during the last few years of my chamber career, my incoming chair would typically ask me about my plans, and I would usually answer by suggesting a likely window for my retirement, such as, "There's an 80% likelihood I won't retire before 65 and an 80% likelihood I won't stay past 67." With each advancing year, my window tightened until I was able to say more definitively that I was planning to retire "sometime in the fall of next year." The three top officers and I agreed that those conversations would remain highly confidential.

About 18 months before my target date, we decided to confide in one more person – the board member who was being recruited to be chair-elect of our board and would serve as board chair during the first year of my successor. My sitting board chair, a thorough corporate executive who took his chamber responsibilities seriously, wanted to begin a search about ten months before my target date so it would unfold on an efficient and deliberate timeline. I, however, favored a tighter time frame of no more than six months from announcement to retirement because I knew from previous experience that a longer period would be awkward for me – with friends and co-workers having to express their congratulations and well wishes one too many times. A longer timeline could also be unsettling for the remaining chamber staff waiting to learn who the new CEO would be. A timeline with about six months between my announcement and the announcement of the new CEO was finally settled when a past board chair suggested that I shouldn't be perceived as a lame duck during the state's upcoming legislative session and that my retirement should be announced immediately after the legislature adjourned.

The three top officers who knew of my plans asked me if there would be an internal candidate. I suggested one in particular, our senior vice president of public affairs. They asked me to approach her about her interest and to actively mentor her – not to be selected but to be as prepared as possible to be considered alongside external candidates. I told her of that strategy and began involving her in additional administrative duties outside her more specialized public affairs function. While my board officers wanted to observe her in higher-profile settings (board meetings, speeches, legislative testimony), I was limited in how much additional exposure I could offer her without giving the impression to board members and other staff that she was my preferred candidate.

As my retirement was announced, a search committee of eight top CEOs – four male and four female – was formed, and a search firm was hired to conduct a national search. The internal candidate and I had candid conversations during the search process, and I gave her suggestions about her interviews with the committee, how to deal with rumors and how to respond to staff curiosity. However, I told her and the committee that while I had great confidence in her abilities and I didn't know anyone who I thought would be more likely to succeed in the position I was vacating, the search process might reveal candidates I didn't know and whose backgrounds and skill sets would appeal to the search committee.

As a practical matter, any effort on my part or the perception of effort on my part to lobby the search committee on her behalf could have backfired – on her. While the board had been very supportive of my tenure and gave me a very gracious send-off, the chamber was clearly their chamber. Any perceived intrusion by me in the process could meet with an adverse reaction. I kept an arms-length distance from the search, avoided rumors with people outside the chamber about various candidates and declined to state a preference. Near the end of the search, the chair asked me to meet with the four finalists and to join the final committee conference call to share my observations about the two remaining contenders: the internal candidate and one remaining external candidate.

Chamber CEOs who are retiring after investing years of sweat equity in their organizations naturally want to perpetuate their programs and policies. However, I think it's important to step back and be conspicuous in keeping a distance from the process. If an internal candidate is the preferred candidate of the retiring CEO and he/she emerges from a thorough and independent search process, that person starts with a built-in authority of earning the position on merit and not through manipulation by the out-going CEO or through political favoritism.

One additional point should be noted. As the search was underway, the committee quietly contacted several important stakeholders (legislators, local chamber execs and a few key chamber investors) about the final two candidates. While a chamber never wants to seek permission from outside parties, such as a mayor or governor, to hire its exec, having as much buy-in as possible from key leaders will smooth the transition and pave the way for the new exec to be effective from Day One. That quiet, confidential outreach might also uncover some unforeseen, damaging issue that might otherwise erupt only after the search is complete and the new CEO announced.

I've been asked if I thought the cost of a search firm (typically about one-third of the incoming CEO's first year compensation) was worth the money, and I've answered, yes. I would recommend it again, even knowing the outcome. While the winning candidate was literally right down the hall from me, the open search process and a serious effort to identify the best candidates for the job gave her the credibility she deserved as she assumed the role. And the process provided the search committee a greater awareness of the current market for chamber CEOs and the talent pool that could be tapped.

I've been asked if I thought the cost of a search firm (typically about one-third of the incoming CEO's first year compensation) was worth the money, and I've answered, yes.

No two succession scenarios are the same, but if a chamber exec has the good fortune to leave on his/her own terms, it's best for the organization for the CEO to keep a distance from the choice of a successor unless explicitly invited to participate in a specific way.

A transition in CEOs is an excellent time to take stock of the chamber and why it exists. Lew Ebert of the Council of State Chambers offers this checklist of pre-search items:

- Take an inventory to determine the state of your chamber.

- Focus on the "why." Create clarity around the chamber vision/mission/purpose.

- Determine if the executive committee and board are 100% focused and in agreement. Are you sure? Leaders have lots of opinions, not always well founded.

- Solicit stakeholder feedback, perhaps with a survey. It's a good opportunity to identify expectations, concerns and aspirations.

- Define the state of the business community in your community or state. Is it on the right track or wrong track? Is it competitive with other communities or states?

- Define the organization's strategy, plan and direction that your new CEO will need to execute.

- Decide where you want the organization to be in five to ten years.

- Consider what big things are possible. What's your BHAG (big hairy audacious goal) for the organization and for your community or state?

- Conduct an operations assessment. What's the revenue trajectory, and what's in the reserves? Benchmark these against other organizations.

- Consider whether there is alignment in the business community. Do other groups that represent major companies in your community or state support working together to accomplish compatible priorities?

- Assess your opposition. Who's working against your vision for the future? What's their annual budget and how does that compare with the chamber budget?

Completing all of these things is recommended before a search to ensure there is clarity among chamber leaders on their central vision, mission and goals. Clarifying these items will increase the leaders' prospects for a successful search to find the individual who would best implement the organization's vision.

■ ■ ■

Managing an effective chamber requires tough decisions, including some occasions of having to ask an employee to resign or be terminated. As author Jim Collins puts it, "It is better to first get the right people on the bus, the wrong people off the bus, and the right people in the right seats" before you can figure out where to drive. Making the tough decisions about who sits in what seats on the bus is a critical part of being a chamber executive and building a high-performance, catalytic chamber.

CONCLUSION

In putting together some of my observations about life in Chamber World, I have reflected on the special nature of chambers of commerce and the unique role chamber professionals play in their communities. In some cases, I've borrowed from the thoughts of other chamber leaders to project current trends and imagine the demands that chambers and chamber executives will face in the years ahead. I've tried to avoid being dogmatic or instructive. This isn't meant to be a *Chamber Management 101* textbook with a set of ten magic rules for running a chamber. Instead, it is my personal observations offered from the vantage point of managing three very different chambers and observing countless other chambers during more than four decades in and around the chamber business. I have offered these experiences in the hope they will prompt readers – even when surely disagreeing with my particular approach to certain situations – to reflect on their own chamber experiences and question, adjust and/or affirm their own thoughts about how and why they do what they do to strengthen their chambers and communities.

Chambers Aren't Going Anywhere

The citizens of our communities will always imagine a better day for themselves. While some of those people will have a vague sense of hoping for a better life for their children and grandchildren, others will develop more focused aspirations for achieving greater levels of economic prosperity and livability. To the extent these hopes and dreams take root in a community and within its business community, there will emerge a desire to act and to use associations – often chambers of commerce – for collective action. I have suggested to local chamber leaders that if a chamber suddenly disappeared from its community, someone or some group of business people in the community would be working to create one by the end of the week.

There will always be business leaders motivated to act on a community's aspirations but either because of their personal limitations such as holding a pressure-filled day job or the recognition that special skills are needed to pursue their civic aspirations, they will seek out people with the personal capacity and professional skills to provide leadership to pursue those aspirations. That's where chamber executives come in.

The professional occupation of chamber executive doesn't have strict educational prerequisites, licensure requirements or a professional designation as tightly defined as the centuries-old professions of lawyer, doctor or clergy. In that sense it's a relatively recent profession. But it has firmly established itself in modern life and continues to evolve in our information-based society. And while the majority of chamber executives find themselves in our occupation by way of an unplanned career path, and while their educational and professional backgrounds are far more varied than certain technical professions, the demand for skills needed to provide catalytic leadership for business, political and civic leaders while occupying a structurally subservient role within their organizations makes the occupation of chamber executive a distinct profession.

Horseshoes vs. Chess

I chose the analogy of playing horseshoes vs. chess to illustrate the contrast between the all-too-common and often dismissive attitude by some civic leaders that anyone can run a chamber (playing horseshoes) vs. the distinct professional challenge and opportunity of managing a chamber (playing chess). The game of horseshoes implies that managing a chamber is like a simple attempt to step up without any particular preparation or physical skill, toss a horseshoe and get a ringer – or at least get close to the stake. Chess, on the other hand, reflects the complexity of modern communities. Chess requires experience, concentration, the ability to visualize multiple scenarios for advancing and the ability to plan a sequence of two, three or four moves that will gain advantage over one's opponent. The opponent in this analogy is the collection of barriers (apathy, ignorance, conflict, jealousies, competition, lack of resolve) that keep a chamber and its community from advancing as it seeks to gain economic and cultural prosperity. Achieving that prosperity for one's community will be increasingly complex in the future and will require the calculated, multi-dimensional strategies of a focused chess player.

Major Forces are Shaping Communities and Chambers

Powerful overarching trends are profoundly shaping our communities, our chambers and our profession and will likely continue long into the foreseeable future. Leaning on the work of ACCE and other chamber observers, I have attempted to describe some of those trends: the changing nature of belonging to a group, the dizzying advancements in communications and technology, the issues of scarcity and abundance, the impact of globalization, the nature of demographic shifts, the reality of political and social fragmentation, the need to consciously align available resources with our missions, the value of providing catalytic leadership, and the reality of government's limitations for solving our problems. Taken together, they describe a future of accelerating change and greater complexity which chambers will have to navigate. They also help define the incredible opportunities that lie ahead for chambers and chamber executives.

As I completed this manuscript, the COVID-19 virus suddenly and dramatically altered our personal lives, our chambers, our communities and our globe. To an uncanny extent, it and our reactions to it vividly illustrate every one of the trends – the Nine Influences – cited earlier and it inflicted, practically overnight, a seismic impact on chambers across the country. As I recently told the very talented chamber exec who succeeded me at the Kentucky Chamber, "You've experienced more disruption of the chamber in 30 days – in finances, office operations, events, programs, even your mission – than I did in 15 years!"

Chambers Will Have to Adapt

Chambers that strive to be relevant, effective and consequential will have to recognize and adapt to these major trends affecting their communities. Chambers that can help create visions for their respective communities, develop actionable plans for pursuing those visions and help their communities navigate the increasing pace of change and complex issues shaping our lives will achieve their best and highest purpose within their communities. Not insignificantly, they will also be able to attract greater financial support for their causes.

The basic business model of chamber members paying dues to affiliate and fees for add-on services will need to transition toward a more diversified revenue model that includes traditional dues, creative non-dues revenue through fee-based services and strategic, cause-based fundraising. Because of tighter corporate budgets for civic engagement, greater expectations by businesses for direct returns on their chamber investments and the increasing amount of accumulated private wealth in America, chambers that are striving to grow will need to look beyond incremental increases in dues revenue and work to attract greater investments through targeted sponsorships, focused fundraising campaigns, charitable donations to their foundations and other cause-based contributions. Chambers will have to make specific adjustments to their internal operations to create a culture of intentional and continuous – rather than ad hoc and reactive – fundraising.

Chamber Professionals Will Have to Adapt

Chamber executives will be called upon to lead their chambers in transitioning from the manic activity of selling pancakes and coordinating parades to higher levels of organizational maturity, including but not limited to elevating the civic dialogue of their communities and engaging proactively in the public policy arena. Specialized skills and ongoing professional development will be required of chamber professionals to stay abreast of economic and social trends, effectively lead their chambers and help their communities navigate rapid change and increasing complexity. Highly motivated chambers looking to employ professional chamber executives will likely place a greater premium on the relevant background, specific personality traits, a more tightly defined skill set and a personal commitment to continuous professional development when selecting their chief executives.

Within the chamber profession, opportunities for professional growth and peer-to-peer interaction will need to expand as expectations by chambers and chamber executives grow and professional certifications gain stature and currency. If indeed the chamber profession is sometimes limited by the low expectations of our communities and chambers, it is up to us as chamber professionals to collectively raise that bar through our own professionalism and skilled performance. It's my sincere hope that this collection of reflections on a chamber career contributes to raising that bar.

A Noble Calling and a Profound Opportunity

Being a chamber executive can be an occupational stepping stone, a professional career or, in its fullest sense, a calling. A chamber executive who is passionate about seeing his/her community grow and prosper can approach the role of chamber executive with great zeal and take enormous pride in the accomplishments – some tangible, others intangible – that one can attain during a chamber career. Those accomplishments can serve as a virtual trophy case of one's personal and professional life story.

Being a chamber executive can be an occupational stepping stone, a professional career or, in its fullest sense, a calling.

What is at the heart of our life's work? It's certainly not serving as a mere caretaker to keep the doors open and to keep our chambers in the black. Our best and highest role as a chamber executive is to provide catalytic leadership and to simultaneously serve our communities – all while focused on the goals of economic prosperity and community development.

Those of us who have been given the profound opportunity to occupy a role as a chamber executive are truly blessed. Here's hoping the next generation of chamber leaders will taste the sweet satisfaction and professional accomplishments that come from such an incredible personal journey.

YOUR GIFT TO A CHAMBER COLLEAGUE!

If you found *Horseshoes vs. Chess* thought-provoking and helpful, consider ordering a copy for your favorite chamber colleagues, a few key board members, your staff, your incoming board chair or a chamber search committee. For chamber professionals, it hopefully provides positive affirmation of the important work you do every day and for chamber volunteers - especially those coming into new chamber roles - it offers a valuable glimpse inside Chamber World. Special bulk discounts are available for orders of five or more by emailing dave@chamberdave.com.

ABOUT THE AUTHOR

A veteran chamber executive and former mayor, Dave Adkisson, CCE, served as the CEO of three chambers: his hometown chamber in Owensboro, KY; the metro Birmingham (AL) Regional Chamber and the Kentucky (state) Chamber. On the national level, he served as the 2010 chairman of the board of the Association of Chamber of Commerce Executives (ACCE), was the 2014 chairman of the board of the Council of State Chambers (COSC), was a founder of the national State Chamber Policy Center, served six years on the board of the U. S. Chamber and served as the chairman of the U.S. Chamber's education policy committee. He is a past chair of the ACCE Foundation. Together, he spent more than 30 years in the chamber field.

Adkisson retired from the Kentucky Chamber of Commerce in 2019 after 15 years as president and CEO. During his tenure the Chamber was routinely ranked as the top lobbying organization in Kentucky, tripled its budget, doubled its staff and was named the 2017 State Chamber of the Year. In addition to achieving several landmark legislative victories, Adkisson created the Kentucky Chamber Workforce Center and the Leadership Institute for School Principals, a program which has invested more than $3 million in executive leadership training for school principals.

Earlier in his career, he was elected mayor of Owensboro, KY at age 34 and re-elected four years later without opposition. He championed the creation of the RiverPark (performing arts) Center on the Owensboro riverfront, the Mid-America Airpark, a city-county workforce center and the 13-mile-long Greenbelt Park which was later named in his honor. He was a co-founder of Leadership Kentucky and is a former chairman of the Kentucky Advocates for Higher Education. He serves on the board of the Kentucky American Water Company.

Originally from Owensboro, Adkisson received his B.A. in philosophy and political science from Georgetown College, where he is the immediate past chairman of the board of trustees, and earned his masters in ethics from Harvard University. He was the 2019 recipient of Leadership Kentucky's "Flame of Excellence" award and in 2020, was one of two recipients of ACCE's Life Member Award. He and his wife, Bonnie, reside in Lexington, KY, along with their two children and three grandchildren.

You can email Dave at dave@chamberdave.com or by visiting his website at www.chamberdave.com.